REFORMING SOCIAL REGULATION

SAGE FOCUS EDITIONS

1. **POLICE AND SOCIETY**, edited by David H. Bayley ● 2. **WHY NATIONS ACT**, edited by Maurice A. East, Stephen A. Salmore, and Charles F. Hermann ● 3. **EVALUATION RESEARCH METHODS**, edited by Leonard Rutman ● 4. **SOCIAL SCIENTISTS AS ADVOCATES**, edited by George H. Weber and George J. McCall ● 5. **DYNAMICS OF GROUP DECISIONS**, edited by Hermann Brandstatter, James H. Davis, and Heinz Schuler ● 6. **NATURAL ORDER**, edited by Barry Barnes and Steven Shapin ● 7. **CONFLICT AND CONTROL**, edited by Arthur J. Vidich and Ronald M. Glassman ● 8. **CONTROVERSY**, edited by Dorothy Nelkin ● 9. **BATTERED WOMEN**, edited by Donna M. Moore ● 10. **CRIMINOLOGY**, edited by Edward Sagarin ● 11. **TO AUGUR WELL**, edited by J. David Singer and Michael D. Wallace ● 12. **IMPROVING EVALUATIONS**, edited by Lois-ellin Datta and Robert Perloff ● 13. **IMAGES OF INFORMATION**, edited by Jon Wagner ● 14. **CHURCHES AND POLITICS IN LATIN AMERICA**, edited by Daniel H. Levine ● 15. **EDUCATIONAL TESTING AND EVALUATION**, edited by Eva L. Baker and Edys S. Quellmalz ● 16. **IMPROVING POLICY ANALYSIS**, edited by Stuart S. Nagel ● 17. **POWER STRUCTURE RESEARCH**, edited by G. William Domhoff ● 18. **AGING AND SOCIETY**, edited by Edgar F. Borgatta and Neil G. McCluskey ● 19. **CENTRE AND PERIPHERY**, edited by Jean Gottmann ● 20. **THE ELECTORATE RECONSIDERED**, edited by John C. Pierce and John L. Sullivan ● 21. **THE BLACK WOMAN**, edited by La Frances Rodgers-Rose ● 22. **MAKING BUREAUCRACIES WORK**, edited by Carol H. Weiss and Allen H. Barton ● 23. **RADICAL CRIMINOLOGY**, edited by James A. Inciardi ● 24. **DUAL-CAREER COUPLES**, edited by Fran Pepitone-Rockwell ● 25. **POLICY IMPLEMENTATION**, edited by John Brigham and Don W. Brown ● 26. **CONTEMPORARY BLACK THOUGHT**, edited by Molefi Kete Asante and Abdulai S. Vandi ● 27. **HISTORY AND CRIME**, edited by James A. Inciardi and Charles E. Faupel ● 28. **THE FUTURE OF EDUCATION**, edited by Kathryn Cirincione-Coles ● 29. **IMPROVING SCHOOLS**, edited by Rolf Lehming and Michael Kane ● 30. **KNOWLEDGE AND POWER IN A GLOBAL SOCIETY**, edited by William M. Evan ● 31. **BLACK MEN**, edited by Lawrence E. Gary ● 32. **MAJOR CRIMINAL JUSTICE SYSTEMS**, edited by George F. Cole, Stanislaw J. Frankowski, and Marc G. Gertz ● 33. **ANALYZING ELECTORAL HISTORY**, edited by Jerome M. Clubb, William H. Flanigan, and Nancy H. Zingale ● 34. **ASSESSING MARRIAGE**, edited by Erik E. Filsinger and Robert A. Lewis ● 35. **THE KNOWLEDGE CYCLE**, edited by Robert F. Rich ● 36. **IMPACTS OF RACISM ON WHITE AMERICANS**, edited by Benjamin P. Bowser and Raymond G. Hunt ● 37. **WORLD SYSTEM STRUCTURE**, edited by W. Ladd Hollist and James N. Rosenau ● 38. **WOMEN AND WORLD CHANGE**, edited by Naomi Black and Ann Baker Cottrell ● 39. **ENVIRONMENTAL CRIMINOLOGY**, edited by Paul J. Brantingham and Patricia L. Brantingham ● 40. **GOVERNING THROUGH COURTS**, edited by Richard A.L. Gambitta, Marlynn L. May, and James C. Foster ● 41. **BLACK FAMILIES**, edited by Harriette Pipes McAdoo ● 42. **EFFECTIVE SCHOOL DESEGREGATION**, edited by Willis D. Hawley ● 43. **AGING AND RETIREMENT**, edited by Neil G. McCluskey and Edgar F. Borgatta ● 44. **MODERN INDUSTRIAL CITIES**, edited by Bruce M. Stave ● 45. **LIVES IN STRESS**, edited by Deborah Belle ● 46. **FAMILY RELATIONSHIPS**, edited by F. Ivan Nye ● 47. **MEXICO'S POLITICAL ECONOMY**, edited by Jorge I. Dominguez ● 48. **STRATEGIES OF POLITICAL INQUIRY**, edited by Elinor Ostrom ● 49. **REFORMING SOCIAL REGULATION**, edited by LeRoy Graymer and Frederick Thompson ● 50. **CUBA**, edited by Jorge I. Dominguez ● 51. **SOCIAL CONTROL**, edited by Jack P. Gibbs ● 52. **ENERGY AND TRANSPORT**, edited by George H. Daniels, Jr., and Mark H. Rose ● 53. **GLOBAL POLICY STUDIES**, edited by Gary K. Bertsch

Reforming Social Regulation

Alternative Public Policy Strategies

Edited by

LeRoy Graymer
Frederick Thompson

SAGE PUBLICATIONS
Beverly Hills / London / New Delhi

For information address:

SAGE Publications, Inc.
275 South Beverly Drive
Beverly Hills, California 90212

SAGE Publications India Pvt. Ltd.
C-236 Defence Colony
New Delhi 110 024, India

SAGE Publications Ltd
28 Banner Street
London EC1Y 8QE, England

Printed in the United States of America

Library of Congress Cataloging in Publication Data
Main entry under title:

Reforming social regulation.

(Sage focus editions ; 49)
Papers from a conference held in 1981, which was sponsored by UCLA Extension.
1. Social legislation — United States — Congresses. 2. Trade regulation — United States — Congresses.
I. Graymer, LeRoy, 1932- . II. Thompson, Frederick. III. University of California, Los Angeles. University Extension.
KF3300.A75R34 344.73 82-5792
ISBN 0-8039-1845-3 347.304 AACR2
ISBN 0-8039-1846-1 (pbk.)

FIRST PRINTING

Contents

Acknowledgments

The genesis of this book was a conference entitled "Reforming Government Regulation: Alternative Strategies to Social Regulatory Policy," which was held in 1981. The conference was sponsored by UCLA Extension and coordinated by LeRoy Graymer in his position as head of the Public Policy Program, Department of Humanities and Social Sciences. Appreciation is extended to several people within UCLA Extension for the support, encouragement, and generous assistance that made both the conference and this book possible: the late Philip Frandson, Dean; Lois Smith-Bupp, Director, Department of Humanities and Social Sciences; and Warren Pelton, Director, Department of Management, Labor and Business.

Thanks is also given to Joy Gilliam for her assistance in editing the conference materials and copy editing the book manuscript, and to Ann Mine for her extraordinary contributions as Program Representative for the Public Policy Program.

1

Introduction

LeROY GRAYMER
FREDERICK THOMPSON

Is the new wave of interest in reforming government regulation merely rhetoric designed to capture the current political mood, or are there intrinsically interesting and important public policy questions regarding regulatory processes that deserve serious attention and scholarly investigation? The fact is that the terms *regulatory reform* and *deregulation* have become part of the political language of the day precisely because government regulation has become an increasingly significant factor in economic, social, and political transactions in the United States. As the scope of regulations increases and their consequences affect more individuals and segments of our economy, it is natural that political attention to regulatory impacts, costs, and achievements would increase. Before the 1960s most regulatory activity was aimed at specific industries, rarely involving broader publics. During the last ten to fifteen years, however, the scope of regulatory activities has expanded greatly. Also, the consequences of these new regulations are now observable, so that specific questions can be raised about the effectiveness, appropriateness, and costs of the regulatory methods that have been instituted in an effort to achieve desirable social goals.

Before proceeding with this discussion it is necessary to clarify which aspects of government regulatory activity will be addressed in this book. The "new social regulation" is an imprecise category, which is probably most easily characterized by what it is *not*. The other type of regulation, usually entitled *economic regulation*, refers primarily to those efforts by government to correct or offset problems related to monopoly practices in the free-market economy. Such regulations were originally instituted to redress the grievances occurring when large or whole segments of markets were controlled by monopolies or cartels. A few giant firms could dictate prices and prevent would-be competitors from entering the market or surviving in it. Muckrakers such as Frank Norris, author of *The Octopus,* dramatized the stranglehold that railroad monopolies had over farmers in getting products to markets. Revelation of the consequences of such concentrated power resulted in the creation of several independent federal commissions to regulate the practices of monopoly industries. The changing structure of political power occurring in the United States during the late nineteenth and early twentieth centuries provided a receptive context for adoption of these regulations. In some instances, the rationale of economic regulation was different. The government fostered or cooperated in the creation of monopolies or cartels in such industries as the airlines and public utilities to encourage development of certain kinds of new economic activity. National monopolies were acknowledged as necessities. At the same time, they were regulated to assure that their activities would serve the "public interest."

Much of the focus of deregulation in recent years has been on the outdated and, in many cases, counterproductive, activities of these agencies. For example, the Interstate Commerce Commission, established in 1887 to deal with railroad monopolies and subsequently surface transportation, had become a mechanism for limiting market entry (competition) and fixing prices. As surface transportation became more diversified, less regulation would mean greater competition. Similarly, the airline industry, by 1980, was far from an infant industry in need of protection.

What is now characterized as *social or protective regulation* has a shorter history than economic regulation, and deals with a much more diffuse set of concerns. Water quality, air pollution controls, consumer product safety — including food, drug, and medical device regulation — and occupational health and safety are the major concerns of social regulatory policies. While many of these areas (such as food and drug and occupational safety) have been subject to government regulation for some time, the period from the mid-1960s through the 1970s witnessed a dramatic increase in regulatory activity relevant to broad social and protective concerns. Advocates for federal legislation to increase regulation in these areas found the political climate receptive during an era of relative prosperity.

The enormous increase in protective regulations during this period reflects how important dramatization is to political action. Ralph Nader's *Unsafe at Any Speed* took on the giant of the automobile industry and the publicity the book received forced the government into taking action to regulate auto safety. Earth Day was the culmination of several years of political mobilization to dramatize how America's rivers were not only devoid of beneficial life and repulsive to our aesthetic senses, but a source of poison and disease. Smog in industrialized regions — and surrounding areas — became a symbol of environmental concern that everyone could understand. Occupational hazards, with effects well beyond the localized ones of mining accidents, were brought to public attention: Asbestos and chemicals used in both industry and the home were found to contain carcinogens. It seemed that hardly a day passed without reports of some prospective new source of cancer-causing materials invisibly invading our work places and private lives. Organized political action groups became skillful at focusing attention on these threats to our lives and society.

This kind of public awareness and mobilization emerged at a time when the United States was experiencing economic prosperity and had successfully landed a man on the moon. It was difficult for any elected official, even if so inclined, to argue that saving human lives and ensuring a safe and decent environment for succeeding generations should take a lower priority than space exploration. Support for social regulatory action was found among many Republicans as well as among traditionally liberal Democrat and labor leaders.

There is no doubt that in a number of areas the newly established regulatory agencies dealt successfully with real problems. For example, prior to the establishment of the Mine Enforcement and Safety Agency (MESA) in 1969, there were 100 deaths attributable to mine-related accidents and illness for each 10,000 man years worked, a death rate nearly 8 times higher than that in the next most dangerous industry, railroading. The rate is now half what it was before the establishment of MESA.

On the other hand, that some people are dissatisfied with social regulation is not surprising: Broad powers have been delegated to regulatory agencies and any exercise of broad power necessarily has an adverse effect on the interests of many, therefore inducing resistance and attack. Indeed, bitter opposition is frequently evidence of the effectiveness of a public agency. The significant question now is whether the growing dissatisfaction with the new social regulation reflects the natural opposition of those who are adversely affected by it, whether it is simply evidence of a swing of the political pendulum, or whether it is indicative of fundamental flaws in the design and execution of regulatory programs.

While political analysts might provide theories about the reasons why criticism of regulation is surfacing at this particular time, that is not our purpose here. This book addresses questions that have been raised about the appropriateness of the regulatory strategies used in pursuing socially desirable objectives. That is, are the regulations now in place the most effective and efficient ways to achieve the desired goals, or do they impose unnecessary costs? At a time when concerns about economic productivity and competitiveness in the world economy dominate our attention, it is incumbent on the public sector to search for the most efficient ways to govern. When government itself faces a crisis of confidence, its ability to maintain programs may depend on our ingenuity in designing more efficient and effective instruments for achieving social goals.

This book is designed to accomplish four major purposes: (1) to identify and diagnose problems associated with the existing regulatory regime; (2) to examine innovative alternative approaches for achieving the goals of the new social regulation; (3) to examine efforts to regulate regulation — that is, to subject the process of generating new or expanded regulations to systematic critical review; and (4) to address the issue of political feasibility associated with efforts to reform and improve regulatory activity.

All of the chapters contained in this book were prepared by leading authorities of regulatory policy who participated in a national conference entitled "Reforming Government Regulation: Alternative Strategies to Social Regulatory Policy." The chapters by Eugene Bardach and Robert A. Kagan, Robert W. Hahn and Roger G. Noll, Alfred E. Kahn, William A. Niskanen, and David Harrison, Jr., and Paul R. Portney were presented, in slightly different form, at the conference. David Leo Weimer has contributed a study focusing on drug regulation, a topic that was not covered in detail at the meeting.

In addition to the insights presented by the major speakers at the conference, many valuable ideas, comments, and caveats were offered during formal and informal discussions. Prepared critiques of the papers offered exceedingly important ideas, and some of these presentations have been edited and included as chapters in this volume. The editors' introductory and concluding material also incorporates many of the points that were raised in order to add to an understanding of the issues.

David Leo Weimer's analysis in Chapter 2 of regulation by the Food and Drug Administration (FDA) reveals several factors that can lead to what seem to be highly restrictive practices by regulatory agencies. Ideally, federal regulators would control or outlaw only those products that all fully informed people would wish to avoid. However, when not everyone wants to avoid the same things, regulators are imposing a cost upon anyone preferring an outlawed option. For example, the FDA's withholding of a drug from the marketplace while awaiting a high degree of assurance against risks may cause severe consequences for those not having access to the benefits of the medication. In no other area of the new social regulation is this type of trade-off more dramatic.

Furthermore, Weimer argues that decision making within the FDA has been heavily tipped toward avoiding or delaying approvals. Since it would be far more damaging to authorize the sale of a drug that later was found to produce harmful side effects than to prevent the sale of a drug that might do considerable good, the FDA tends not to authorize the sale of a drug unless it has nearly perfect information about its possible side effects.

Weimer's examination of the way drug regulation functions also helps us to understand the political and legal context in which regulatory agencies function. Reforming the social regulatory structure requires an understanding of the forces that impinge on regulators, as well as the latitude and restrictions of the mandate under which agencies operate.

In Chapter 3, William A. Niskanen focuses on the complex interaction of several different kinds of regulatory policies on the automobile industry. He argues that not only are several of the individual regulations unsuccessful in achieving desired outcomes at reasonable costs, they frequently function at cross purposes. Fuel economy standards have had the effect of reducing safety, while safety and emissions standards result in reduced fuel economy. In particular, Niskanen criticizes the regulators' failure to develop consistent objectives, their overreliance on design standards and the uniform application of performance standards, their failure to consider alternatives to regulation, and their failure to target enforcement efforts where the payoff would be greatest. He attributes these failures to flaws in the design of the regulatory apparatus — flaws that lead to excess standardization, caution, and inflexibility.

Michael E. Levine and John Mendeloff challenge several of Niskanen's claims about the magnitude of benefits and costs associated with various regulations. In particular, Levine rejects the claim that fuel economy standards had a substantial adverse effect on the industry, although he would agree with Niskanen that these standards ought now to be withdrawn. Mendeloff questions Niskanen's claim that a mandatory passive restraint standard is without justification, although he appears to agree that it makes sense to defer a decision to require passive restraints until such time as the alternatives to, and the consequences of, such a requirement are better understood.

Despite Levine and Mendeloff's disagreements with Niskanen, all three of these authors agree on one key point: The *methods* used to deal with the problems addressed by the new social regulation are often inappropriate, frequently contradictory, and fail to achieve goals in the most efficient manner. Moreover, they appear to agree in their diagnosis of the source of these failings. In Chapters 4 and 5 Mendeloff and Levine set forth their diagnoses of the main difficulties associated with existing automobile regulation strategies and give some clues as to the possible reforms that could be developed.

In Chapter 6, Robert W. Hahn and Roger G. Noll examine one of the efforts to design regulatory schemes that avoid some of the costs and organizational problems associated with command-and-control approaches to regulation. Tradable emissions permits would introduce a system under which the socially desired goal of limiting emissions would be administered through a market system. Permits for emissions would have an economic value and holders would find it economically advantageous to limit emissions, thus reducing the need to hold permits. The chapter addresses several of the concerns and objections to this approach and offers some promising preliminary results based on analysis of the Los Angeles air basin. The efforts by the Environmental Protection Agency (EPA) to experiment with alternatives to standard setting and direct regulation of site pollution depend on the kind of research reflected in this chapter.

Chapter 7 broadens and continues the discussion of tradable emissions permits. James E. Krier provides an overview of several marketlike approaches to pollution control, assesses the legal issues associated with the use of tradable permits, and comments on the feasibility of such an approach. Roy N. Gamse, writing from experience gained in the relevant federal regulatory agency (EPA), explains how the proposed tradable permits scheme would fit within the agency's program to promote marketlike approaches to all pollution problems. Gamse also discusses the political and administrative obstacles to implementing these strategies. Finally, W. R. Z. Willey raises some serious challenges to the use of tradable permits. For both political and technical reasons he is concerned that the goals of protecting air quality standards cannot be achieved on the basis of what is now known. Thus, he calls for experiments with alternatives to assess their potential for achieving the desired social objectives more effectively and efficiently.

Much of discussion about the new social regulation, as well as the alternatives to regulation, is conducted at the macro level. One finds little discussion of the practical details of the activities and tasks performed by the regulators, their interactions with private-sector organizations, or the behavior of their counterparts in the private sector. If one of the fundamental problems with the new social regulation is with its means and not its ends, what is needed is careful, empirically based institutional and organizational analysis and design.

Based upon an extensive field investigation of the interaction between regulators and regulated organizations, Eugene Bardach and Robert A. Kagan, in Chapter 10, explain the institutional basis for much of the inflexibility and unreasonableness of the regulatory inspectorate and assess the competence of industry personnel to identify and to solve the problems that the new social regulation was intended to treat. Their research reinforces Weimer's conclusion that bureaucratic risk avoidance leads to overregulation and to inflexibility on the part of regulatory agencies. The chapter by Bardach and Kagan also presents a reasoned argument for employing a combination of private, quasi-private, and public-private regulatory schemes.

To say that better methods exist is not, however, to say that they will be adopted. In Chapter 11, David Harrison, Jr., and Paul R. Portney survey the attempts that have been made, and the proposals offered, to improve regulatory methods by changing the regulatory decision-making process, by setting performance standards for the regulators to meet, and by changing the incentives facing the regulators to motivate them to make better decisions. In addition, the authors review proposals to alter the enabling legislation under which regulations are promulgated and to institute major structural reforms that would shift the basis of control over the regulatory process to the executive office or to Congress. These latter reform proposals include the so-called omnibus proposals, regulatory cost accounting and budgeting proposals, and legislative veto proposals.

The political will and ability to capture a place on the public agenda is critical not only to the enactment of new legislation, but to the reform and restructuring of existing governmental practices. All of the good analyses and prescriptions will be wasted if their promulgators lack the understanding of how to negotiate the political environment. This entails an understanding of the broader political context as well as the workings of the political process. Alfred E. Kahn, whose scholarly work has for years addressed the theory of government regulation, also has functioned in the political environment as a leader in regulatory reform. In Chapter 12 he addresses the conditions necessary to institute political reform. From his intellectual and practical experience with reform in areas of economic regulation he draws important lessons for how changes might be brought about in the areas of social and protective regulations.

The final chapter draws on the several contributors to the book and the broader literature on regulation, economics, and political science to analyze the prospects for reforming the new social regulation.

Public support for maintaining a cleaner and safer environment remains strong. At the same time, there is stiff competition for economic resources and general impatience with the intrusiveness and inefficiencies generated by government regulations. Designing public policies that can reconcile these competing demands and sometimes conflicting desires is not an easy task. It is encouraging to find research and experience that offer prospects for continuing to pursue some of the objectives of social regulations, while promising to reduce some of the unnecessary and counterproductive effects of regulation strategies adopted earlier. This book attempts to bring some of that creative thinking and analysis to this task.

PART I

Diagnosis and Prescription
Problems with the Existing Regulatory Regime

2

Organizational Incentives

Safe – and Available – Drugs

DAVID LEO WEIMER

Diantha Ain, of Simi Valley, California, suffered so much pain from a ruptured spinal disk that she could hardly walk. Ahead of her lay the possibility of a four-hour operation to remove the disk and fuse her spine into position by means of pieces of bone removed from her pelvis. But her orthopedist suggested she first try a less drastic procedure — the injection of a substance called chymopapain that might shrink the ruptured disk and give her relief. The 48-year-old housewife took the advice, received the injection, and was able to walk out of the hospital the next day.

But there was one major complication: Mrs. Ain had to go all the way to Vancouver, in Canada, because chymopapain is not approved by the U.S. Food and Drug Administration. . . .

Bernard S. Abrams, a Columbus, Ohio, physicist, flew his daughter Felice to England last year to get sodium valproate —

AUTHOR'S NOTE: Reprinted by permission of the publisher from *Instead of Regulation: Alternatives to Federal Regulatory Agencies,* edited by Robert W. Poole, Jr. (Lexington, MA: Lexington Books, D.C. Heath and Company, Copyright 1981, D.C. Heath and Company).

I would like to thank William M. Wardell and the Center for the Study of Drug Development of the University of Rochester for valuable assistance. Martin M. Eisman, Robert W. Poole, Jr., Lynda Powell, and William Riker made helpful comments. I would also like to thank Peter Barton Hutt for thoughtful comments on an earlier paper on a similar topic. The conclusions and errors, however, are solely mine.

the only medication that could control the 6-year-old's epileptic seizures. He then waged a campaign, including the threat of a class-action suit on behalf of epilepsy victims, that finally helped put the drug on the U.S. market.

— "How Bad the Drug Lag?"
Newsweek, October 9, 1978

Reduction in the loss of life, limb, and health is a laudable goal, pursued by a variety of federal regulatory agencies. In general, at often substantial economic costs to society, these regulatory efforts do improve the health and safety of at least some people without impairing the health and safety of the remainder. There is, however, one very important class of products whose regulation increases safety for some consumers while simultaneously impairing the health of others. Under our current system of regulation of pharmaceuticals, beneficial as well as harmful drugs are precluded from the market.

The Food and Drug Administration (FDA) has statutory responsibility for ensuring that pharmaceuticals marketed in the United States are safe and effective for the use for which they are labeled. In addition, the agency is responsible for promoting safety and quality standards for the food and cosmetics industries. The FDA's endeavors in regulating these industries have produced uncertain benefits at considerable cost. Although reviewing all of the FDA's activities would be fruitful, its regulation of pharmaceuticals deserves special attention, both because that regulation has such critical consequences for the health and safety of the public, and because the task involves especially complex cost-benefit calculations. Furthermore, any suggestions of alternative solutions for providing the public with safe and effective drugs would, very probably, be applicable in principle to the food and cosmetics industries.

Because any therapeutically active drug cannot be totally safe, the absolute standards of safety and efficacy implied by U.S. law are unrealistic. A more reasonable approach, one actually employed by the FDA, is to consider efficacy relative to safety: Greater levels of risk are tolerated for drugs offering greater potential benefits. The benefit-risk concept is borrowed from medical practice, where it describes the calculus physicians use in deciding whether or not to administer specific drugs to specific patients. If the benefits expected from administration of the drug outweigh the perceived risks, the drug will be given to the patient. Further, if alternative drugs are available, the one with the most favorable benefit-risk ratio will be selected for the patient.

There are serious problems, however, in applying the benefit-risk criterion to decisions concerning the availability of drugs to society rather than to individuals. The societal benefit-risk ratio may be unfavorable for the population as a whole yet be very favorable for specific groups of patients. In such situations, an overly conservative or inflexible application of the benefit-risk criterion would block the availability of a drug that is beneficial, perhaps lifesaving, to some groups of patients. These forgone benefits are clearly one cost of attempting to achieve greater safety for the population as a whole through regulation. If physicians, in the absense of regulation, prescribed controversial drugs only to patient groups with favorable benefit-risk ratios, regulatory action would actually represent a net loss in the aggregate health of the population.

Central to our current system of pharmaceutical regulation is the power of the FDA to grant or withhold permission for marketing. For every drug, regulatory action will result in one of two types of harm.[1] If a drug is allowed to be marketed, harm will result to some people—either directly, through adverse reactions, or indirectly, by displacing more efficacious treatment. If a drug is not allowed on the market, harm will result to some people, who are denied therapeutic benefit. Under our current regulatory structure, the best the FDA can attempt to do is estimate the magnitude of these harms and make the decision generating the lesser harm. Theoretically, equal weight should be given to each type of harm. But the political environment in which the FDA operates encourages it to be more careful about inflicting harm through approvals than through denials. As David Seidman points out, the victims of adverse reactions are much more easily identified than those suffering because drugs beneficial to them have not been approved.[2] The FDA frequently has to defend its approval decisions before congressional oversight committees, but almost never has to defend its decisions to prohibit marketing.[3] In light of this political pressure, it would be surprising if the FDA were not overly cautious in approving new drugs. Similarly, the political environment has led the FDA to adopt even more extensive regulations aimed at reducing the harm from approved drugs.

Federal Drug Regulation: Legislative Landmarks

Over the last 75 years, federal regulation of pharmaceuticals has been increasing at an accelerating rate. During this time, 3 legislative landmarks have marked changes in regulatory philosophy: the Pure Food and Drugs Act of 1906, the Food, Drug, and Cosmetic Act of 1938, and the Kefauver-Harris Amendments of 1962.

These legislative landmarks share a number of similarities. After years of inconclusive debate, each was passed speedily in the wake of public outcry and newfound presidential support accompanying sensational incidents. Each aroused both opponents and proponents among the industries being regulated. The issues each law addressed were kept before the public prior to passage by the sustained efforts of a small number of individuals or groups. Most significant, each law substantially increased the role of the federal government in the regulation of pharmaceuticals.

The Pure Food and Drugs Act of 1906 was the culmination of a long campaign led by Dr. Harvey Wiley, then director of the Division of Chemistry of the U.S. Department of Agriculture, against the misbranding and adulteration of food and drugs. Wiley initiated the move for national legislation by drawing attention to the increasing use of food preservatives and the fraudulent adulteration of foods that was occurring at the turn of the century. The effort soon expanded to include patent medicines, which often contained, without warning to consumers, harmful or addictive substances. Magazines such as *Ladies Home Journal* and *Collier's* ran exposés drawing attention to the abuses of the patent- and proprietary-medicine trades.[4] Although the efforts of Wiley and other reformers led to a steady stream of pure food and drug bills, beginning in 1900, legislation seemed to be always just beyond reach.

As might be expected, major opposition to the bills came from several of the industries that would be subject to regulation. The patent-medicine trade and the rectifiers of whiskey became the dominant opponents of legislation. Other manufacturers falling under the proposed legislation became leading proponents. Cream of tartar manufacturers saw labeling requirements as a way to gain advantage over sellers of powder of alum.[5] Drug manufacturers with products appearing in the National Formulary and the United States Pharmacopoeia, and even some of the larger patent- and proprietary-medicine manufacturers, saw pure drug legislation as a way of eliminating the competition of nostrum sellers.

A breakthrough toward pure food and drug regulation did not occur until 1906, when President Theodore Roosevelt began applying pressure on congressional leaders. Before 1906, Roosevelt had not provided active support for such legislation. In that year, however, Upton Sinclair's *The Jungle* appeared. Roosevelt was shocked, not only by Sinclair's book, but also by the reaction of meat packers to corroboration provided by an independent investigation he had initiated. With Roosevelt's support, a pure food and drug act was passed by Congress on June 30, 1906.

The act defined *drug* as any medicine or preparation "recognized in the United States Pharmacopoeia or National Formulary for internal or external use, and any substance or mixture of substances intended to be used for the cure, mitigation, or prevention of disease in either man or other animals."[6] Under the act, a drug was considered adulterated if either its strength or its purity fell below the professed standard of quality under which it was sold, or if it had a different strength, quality, or purity from that specified in the United States Pharmacopoeia or National Formulary and was not so labeled. The act considered a drug misbranded if it was offered for sale under the name of another drug or if its package failed to bear a label indicating the quantity or proportion of any alcohol, morphine, opium, cocaine, heroin, alpha or beta eucaine, chloroform, cannabis indica, chloral hydrate, or acetanilide. A drug was also considered misbranded if its labeling was false or misleading in any particular. The Bureau of Chemistry of the Department of Agriculture was given authority to examine food and drugs transported or sold in interstate or foreign trade to determine whether they were adulterated or misbranded. Individual shipments found to be adulterated, misbranded, or of a "poisonous or deleterious character" could be seized for confiscation by a process of libel for condemnation in the federal courts. The power to make rules and regulations for implementing the act was given jointly to the secretaries of the Departments of Treasury, Agriculture, and Commerce and Labor.

The Food and Drug Administration, established by the Department of Agriculture in 1927 to take over the regulatory activities of the Bureau of Chemistry, had little success in controlling the large number of nostrums that were being sold widely. Although a 1912 amendment to the 1906 act attempted to strengthen control over labeling, the FDA still had to show that therapeutic claims were false and fraudulent in order for a drug to be deemed misbranded. Showing fraudulent intent was extremely difficult. Even when the FDA was successful, the seller simply shifted the offending claims from labeling to radio, newspaper, or direct-mail advertising, which were not subject to FDA regulation.

There was small but growing public support for stronger federal food and drug legislation in the early 1930s. Consumer advocates Arthur Kallet and F. J. Schlink drew public attention to the weakness of the FDA in their popular book, *100,000,000 Guinea Pigs*.[7] At its 1930 national convention, the American Pharmaceutical Manufacturers Association, representing the more scientifically advanced drug manufacturers, called for federal legislation that would allow the Department of Agriculture to control the advertising of drug products.[8] The sustained effort for new legislation, however, came from the FDA itself. In 1933, Walter Campbell, chief of the FDA, with the support of Assistant Secretary of Agriculture Rexford Tugwell, began a five-year campaign to secure new legislation. Although they were able to keep legislative proposals before the Congress during this period through the vigorous advocacy of Senator Royal Copeland, lack of presidential support and opposition from segments of the food, drug, and publishing industries stalled the legislative effort.

After 4 years of inconclusive debate, the public outcry and professional reassessment that followed in the wake of the Elixir Sulfanilamide disaster finally precipitated passage of a new food and drug law.[9] By 1937, sulfanilamide was being used widely for its dramatic curative effects in the treatment of such infectious diseases as gonorrhea and septicemia. In September of that year, without conducting tests to detect toxicity, the Samuel E. Massengill Company began marketing a liquid version of sulfanilamide that used diethylene glycol, a substance generally known to be toxic, as a solvent. Elixir Sulfanilamide proved highly toxic, causing 107 deaths from kidney failure before the FDA was able to account for the 2 batches of the drug that had been distributed. The FDA based its seizures on the charge that Elixir Sulfanilamide was misbranded because "elixir" implied alcoholic content, of which it had none. That the FDA had to rely on this technicality pointed to the inadequacy of the 1906 act. The disaster, and its coverage by the press, generated widespread public interest, which forced congressional action.

The Food, Drug, and Cosmetic Act of 1938 expanded the definition of *drug* to include medical devices and added the Homeopathic Pharmacopoeia as an official standard.[10] Drugs appearing on one of the official compendia had to meet the stated standards of strength, quality, and purity or had to state explicitly, on their labels, the extent of difference. Drugs not appearing in one of the official compendia had to list in their labeling the active ingredients in alphabetical order, as well as the name, quantity, and proportion of 19 specified drugs that were considered potentially dangerous. Additionally, drugs containing any of 17 narcotic and hypnotic ingredients had to list the name, amount, and percentage of each, along with a warning that the drug might be habit-forming. Except for drugs that were to be dispensed only by physicians' prescriptions, the act required that labeling contain adequate information for safe use. A drug would be considered misbranded if it was dangerous to health when used in the dosage or with the frequency or duration prescribed, recommended, or suggested in its labeling.

The FDA was given greater leverage over therapeutic claims made in labeling through a redefinition of misbranding to include any claims that were false or misleading in any particular. The FDA did not, however, gain control over drug advertising. Believing advertising control by the Federal Trade Commission (FTC) would be less onerous, much of the drug trade supported the Wheeler-Lea Amendment as a way to avoid giving advertising control to the FDA.[11] Under the Wheeler-Lea Amendment, harm to consumers would be added to harm to honest competitors as grounds for FTC intervention in cases of false and misleading advertising.

The FDA did gain authority to control the introduction of new drugs into interstate commerce. Manufacturers were required to file applications for new drugs, to report on tests performed to determine their safety, to indicate their composition, and to describe how they would be manufactured. A manufacturer could begin marketing within 60 days of filing the application unless the FDA gave notice that more time was needed for study (up to 180 days) or unless the FDA, after due notice and opportunity for hearing, refused the application because it found that inadequate or inconclusive tests had been conducted, or that the results of the tests showed that the product was unsafe for use under the conditions recommended in the labeling, or the quality control in manufacturing was judged to be inadequate. The FDA was also given authority to suspend applications if new evidence came to light showing the drug to be unsafe or if the application was found to contain any untrue statement of a material fact.

The pharmaceutical industry prospered under the 1938 law. In the 20 years that followed its passage, an avalanche of new drugs flowed from the laboratories of the pharmaceutical manufacturers. Although many of the drugs introduced were close substitutes for ones already on the market (the "me too" drugs), a substantial number represented major medical advances. High profits accompanied the growth in new products. By 1958, the drug industry appeared to be enjoying a rate of profit on invested capital almost twice that of the average for all manufacturing firms.

The apparently high rates of return in the drug industry attracted the attention of Senator Estes Kefauver, chairman of the Subcommittee on Antitrust and Monopoly of the Committee of the Judiciary.[12] In December 1959, Kefauver began investigative hearings into the pricing practices of the pharmaceutical companies. The skill with which he conducted these hearings caught many drug companies, as well as the newly formed Pharmaceutical Manufacturers Association (PMA), off guard.[13] Drawing attention to high markups on specific drug products, Kefauver was able to generate considerable press interest in the hearings. In April 1961, Kefauver concluded 10 months of investigative hearings and introduced a drug bill that had as a primary focus the enhancement of price competition. A major provision called for mandatory licensing of drug patents to manufacturers who were willing to pay royalties of up to 8 percent of sales.

Kefauver was unsuccessful, however, in gaining administration support for his bill. Eventually, criticism from the press and from the AFL-CIO prompted President Kennedy to write a letter to Senator James Eastland, urging action on a weakened version of the bill, which was stuck in the Judiciary Committee. Just as in 1938, it took a pharmacological disaster and the accompanying public furor to bring about the presidential involvement necessary to secure congressional passage of a drug bill.

In July 1962, the press began to report that women who had taken the sedative thalidomide during pregnancy were giving birth to a disproportionate number of children with serious birth defects.[14] Most of the reports were based on experience in Europe, where thalidomide had been on the market since 1957. Thalidomide was not marketed in the United States. In September 1960, the Richardson-Merrell Company, which had bought the rights from the German pharmaceutical company Gruenenthal to market thalidomide in the United States, submitted a new drug application to the FDA for Kevadon, the trade name it intended to use for thalidomide. For more than a year, Richardson-Merrell tried to secure favorable action on its application. The FDA officer handling the application, Dr. Frances Kelsey, withheld approval on the grounds that the application did not meet the standards necessary for certification of safety. While waiting for marketing approval, Richardson-Merrell distributed Kevadon to more than 1200 doctors for clinical testing. This distribution is believed to have caused from 10 to 16 known cases of birth defects in the United States. First reports of these cases fed the growing concern among the public over drug safety that led to passage of the Kefauver-Harris Amendments to the 1938 Food, Drug, and Cosmetic Act.[15]

The Kefauver-Harris Amendments, signed into law by President Kennedy in October 1962, did not contain the mandatory licensing provision for which Kefauver had fought the hardest. Despite drug industry lobbying efforts that persisted right through the Senate-House conference on the bill, a strong advertising provision was included. Prescription drug advertising was required to carry the established, or generic, name in type at least half as large as the trade or brand name. The quantity of each ingredient in drugs was required to be displayed in the advertising to the same extent that it had to appear in labeling. Advertising for prescription drugs also had to show "such other information in brief summary relating to side effects, contraindications, and effectiveness as shall be issued by the Secretary [of HEW]."[16] Enforcement of prescription drug advertising regulations was shifted from the FTC to the FDA, and the secretary of the Department of Health, Education and Welfare was given authority to review and revise the established names given to drugs in the official compendia.[17]

The amendments specified that the FDA must certify drugs as effective as well as safe under the conditions of use prescribed, recommended, or suggested in their labeling. The new drug application (NDA) was required to show "substantial evidence" of safety and efficacy. Substantial evidence was defined as "consisting of adequate and well-controlled investigations, including clinical investigations, by experts qualified by scientific training and experience to evaluate the effectiveness of the drug involved, on the basis of which it could fairly and responsibly be concluded by such experts that the drug will have the effect it purports or is represented to have."[18] The FDA was given 180 days either to accept the NDA or to notify the applicant of the right to a hearing on the application. Once an NDA was accepted, the applicant was required to maintain records of clinical experience or other information related to the drug in accordance with regulations established by the secretary. If the secretary found that a drug posed imminent hazard to the public health, he would have the authority to suspend the NDA.

A totally new provision gave the FDA authority to regulate clinical trials that were conducted prior to submission of the NDA. Manufacturers wishing to begin clinical testing of a drug were now required to submit a notice of claimed investigational exemption for a new drug (IND), which presented preclinical tests justifying the proposed clinical trials, indicated the formal agreement between the manufacturer and the clinical investigators specifying the nature of the trials, and stated the procedures that would be followed in maintaining records of the trials. Additionally, the FDA was granted the right of access to records kept by the clinical investigators.

Although a number of bills intended to reform the regulation of pharmaceuticals have been actively debated in Congress since 1976, including passage of one by the Senate in September 1979, the Kefauver-Harris Amendments continue to provide the basic framework governing the FDA.

The FDA in Action

Fundamental to an understanding of current regulatory practices is an overview of the way the FDA has implemented its authority over the development and promotion of drugs. Regulations related to the determination of safety and efficacy have grown in complexity and comprehensiveness since 1962. So, too, have regulations governing promotion.

How Can a New Drug Get to Market?

Under Section 505 (i) of the 1938 law, the FDA had authority to promulgate regulations governing the distribution of drugs for investigational use. The regulations initially issued by the FDA required that manufacturers keep records of the distribution of drugs for investigational purposes, that investigators sign statements that they had adequate training and facilities to safely conduct the investigations, and that labels contain the statement, "Caution: New Drug; Limited by Federal law to investigational use." These regulations permitted the distribution of thalidomide to more than 1200 physicians. The same furor that led to passage of the 1962 amendments prompted the FDA to revise its regulations for investigational drugs. In August 1962, prior to passage of the Kefauver-Harris Amendments, the FDA published regulations that, in effect, established an IND procedure. They required that only qualified investigators be used, that their qualifications be filed with the FDA, that drugs be tested on humans only after animal testing, that the FDA be kept fully informed of the results of the testing, and that special precautions be taken in testing drugs intended for use by children or pregnant women.[19] This is one of several instances in which proposed legislative changes were anticipated in FDA regulations.

In June 1963, the FDA established a formal IND process. The first step of the process is the submission of an IND application by the drug sponsor that must include all data from preclinical testing on animals, relevant literature on toxicity and pharmacology, and detailed plans for the proposed clinical testing, with protocols for each investigator. After a 30-day wait, the sponsor may begin clinical testing if the FDA has not rejected the IND. At intervals not exceeding 1 year, the sponsor must submit progress reports to the FDA. Any findings that suggest significant side effects must be reported immediately.

Clinical investigation is divided into three phases. Phase I involves the administration of the drug to a small number of healthy subjects to determine the range of safe doses and the nature of the pharmacological actions of the drug in the human body. Phase II involves detailed, controlled studies involving a small group of patients to gain information about the efficacy of the drug in treating a specific disease and the safety associated with its use. During Phase III, longer-term studies are completed to gain further information about safety and efficacy. The Phase III studies typically involve a substantial number of patients treated in a clinical setting. After completion of these three phases, the sponsor prepares and submits an NDA if the results suggest that substantial evidence of safety and efficacy has been developed.

With the appointment of a new FDA commissioner in 1966, the regulations governing the IND process became more detailed.[20] At the same time, the FDA was faced with the task of determining the efficacy of all the drugs whose NDAs had been approved between 1938 and 1962. Lacking sufficient scientific human resources to complete this task, the FDA contracted in 1966 with the National

Academy of Sciences and its research arm, the National Research Council, for a review of the efficacy of the approximately 4,000 drug products introduced during this period.[21]. The NAS-NRC project involved the participation of approximately 200 experts formed into 30 panels. The panels reviewed 16,573 specific therapeutic claims. Eventually, all of the drug products considered were put into 6 categories: effective, probably effective, possibly effective, effective but not for all recommended uses, ineffective as a fixed combination, and ineffective. Drugs for which substantial evidence was believed to exist were classified as effective, while those for which no substantial evidence was believed to exist were classified as ineffective. Manufacturers whose drugs were found probably effective were given 12 months to submit additional evidence before the FDA withdrew their NDAs. Manufacturers of possibly effective drugs were given 6 months to submit additional evidence. Manufacturers of ineffective drugs were given 30 days. Manufacturers that did not meet the deadlines were required to begin new clinical tests to demonstrate the efficacy of their products.

By the end of 1970, about 7 percent of the prescription drugs reviewed were found to lack substantial evidence of efficacy for any claim.[22] Because many of these drugs enjoyed considerable sales, efforts by the FDA to remove them from the market were vigorously opposed by their manufacturers. Faced with the prospect of having to grant hearings to manufacturers whose products were ordered withdrawn, the FDA decided to issue stringent regulations defining substantial evidence in order to limit the range of evidence that would have to be considered in hearings. It also developed a two-stage system of summary judgment that severely restricted the number of hearings that would have to be held prior to withdrawal of an NDA.[23]

Regulations defining adequate and well-controlled clinical investigations were published in final form in the *Federal Register* on May 8, 1970. To be considered adequate and well controlled, studies were required to have protocols and reports of results that included clear statements of objectives, adequate assurance of suitability of the selected subjects for the study, assignment of subjects to test groups in such a way as to minimize bias and ensure comparability between treatment and control groups, and discussion of the methods used to minimize bias on the part of subjects and observers. Four types of control groups were recognized: no treatment, placebo treatment, active treatment, and historical comparison. The last group would be recognized as acceptable only in limited circumstances. Uncontrolled studies or partially controlled studies were declared unacceptable as the sole basis for approving claims of effectiveness.[24]

Regulations related to standards for clinical research became more extensive in the 1970s. In March 1971 the FDA required that IND holders have their research initially approved and regularly monitored by institutional review boards (IRBs). During the 1960s, the National Institutes of Health began requiring that researchers receiving grants or contracts for projects involving human subjects have their research proposals reviewed by boards consisting of physicians, scientists, and others. The 1971 regulations extended the coverage of the IRBs to all drug research, thus adding local monitoring of clinical research to that already provided for in the IND process. In August 1978, the FDA proposed regulations that would extend the responsibility of the IRBs to ensure that protocols conform to FDA standards.[25] The regulations established stricter standards of patient supervision by investigators and extended IRB coverage to all products regulated by the FDA. Included are medical devices, which became subject to premarketing clearance after passage of legislation in 1976.

The FDA has taken a number of steps over the years in response to the criticism that the IND-NDA process is overly burdensome. Beginning in 1969, the FDA allowed manufacturers to submit abbreviated NDAs if they wished to market drugs that had already been sponsored through the NDA process by other manufacturers.[26] In 1971, the FDA participated in a joint effort with the Pharmaceutical Manufacturers Association to set guidelines for preparation of IND and NDA submissions.[27] In 1974, in response to criticism that the FDA was taking too long to approve the NDAs of drugs with potentially large therapeutic impacts, the FDA implemented a drug classification system. Under this system, the FDA identifies drugs that it believes have potential for providing therapeutic breakthroughs and attempts to speed up the processing of their NDAs. Although the average processing time from submission to approval has continued to increase since 1974, the average for the drugs put on the fast track has remained constant.[28]

Perhaps the regulatory trend with the greatest potential impact on the IND-NDA process is the move by the FDA to increase the use of postmarketing studies. A major criticism of the current system of new drug regulation is that it places too much emphasis on premarketing studies for the determination of safety and efficacy. Some observers advocate greater reliance on postmarketing studies as substitutes for portions of the premarketing studies now required, while others view postmarketing studies as necessary complements to the existing system. Beginning with the Kennedy-Javits bill in 1975, all the major proposals for drug-reform legislation have called for greater use of postmarketing studies. Since 1970, the FDA, in several instances, has imposed postmarketing studies as conditions for marketing approval.[29] If the current regulatory trend continues, eventual passage of the legislative proposals calling for the greater use of postmarketing studies will be largely irrelevant.

The aggregate impact of the IND-NDA regulations issued since 1962 has been to increase the time and money manufacturers must invest in bringing new drugs to market and to delay or inhibit consumer access to potentially beneficial products. The NDA submissions often run between 50,000 and 100,000 pages per drug, with summaries of 4,000 to 5,000 pages.[30] In October 1979, the FDA published a concept paper suggesting revisions of the IND-NDA regulations.[31] Many of the proposals would further increase the amount of material that manufacturers must submit during the IND-NDA process. These changes, and the prospect of postmarketing studies becoming a mandatory fourth phase in the IND-NDA process, point to even higher costs of bringing new drugs to the market in the future.

What Can Be Said About a Drug?

Promotional activity can be divided into three categories: labeling, general advertising, and direct contact. Although it is defined more comprehensively for regulatory purposes, labeling refers to information provided by the manufacturer and distributed with the drug. General advertising consists of information about the drug that is disseminated through the print and broadcast media. For prescription drugs it is limited almost exclusively to publications directed at physicians, while for over-the-counter drugs it appears in the mass media. Promotion through direct contact involves the provision of information about drugs directly to health professionals on an individual basis. Direct mailings, distribution of free samples, and, most important, the activities of drug company detail people (salespersons), who personally visit doctors and pharmacists, are the elements of direct-contact promotion. Because most direct-contact promotion falls under the scope of regulations governing labeling and general advertising, it will not be considered explicitly in our discussion of the evolution of controls over promotion.[32]

The Pure Food and Drug Act prohibited labeling that was false or misleading. In 1911, the Supreme Court ruled, in United States v. Johnson, that the 1906 law did not apply to claims about therapeutic or curative effects.[33] In response, in 1912, Congress passed the Sherley Amendment, which prohibited false and fraudulent curative or therapeutic claims in labeling.

Between 1930 and 1962, the FDA issued a number of regulations that extended its control over labeling. In November 1948, the FDA issued regulations that defined labeling to include all written, printed, and graphic material used in the promotion of drugs, whether or not the promotional material accompanied the drug in the same interstate shipment. These regulations had the effect of expanding the definition of labeling to include direct-mail advertising and information distributed by detail people. In December 1960, the FDA issued regulations that required labeling to include notice of any hazards, contraindications, side effects, and precautions relevant to all conditions for which the drug is advertised or represented. In the following year, regulations were published requiring that each package of a prescription drug contain complete information for physicians. As the FDA was unable to regulate advertising directly, the physician package insert represented an attempt to provide an alternative source of information to prescribing physicians. Such an approach is of questionable effectiveness, because the package insert usually goes to the pharmacist rather than to the physician. However, the package inserts are compiled in the *Physician's Desk Reference*, a major source of drug information that is distributed to most physicians.

In the five years following the 1962 amendments, the FDA issued a number of regulations under the authority it gained to regulate the advertising of prescription drugs.[34] The first regulations were intended to make advertising and labeling consistent in content. "Fair balance" was required in the presentation of the information on effectiveness, side effects, and contraindications. The presentation of the information was also considered. Information on side effects and contraindications was to be given equal prominence with other information presented in the advertisement. Although the 1962 amendments refer to full disclosure of effectiveness, side effects, and contraindications in "brief summary," the FDA has required that fair balance be maintained throughout the advertisement.

In 1967 the FDA issued regulations that further specified the form and content of prescription drug advertisements. A total of 34 practices that could cause an advertisement to be considered misleading or false were listed. In the same year the FDA stepped up its enforcement of advertising regulations. Companies found to be making false, misleading, and unsupportable claims were forced to write corrective letters ("dear doctor letters") to all practicing physicians. By fiscal year 1974, the FDA was annually reviewing more than 20,000 advertisments. More than 450 were in-depth reviews, and more than 300 corrective actions were taken.[35]

In June 1979, after 5 years of debate and public comment, the FDA issued comprehensive regulations covering the content and format of labeling and prescription drug advertising. The regulations cover 6 pages and the commissioner's comments 28 pages in the *Federal Register.*[36]

A major change in the regulations governing prescription drug advertising is the prohibition of claims or suggestions that the advertised drug is safer or more effective than some other drug, unless the difference has been demonstrated by substantial evidence. Comparative claims must now be approved as part of the labeling submitted with a new drug application. Additionally, manufacturers are neither allowed to refer to published studies as evidence of relative effectiveness or safety nor permitted to give quantitative statements of effectiveness or safety, unless such information has been approved in the new drug application. By requiring that information of this sort be used only if it has been approved for labeling, those regulations have the effect of establishing a preclearance procedure for comaprative claims.

One other area of regulatory activity related to promotion deserves note: the move toward mandatory patient package inserts for prescription drugs. Prior to 1938, any drug, with the exception of certain narcotics, could be purchased without a prescription. Under the 1938 law, the FDA created the distinction between over-the-counter and prescription drugs through the regulations it established for implementing its authority to waive labeling requirements.[37] If a drug was limited to distribution by physicians and its labeling contained language not likely to be understood by laypersons, it was exempted from the 1938 law's requirements for adequate directions for use and warning. In 1951, the distinction created administratively by the FDA was built into the Food, Drug, and Costmetic Act with the Durham-Humphrey Amendment. With creation of the prescription drug category came the ethical standard that they would not be promoted to laypersons. [38]

During the last ten years, the belief that patients should not be provided information about prescription drugs except through their physicians has been challenged. Since 1976, the major proposals for drug-reform legislation have included provisions requiring patient package inserts for virtually all drugs. Not wanting to be beat to the punch, the FDA has proposed general regulations requiring patient package inserts as a standard component of prescription drug labeling.[39]

This brief history of federal drug regulation suggests that the FDA must not be viewed simply as an administrative body implementing the will of Congress as expressed in law. The FDA played an active part in generating support for the 1938 law. In creating the prescription drug category, in issuing clinical testing standards in 1962, in moving toward postmarketing studies, and in proposing mandatory patient package inserts, the FDA has anticipated legislation through its regulations. The expansion appears to feed upon itself.[40] Although each step in the expansion may appear reasonable by itself, the aggregate effect may be unreasonable.

FDA Activity: Benefits and Risks

Since the 1970s, the FDA has been caught in a cross fire of criticism. On one side are consumer advocates and a number of congressional committee and subcommittee chair-persons who believe the FDA allows too many unsafe and ineffective drugs to reach the market. On the other side is the pharmaceutical industry, supported by a substantial body of academic research, arguing that the FDA is too cautious in approving new drugs. As if these critics were not enough, the FDA has faced a steady stream of executive branch studies that have drawn attention to a variety of administrative failings. Are the conflicting criticisms simply an indication that the FDA must balance competing interests better in making the right decisions for society? Do the administrative criticisms suggest that we could expect substantially better regulatory decisions if the FDA had better personnel? Neither question can be answered affirmatively.

The Premarketing Dilemma

Before outlining specific criticisms related to the outcome of FDA decision making, a more fundamental proposition must be considered. There is a divergence between what reasonably can be known and what must be known for the operation of a system of premarketing clearance of new drugs that would neither deprive consumers of beneficial drugs nor confront them with many harmful or ineffective ones. Perceiving this divergence, a number of researchers have recommended greater reliance on postmarketing surveillance as a substitute for the later stages of the NDA process.[41] A simple, hypothetical, stylized example illustrates the nature of the problems arising from the divergence. The hypothetical risks and benefits of drug X are displayed in Table 2.1. For illustrative purposes, numerical cost and benefit figures have been utilized. It must be emphasized, however, that objective quantitative measures of health costs and benefits are, of necessity, arbitrary, since the analyst cannot know the value individuals place on their health. The first row of Table 2.1 lists the expected values of the benefits resulting from administration of the drug to individuals in each of the patient groups. The second row lists the probabilities that individuals in each of the patient groups will suffer a particular harmful side effect from drug X. Assuming that the probability of this particular side effect is the only risk involved in the use of drug X, its benefit-risk ratio can be calculated by dividing the expected value of benefits by the probability of the side effect occurring for the relevant population group. It is further assumed that, after considering the seriousness of the disease that drug X is intended to treat, the nature of the side effect, and possible alternative treatment methods, the FDA decides that Phase III studies must find a benefit-risk ratio greater than 20 for approval of the NDA for drug X. In light of the information provided in Table 2.1 will the NDA be approved?

First, consider the scenario in which the FDA has a suspicion prior to the planning of Phase III trials that patients in Group C have a predisposition to the side effect. Assume that sufficiently large samples are drawn from each of the patient groups so that accurate estimates of the benefits and risks for each of the groups can be made. Although the benefit-risk ratio for the patient population as a whole is less than the cutoff set by the FDA, the benefit-risk ratios for patient Groups A and B are favorable. Under our current regulatory framework, the best decision the FDA could make would be to allow

TABLE 2.1 Benefits and Risks of Drug X

	Group A	*Group B*	*Group C*	*Total Patient Population*
Expected value of benefits to patient	22	82	22	28
Probability of side effects (percentage)	1	1	11	2
Benefit-risk ratio (expected value of benefits per 1% chance of side effects)	22	82	2	14
Percentage of patient population	80	10	10	100

marketing of drug X with a contraindication for patient Group C. Assuming that no patients in Group C would elect to take the drug after being informed of the benefits and risks they would face, a "socially optimal" regulatory decision has been made. (Of course, it must be pointed out that the assignment of numerical risks and benefits is subjective, as is the FDA determination that benefit-risk ratios of less than 20 are unacceptable. Because consideration of what is socially optimal is based upon these subjective calculations, the concept is useful only for explanatory purposes.) A number of factors, however, hinder obtaining the information needed for such decision making. Of greatest relevance to our example is the difficulty of adequately designing Phase III studies so as to detect the differential responses of patient groups. Another factor is the problem of securing sufficient sample sizes for the accurate estimation of the true risks and benefits.

The example assumed that the Phase III studies would lead to estimates of the benefits and risks for each of the patient groups. It is unlikely, however, that Phase III studies would produce such disaggregated estimates unless the possibility of differential responses by specific patient groups was anticipated at the time the studies were designed. There are three sources of intuition about differential responses: animal tests, pharmacological theory, and early clinical studies.

The FDA requires that all new drugs be tested in at least two species of animals prior to testing in humans. Although the results of animal tests provide some indication of the harmful effects that might be expected to occur in humans, they can vary greatly from species to species and often give grossly incorrect predictions for humans. For example, the beneficial drugs digitalis and penicillin are highly toxic to a number of typically used laboratory animals.[42] The methodologies for predicting efficacy, teratogenicity, carcinogenicity, and mutagenicity are much less certain and even more highly sensitive to interspecies variation.

Pharmacological theory provides another source for intuition about likely differential responses from patient groups. Sometimes knowledge of the actions of previously tested drugs can be used to predict the probable actions of chemically similar new drugs. The growing knowledge about the way the human body processes drugs, provided by pharmacokinetics, can sometimes lead to predictions about differential responses. Nevertheless, when it comes to predicting the actions of new chemical entities in humans, pharmacology is still basically a process of trial and error.

The third source of intuition about differential responses is the early stages of clinical testing in humans. Perceptive analysis of apparently deviant responses to the drug being investigated may suggest hypotheses about differential responses that can be incorporated into the Phase III studies. A serious limitation, however, is that early clinical testing is usually restricted to nonrepresentative samples of the patient population: Phase I trials usually involve healthy volunteers, while Phase II trials involve a small number of patients chosen to minimize the probability of false-negative results. Side effects that are limited to a small segment of the patient population are therefore unlikely to be encountered in the early phases of clinical testing.

Returning to our example, assume that the differential respones of patient Group C to drug X was neither anticipated in the design of Phase III studies nor fortuitiously discovered in the analysis of the data that are generated. If the Phase III studies were based on a random sample of the total patient population, a benefit-risk ratio of 14 would be estimated. Under the cutoff of 20 established by the FDA, drug X would not be approved for marketing. So long as there were patients who would elect to take drug X after being informed of the benefits and risks associated with the regulatory decision not to allow marketing would be socially inefficient. Withholding of permission for marketing would harm not only the patients who viewed a benefit-risk ratio of 14 as acceptable but also the patients who would choose the drug in the future in the event that postmarketing surveillance yielded estimates of the benefit-risk ratios for the different patient groups. There is also the possibility that the estimated benefit-risk ratio will either underestimate or overestimate the ratio for the total patient population, depending on the degree to which Group B and Group C patients are over- or underrepresented in the studies.

So far it has been assumed that the Phase III studies would produce reliable estimates of the benefits and risks of drug X either for the entire patient population or for specified patient groups. Underestimated benefits or overestimated risks can lead to incorrect decisions to deny permission for marketing; overestimation of benefits or underestimation of risks can lead to incorrect decisions to grant permission for marketing. In the former case, the drug may never reach the market. In the latter case, more reliable estimates of benefits and risks are likely to be developed slowly in the absence of postmarketing surveillance.

The reliability of the estimates of benefits and risks depends on the number of patients in the studies. For well-designed investigations, larger samples of patients allow greater reliability in the estimation. Increasing sample size, however, invariably increases costs. Larger studies not only are more costly in terms of expenditures but typically take longer to complete. There is also an important ethical issue involved. The FDA places the greatest weight on results from placebo-controlled studies. In such studies, increased sample size means that more patients will be denied treatment. Using the existing treatment of choice as a control, rather than using a placebo, reduces the ethical problem in most situations but requires a different approach to the interpretation of statistical findings by the FDA.[43] For very rare side effects, enormous sample sizes well beyond the scale of current Phase III studies would be required for reliable estimates of incidence.[44]

Cases in Point

Operation of the premarketing clearance system confronts the FDA with a difficult choice: Unreliable estimates of benefits and risks lead to incorrect decisions, while efforts to increase reliability slow the introduction of beneficial drugs and discourage innovation.

The FDA's handling of two specific drugs, azaribine (Triazure) and cyanoacrylate, highlights the policy problems in current drug safety regulation that lead to poor decisions. The first case illustrates the type of congressional response that is likely to arise when the FDA attempts to facilitate early introduction of potentially beneficial drugs. The second illustrates the inflexibility often exhibited by the FDA.

During the 1960s, the drug methotrexate was introduced and eventually approved as a treatment for severe psoriasis. Although highly effective, it sometimes caused liver damage and death. An NDA for Triazure, an alternative treatment, was submitted in 1969. Additional Phase III testing, completed in 1972, indicated that Triazure was highly effective, without apparent liver toxicity. It appeared, however, that it might involve a rather high risk of thromboembolism. Because Triazure was highly effective for many patients who could not take methotrexate, the FDA gave marketing approval in 1975 on the condition that a postmarketing study be conducted by the distributor. When the study found that thromboembolisms of a more serious nature than had been previously encountered were occurring, the FDA withdrew marketing permission.

A month after Triazure was withdrawn from the market, the FDA was forced to defend its initial approval of the NDA before the House Subcommittee on Intergovernmental Relations and Human Resources.[45] The subcommittee chairman began by stating that the purpose of the hearing was to determine whether the FDA was adequately enforcing safety requirements. At the conclusion of the hearing, the chairman voiced his belief that the way Triazure was regulated indicated that protection of the patient was not the FDA's primary concern. After reviewing the Triazure evidence, Seymour Shubin reached a different conclusion:

> In summary, Triazure was, and is, an effective drug for a potentially lethal disease. The only alternative on the market for crippling psoriasis — methotrexate — is a highly toxic anticancer drug that can cause serious side effects, including death. The promising new therapy, methoxsalen plus UV light, is still experimental and will, in any case, not work in some patients who do respond to Triazure.
>
> The estimates made, prior to marketing, of risk of thromboembolism have held up, although there has been a shift in the direction of more arterial and fewer venous thromboses. There are still no good data on how many of these events are related to the disease as

> opposed to the treatment. Even if the most pessimistic estimates are true, and all the trouble seen is due to the drug, there are experienced dermatologists and pitifully sick patients who consider the risk worth taking. . . .
>
> Must our drug regulatory decisions be determined by those who err on the side of therapeutic nihilism?[46]

The FDA showed a desirable degree of flexibility in its initial decision to approve the NDA for Triazure with post-marketing surveillance requirements, but the negative congressional reaction suggests that such flexibility, even if technically desirable, is politically hazardous.

The handling of cyanoacrylate, or tissue glue, illustrates the extent to which the FDA can be inflexible. Cyanoacrylate is a type of glue that, when applied to bleeding tissue in an aerosol spray, forms a temporary seal beneath which natural healing takes place.[47] It can be applied to hemorrhages of internal organs, either directly or through the use of an endoscope. Experimentally available for more than 25 years, cyanoacrylate proved highly effective in treating critically wounded soliders during the Vietnam war. It was also used at Walter Reed Army Institute of Research. No significant harmful side effects have been detected in conjunction with the extensive and extended use of cyanoacrylate by the military, physicians in Europe, and U.S. clinical researchers.

Despite the accumulated evidence that cyanoacrylate is safe and effective in clinical use, manufacturers have been unsuccessful in securing marketing permission from the FDA. In the late 1960s, the FDA suspended the INDs for all types of cyanoacrylate when one of the three types being studied showed signs of tissue toxicity. Eventually, the FDA granted INDs allowing researchers to administer cyanoacrylate of the types not exhibiting tissue toxicity to dental patients who were already dying from some other disease. In 1972, however, the INDs were withdrawn by the FDA when it was discovered that laboratory animals implanted with large quantities of cyanoacrylate sometimes developed malignant tumors. The methodology employed, however, would have produced malignant tumors from almost any foreign substance. Additionally, cyanoacrylate, which is used in very small quantities, does not concentrate in body tissues. Animal tests using different methodologies failed to produce evidence of carcinogenicity. Nevertheless, it was three years before the FDA again granted INDs for clinical research with cyanoacrylate. The FDA has yet to grant permission to market the product. Even if permission is granted, it will be only for indications specifically investigated under the INDs. In other words, the manufacturer would not be allowed to promote cyanoacrylate for general surgical use without repeating the IND-NDA process.

The Costs of Inflexibility

One explanation for the evolution of highly specific regulations defining substantial evidence is the role such specifications play in reducing the number of issues that must be resolved by the FDA through costly administrative hearings. Once the regulations are in place, the possibility of hostile congressional oversight encourages the FDA to be inflexible in their application. The FDA is much more vulnerable to criticism when unanticipated side effects are discovered after marketing has begun if it did not strictly adhere to its regulations in approving the NDA. This inflexibility can dramatically slow down the introduction of beneficial drugs to American patients. The delay is particularly frustrating to members of the scientific community who perceive a divergence between reasonable levels of scientific evidence and regulatory standards. Consider the following exchange that recently occurred between the renowned pharmacologists Dr. Louis Lasagna and Dr. Marian Finkel, associate director of new drug evaluation in the FDA's Bureau of Drugs:

Dr. Lasagna: Dr. Finkel, what happens when anybody with half a brain knows that the drug is effective but we can't prove it? As in the case of propranolol and sodium valproate. I think the public would be very dismayed to find out that drugs which have been shown to be effective in treating hypertension and epilepsy are not available on the market due to cumbersome regulations promulgated by the FDA.

Dr. Finkel: Not true, Dr. Lasagna. At the time of the drugs controversy, the FDA admitted to the public that although the drugs were probably effective, the clinical studies used to assess the effectiveness of the drugs did not meet the FDA's "well-controlled and adequate regulations" as specified in the 1970 regulations. The problem with the trials was that the investigators had chosen to use historical control. This type of control was not adequate for the clinical investigations and therefore all studies on these drugs which used such types of controls could not be considered to be well controlled and adequate. The law does clearly define what a well-controlled and adequate study is.[48]

The FDA eventually approved NDAs for propranolol and sodium valproate — in both cases, years after they were approved for marketing in Great Britain. Some drugs that have long been drugs of choice in other countries are not yet available in the United States. For example, Dr. William Wardell estimates that alprenolol, a drug useful in preventing heart attacks and coronary death, which has been available in Sweden since 1976, could save at least 10,000 lives per year, with a degree of toxicity that would be small, controllable, and highly acceptable to the patients at risk.[49] Even if Wardell's estimate of the number of lives that could be saved overstates the true number by a factor of 100, the absence of alprenolol in the U.S. market involves an annual loss of life comparable in magnitude to the Elixir Sulfanilamide disaster. Yet little attention is given to these statistical deaths by the public media or by Congress.

The congressional committees that oversee the FDA have been very receptive to the consumer-advocate viewpoint. Adopting the view that the FDA is unduly influenced by the pharmaceutical industry, the consumer advocates believe that countervailing pressure must be exerted on the FDA through the courts and Congress. They believe that the FDA often makes decisions before being presented with sufficiently reliable information and that it approves drugs with benefit-risk ratios that are too slow. Often underlying these criticisms are the general beliefs that Americans take too many drugs and that drug companies devote too much effort to introducing "me too" drugs that do not represent real therapeutic advances.[50] In addition to criticizing the FDA for giving marketing permission for specific drugs, the consumer advocates support a change in the law that would require new drugs be shown to be substantially safer or more effective than available drugs in the same therapeutic category.[51]

With few exceptions, oversight hearings on specific FDA decisions have been critical of the granting of marketing permission. Consider the statement of former FDA Commissioner Alexander Schmidt:

> In all our history, we are unable to find one instance where a Congressional hearing investigated the failure of FDA to approve a new drug. . . . The message conveyed by this situation could not be clearer. . . . Until perspective is brought to the legislative oversight function, the pressure from Congress for FDA to disapprove new drugs will continue to be felt, and could be a major factor in health care in this country.[52]

One explanation for the congressional focus on therapeutic harms rather than on forgone therapeutic benefits is that the former are highly visible while the latter are, of necessity, speculative. Victims of harmful side effects or their survivors make dramatic witnesses, who can help attract media coverage; those who suffer because some drug that would have been beneficial to them has not been approved by the FDA often do not even know that they have been harmed. Personalized suffering is much more newsworthy than statistical suffering.

It is easy to point to examples of FDA decisions blocking or delaying the availability of specific drugs that appear to offer favorable benefit-risk ratios to patient populations. Even if the FDA were placing comparable weights on the harm caused by allowing the marketing of drugs with adverse side effects and the harm caused by delaying or preventing the marketing of beneficial drugs, some examples of excessive delay would probably occur as a result of the large number of decisions that must be made with imperfect information. A general pattern of excessive delay, however, would support the argument that the FDA is insufficiently sensitive to the harm caused by forgone therapeutic benefits.

One approach to determining whether regulation by the FDA has led to a general pattern of excessive delay is to compare drug availability in the United States and other countries. The first major study involving an international comparison was William Wardell's investigation of new drugs introduced in the United States or Great Britain from 1962 to 1971.[53] Wardell compared the dates and circumstances of introduction of all 180 new drugs (all new chemical entities) in 9 therapeutic areas. Of the 82 drugs that became mutually available, 14 were introduced in the same year in both countries, 43 were introduced in Britain first, and 25 were introduced in the United States first. Britain enjoyed 120 drug years of prior availability, while the United States only enjoyed 59 drug years of prior availability. Of the other 98 drugs that were not mutually available, 73 were exclusively available in Britain, while 21 were exclusively available in the United States. In parallel studies, Wardell found that many of the drugs exclusively available in Great Britain had become the drugs of choice in British teaching hospitals.[54] Of those drugs exclusively available in Great Britain, only 2 were eventually withdrawn from use because of toxicity, and these contributed negligibly to total drug toxicity in Great Britain during the study period.[55] From these studies, Wardell concluded that the United States had lost considerably in forgone therapeutic benefits, while Great Britain had suffered only slightly greater harm from toxicity.

Three successive FDA commissioners have denied the existence of this "drug lag," at the same time claiming that they were abolishing it.[56] The commissioners may have had some success in their latter claim. Wardell repeated the comparison for the five-year period beginning in 1972 and found that the difference between Great Britain and the United States had narrowed somewhat.[57] The gap may have narrowed as much from more conservative practices in Britain, however, as from more realistic regulatory practices in the United States.

In an attempt to measure how much unnecessary delay can be attributed to the FDA, Martin Eisman and William Wardell compared the dates of NDA approval with first-marketing dates in other countries for all the new chemical entities of 9 research-intensive pharmaceutical companies that received NDA approval from 1970 to mid-1979 as well as marketing permission in at least 1 foreign country.[58] On average, the NDAs for the 30 drugs studied were approved 21 months after submission. First-marketing in any country preceded NDA approval by an average of 18 months. First-marketing in countries with more stringent premarket testing requirements preceded NDA approval by an average of 14 months. First-marketing in select countries with strict and sophisticated review systems for determining efficacy and safety (Australia, Great Britain, Sweden, Denmark, Norway, and Finland) preceded NDA approval by an average of 9 months. These estimates are exclusive of delay the companies were willing to attribute to their own actions. Even if the company admissions are viewed as lower bounds, the analysis still suggests that NDA approvals could have been reached at substantially earlier dates.

Not only does delayed marketing inflict harm on patients who would have benefited from the drug, but delay also contributes to a reduction in rates of innovation by reducing the expected returns on investment in research and development. The present value of the revenue stream expected from the introduction of a new drug is smaller the longer marketing is delayed. Increased delay also reduces the rate of return by decreasing the effective patent life of new drugs. In 1966, the average effective patent life (the time remaining from NDA approval to patent expiration) was 13.8 years; the average in 1977 had declined to 9 years.[59]

The cost of bringing a new drug to market has steadily increased. Between 1962 and 1972, it is estimated that research and development costs had increased by a factor of 5.[60] The most methodologically valid estimate of the expected cost of bringing a new drug to market in the United States has been made by Ronald Hansen.[61] He developed his estimate from a weighted random sample of new chemical entities (NCEs) first tested in humans from 1963 to 1975. After taking account of the attrition rate of NCEs at each stage of drug development, Hansen estimated that the average sum of discovery costs and testing expenditures per marketed NCE capitalized to the point of marketing approval was $54 million in 1976 dollars. The $54 million estimate is based on a discount rate of 8 percent. Higher discount rates would yield even higher estimates.

Thus, a profit-maximizing firm would not be expected to invest in the discovery and development of drugs that are likely to generate revenue streams less than the cost of developing and obtaining marketing approval for them ($54 million for the average drug). Ignoring discovery costs, the expected cost of post-IND testing is estimated to be $21 million. The higher these costs, the greater will be the number of "orphan drugs" — beneficial drugs that are not commercially developed because they are likely to have only small markets.[62] Orphan drugs are a side effect of more stringent regulations, which increase the cost of development.

To what extent have the more stringent regulations implemented since 1962 slowed pharmaceutical innovation in the United States? A number of researchers have employed econometric methods in an attempt to answer this question.[63] Using data for the 15-year period ending in 1962, Sam Peltzman estimated the parameters of a demand-pull model for explaining yearly rates of introduction of new chemical entities.[64] Actual introduction of new chemical entities for the 10-year period following 1962 were roughly half the number predicted by Peltzman's model. By comparing the behavior of hospitals, expert panels employed by state public-assistance agencies to approve drugs for formularies, and the American Medical Association's Council on Drugs before and after the 1962 amendments, Peltzman concluded that only a small portion of the decline in the rate of introduction of new chemical entities could be attributed to the FDA's preventing inefficacious drugs from reaching the market.[65] In other words, the regulatory burdens stemming from the 1962 amendments appear to have substantially slowed the rate of introduction of beneficial new drugs.

As an alternative explanation for the decline in the rate of introduction of new chemical entities, the FDA has claimed that pharmacological research and development has reached a natural plateau after the rapid advances of the 1950s, which depleted exploitable knowledge. Martin Baily developed a production-function model relating the rate of introduction of new chemical entities to past investments in research and development, a variable measuring the depletion of research opportunities, and the impact of the 1962 amendments.[66] Baily estimated the parameters of his model using yearly data from 1954 to 1969. He found that the 1962 amendments reduced the rate of introduction of new chemical entities even after statistically controlling for knowledge depletion and past investments in research and development.

Henry Grabowski, John Vernon, and Lacy Thomas have developed an expanded version of Baily's model that allows tests of several additional alternative hypotheses to explain the decline in the rate of introduction of new chemical entities.[67] They estimated the rate of decline in yearly introduction of new chemical entities in Great Britain between 1960 and 1970. They then entered this rate as an explanatory variable in the model of the rate of introduction of new chemical entities in the United States, assuming that it would statistically control for such factors as the depletion of knowledge, industry caution in the wake of the thalidomide tragedy, and increases in the costs of development associated with advances in pharmacological science, which would be expected to have similar impacts in Great Britian and the United States. Estimating parameters for the period 1954 to 1974, they found that the 1962 amendments had a negative impact on the rate of introduction of new chemical entities. Using alternative specifications, they found that increased regulatory stringency also had a negative impact on innovation.

Decreased rates of innovation, loss of freedom of choice, delayed introduction of beneficial drugs, and increased numbers of orphan drugs constitute the major, but often neglected, costs of the system of premarketing clearances as operated by the FDA. The system does provide benefits by reducing the number of unsafe and inefficacious drugs reaching the market, but several of the researchers cited have concluded that the costs of our current regulatory system outweigh its benefits. Even if they are incorrect, it is still appropriate to ask whether there is some way of achieving current levels of benefits at reduced costs.

In developing alternatives to the current system, it is first helpful to consider what would occur if the FDA were simply abolished, with no other changes. It is then possible to suggest institutional and legal changes that would reduce or eliminate incentives for irresponsible behavior in the absence of any regulation. Through such changes physicians and manufacturers would be encouraged to make decisions that broaden the therapeutic options available to consumers without significantly increasing therapeutic risk.

Naive Deregulation: Reactions and Incentives

What would be the consequences of simply abolishing the FDA? Although few have suggested so radical an approach, consideration of the consequences likely to result from deregulation in the absence of any other changes (naive deregulation) provides a framework for analyzing solutions less onerous than bureaucratic regulation. Two questions guide that analysis. First, what reactions might private organizations and individuals tend to develop as substitutes for current regulatory activities? Second, what remaining incentives might lead firms and physicians to socially irresponsible behavior? Mitigation of these incentives is the key to developing effective alternatives to bureaucratic regulation.

We will assume, however, that several major provisions of current drug laws would be retained in other forms. Under general laws against fraud, drugs appearing in one of the official compendia would still be required to meet stated standards of strength, quality, and purity or to explicitly state the extent of the differences on their labels. Drugs not appearing in one of the official compendia would be required to list all active ingredients as well as the quantities and proportions of specific ingredients listed in the 1938 law. Misbranding would still be defined as claims that are false or misleading in any particular. Violators of these provisions would be subject to civil action by parties who could show that the violations caused them harm and to criminal action by state or federal law enforcement agencies.

The removal of FDA intervention in what is now the IND phase would not cede complete discretion to firms in designing and conducting clinical trials. The institutional review boards (IRBs) of the hospitals, clinics, and research centers where the testing is to be conducted would still insist that firms demonstrate that human subjects are not being submitted to undue risks. Although there is danger that some IRBs would be excessively lax in controlling testing, and perhaps would attract industry-sponsored research because of it, several factors encourage responsible behavior. The institution that the IRB represents is subject to charges of malpractice, along with the individual researchers and possibly the drug firm, if injury occurs in the absence of informed consent or from failure to follow appropriate standards of care. These possibilities encourage the proper exercise of professional norms by members of the IRBs.

Although there are no institutional mechanisms currently in place that can replace the role of the FDA in controlling the entry of drugs in the market as readily as the IRBs can replace the role of the FDA in controlling clinical testing, several types of private organizations might be expected to contribute to the prevalence of safe and effective drugs in the marketplace.

Hospitals generally establish lists of drugs that are routinely distributed through their pharmacies. Since 1965, the Joint Commission on Accreditation of Hospitals has required the appointment of formulary committees to act on drug availability and utilization as a precondition for accreditation.[68] Formulary committees typically include representatives of the various medical departments as well as the chief pharmacists of their hospitals. Most operate primarily to standardize the drugs prescribed in order to realize cost savings through competitive bidding, high-volume discounts, and inventory control. Some actively limit the access of drug company detail people to hospital staff members. Formulary committees often publish newsletters that inform the hospital staff about additions to and deletions from the formulary and provide information relevant to safe and effective prescribing.

If the FDA no longer regulated the marketing of new drugs, formulary committees might give greater attention to questions of safety and efficacy. Unlike the individual staff member, who has little time to evaluate promotional information in daily practice, the formulary committee has both the time and the expertise to review scientific evidence relevant to proposed entries in the formulary. Manufacturers wishing to reach the hospital market would find it necessary to present convincing scientific evidence to the formulary committees. During the 1930s, the New York Hospital formulary committee encouraged its clinical staff to conduct comparative tests of drugs they wished the committee to add to the formulary.[69] Formulary committees might again have an incentive to adopt comparative testing and other forms of intrahospital postmarketing surveillance. The development of cummunication networks among hospital formularies, probably drawing on computerized data banks, could help reduce duplication in testing and evaluation.

A number of formularies cover segments of the patient population that are receiving prescription drugs outside of the hospital setting. States have established formularies in an attempt to control reimbursements for drugs under Medicare and Medicaid. Tennessee, for example, operates a computerized information system to monitor prescriptions and also makes bioavailability assessments of drugs listed in its formulary.[70] A more active role by the state formularies would help shield the poor and the aged — the groups least able to act as informed consumers — from unsafe and ineffective drugs. Formularies established by private health insurance providers and health maintenance organizations have potential for covering a substantial portion of the remaining prescriptions written outside of hospitals.

It would not be surprising if medical societies were to play a more active role in the wake of deregulation. Providing information about drugs would be a relatively more valuable service to their members than is now the case. Committees of experts representing each of the various specialties would probably be given responsibility for reviewing therapeutic claims for drugs in their areas. They might also serve as clearinghouses for information about adverse reactions and serendipitous discoveries. In the late nineteenth and early twentieth centuries, the American Medical Association (AMA) and the American Pharmaceutical Association (APA) did, in fact, fight quackery and adulteration, respectively. Furthermore, the AMA's seal-of-acceptance program, which, between 1929 and 1955, required that all drugs advertised in the *Journal of the American Medical Association* be approved by the AMA's Council on Pharmacy and Chemistry, might be reinstated in the absence of similar free services now provided by the FDA.[71] Information services not directly linked to medical societies, such as the *Medical Letter on Drugs and Therapeutics,* would likely expand their scope of operations. Consumer advocate groups could also be relied upon to point out the worst cases of overpromotion.

The *Medical Letter on Drugs and Therapeutics* is particularly relevant to our discussion because it is a prototype of the kind of information services that would likely flourish under deregulation. The *Medical Letter* carries no advertising and derives its revenues totally from subscriptions. It currently has a circulation of about 120,000, with pharmacists, medical students, and pharmaceutical companies, as well as physicians, among subscribers.[72] Taking a consumer orientation, the *Medical Letter* reviews almost all new drugs approved by the FDA each year. Reviews of older drugs also appear sometimes prompted by correspondence with clinicians. An attempt is made to make the reviews, which indicate possible alternative medications, easily readable by busy physicians.

Firms offering certification services might arise to help the more reputable manufacturers distinguish themselves from the rest of the industry. These independent firms might be hired to certify quality control in manufacturing, validity of clinical studies, and truthfulness of therapeutic claims. If the certification firms were successful in establishing their credibility with physicians and consumers, the entire pharmaceutical industry would be forced to seek their services. Although currently hampered by a lack of credibility, trade associations might attempt to play a similar role. At the least, they would help establish minimum standards in testing and advertising for the industry and would probably have some success in disciplining or drawing attention to the unfair practices of the least reputable firms.

A final compensating reaction to deregulation would be a change in the attitude of physicians toward new drugs. Under the current regulatory system, the major information conveyed to doctors by the FDA is through its decision to allow or not to allow marketing. For some classes of patients, the differential responses of the population render erroneous the implicit information conveyed by marketing approval that a drug is safe and effective. The market/no-market dichotomy may encourage doctors to assume a higher level of safety than is warranted, becuase they equate the general safety implied by permission to market with specific safety for all patient groups. Under deregulation, doctors would no longer be encouraged to equate market availability with safety. Hence, greater care in prescribing could conceivably result.

Compensating reactions of the sort outlined above would provide some protection from the promotion and prescription of unsafe and inefficacious drugs. Would they induce manufacturers to invest an adequate amount of resources in testing? Would they be strong enough to discourage deceptive promotional claims? Would they lead doctors to be sufficiently careful in selecting drugs for their patients?

Drug manufacturers are in the best position to discover and disseminate information about their products. Manufacturers make efficient decisions concerning the marketing of their products only if they consider all costs as well as benefits that are likely to result. A major purpose of liability laws is to force manufacturers to include injury costs in their calculations. The courts generally hold manufacturers liable for injuries that they reasonably could have foreseen.[73] Under current laws, however, a number of factors prevent manufacturers from being held liable for the total costs of their marketing decisions. Not all patients will know that their injuries have been caused by a particular drug. It may not be possible for all potential plantiffs to establish legally that their injuries were caused by the drug. High transaction costs are likely to deter those who have suffered only minor injuries from seeking compensation in the courts. These factors are likely to be particularly important in cases in which the injury is caused by an ineffective rather than unsafe drug. To the extent that manufacturers are unlikely to be held liable for all the harm caused by their drugs, they face an insufficiently strong incentive for conducting fully adequate testing and distributing sufficiently detailed information.

Manufacturers currently can be held negligent for failing to conduct "reasonable" premarketing testing, for failing to convey warnings indicated by the medical literature, or for failing to warn of adverse reactions that become known through spontaneous reporting. The courts generally do not hold manufacturers negligent for failing to initiate postmarketing surveillance studies. Although most manufacturers now voluntarily conduct some sort of postmarketing surveillance without being required to do so by the FDA, scientifically valid postmarketing studies are conducted for only a small fraction of marketed drugs. Aside from the lack of legal pressure to do so, these studies are currently not done more often because negative findings are potentially very detrimental to manufacturers, whereas positive findings are likely to be of only marginal value in promotion. Finding that a drug being widely marketed is not as effective as was initially believed (and promoted) or that it has an unanticipated side effect may reduce, or even stop, further sales. Finding the drug to be as effective as was initially believed probably will not substantially increase already high sales. Although it would be easier to exploit commercially the fortuitous discovery of effectiveness for new indications under deregulation, an insufficient amount of postmarketing surveillance might still prevail.

Successful penetration of the market with new drugs depends on developing the perception among physicians that the new drugs are safer or more effective than those already in use. Manufacturers therefore face a strong economic incentive to understate risks and overstate effectiveness in their promotional efforts. Liability laws provide a much stronger counterincentive against understatement of risks than against overstatement of effectiveness. One way to estimate the likely extent of the overstatement of effectiveness is to look at the claims made for products introduced prior to the 1962 amendments. The NAS-NRC study of drugs introduced between 1938 and 1962 found that only 7 percent of the drugs had no substantial evidence of effectiveness. Almost 15 percent of the therapeutic claims reviewed, however, were found to be supported by no acceptable evidence. An additional 35 percent of the claims made were supported by little evidence of effectiveness.[74] The high percentage of unsupported or poorly supported claims suggests widespread overpromotion.

Whereas formularies can be expected to reduce the impact of overpromotion on physicians practicing in institutional settings, physicians in private practice would be more vulnerable. Unfortunately, the editorial boards of the most widely distributed medical journals have largely abdicated responsibility for ensuring that advertising is balanced and accurate. The reason is economic. The majority of medical journals receive large percentages of their revenues from drug advertisements. In fact, 24 of the 28 medical journals with the largest circulations are supported entirely by advertising revenue and are distributed free to physicians.[75] In 1955, the *Journal of the American Medical Association* abolished its seal-of-acceptance program because, although popular with most physicians, it was found to be holding back the growth of advertising revenue.[76] In view of these economic incentives, substantially greater editorial control over advertising may not occur under deregulation. Consequently, pharmaceutical advertising directed toward physicians may contain excessive claims of efficacy. Some analysts, however, have suggested that the seal-of-acceptance program was abolished not because of difficulties it posed for establishing advertising revenues but because it had to compete with similar, but free, services operated by the

FDA.[77] If this is the case, a seal-of-acceptance program might again be developed in the absence of the FDA.

Just as our liability laws should encourage manufacturers to take into consideration the full costs of their decisions concerning the discovery and transmission of information, liability laws should also encourage physicians to consider the full costs of their prescribing decisions. Physicians should be held liable for injuries that result when they fail to heed the direction, precautions, warnings, and contraindications provided by the manufacturer. Yet, in most jurisdictions, physicians can avoid liability if they have followed the standard of professional care prevalent in their community.[78] Thus the plaintiff is forced to establish that reasonable physicians in the community would have acted on the information supplied by the manufacturer. The actions of a reasonable physician in the community also serve as the standard for determining whether physicians have secured informed consent. The community standard may be considered acceptable in determining whether informed consent was adequate in light of the voluntary and special nature of the relationship between physician and patient; because it encourages ignorance about important information that is relevant to safe and effective prescribing, it should not be viewed as satisfactory in determining liability for drug injuries exclusive of the issue of informed consent.

A second problem in physician behavior is related to the "public good" nature of information about side effects. Physicians bear the full cost of making efforts to report suspected adverse reactions to manufacturers, whereas the benefits accrue primarily to others, making underreporting by physicians likely. Furthermore, physicians may view the reporting of adverse reactions as an admission of treatment-induced injury that increases their chances of being sued for malpractice. Perhaps underreporting resulting from the latter factor would be reduced by establishing procedures, possibly developed by a consumer group, for anonymous reporting.

In summary, naive deregulation would not leave the public totally unprotected. The incentives provided by civil liability for injury and the reactions of private organizations would provide considerable protection to consumers from exposure to unsafe and inefficacious drugs. Nevertheless, insufficient care in prescribing, underinvestment in postmarketing surveillance, and excessive claims of efficacy (including underreporting of adverse reactions) might still occur. Institutional changes in the pharmaceutical marketplace should be directed at mitigating these deficiencies.

Improving the System of Incentives

How can the system of incentives that would prevail under deregulation be improved without resorting to the creation of centralized bureaucratic institutions? Several problems underlie any attempt to devise alternative legal and institutional mechanisms.[79] First, whether any given set of proposals seems adequate depends on one's personal assessment of the amount of extra safety, if any, that would result and the magnitude of disadvantages that would accompany any particular policy. Second, evaluating the adequacy of alternative policies ultimately involves personal value judgments about the worth of additional safety, the cost or retarded rates of innovation, and other costs associated with implementing the chosen policy. Because the worth of additional safety is, of necessity, an individual judgment, proposals that give individuals greater opportunites to make that calculation deserve particular attention. For those who might judge the implications of these legal and nonbureaucratic solutions inadequate, several supplementary proposals will be considered. It must be emphasized, however, that any interventionist policy carries with it subtle repercussions and costs that are often unforeseen in the initial estimation of its potential benefits. The three problem areas — insufficient care in prescribing by physicians, insufficient investment in postmarketing studies, and excessive claims of efficacy and safety — will provide the focus for proposing policy alternatives.

Physicians' Care

As suggested by Richard Merrill, the community standard of care should no longer be allowed as a defense against negligence in injury cases involving drugs.[80] Failure to follow the directions, contraindications, warnings, and precautions provided by the manufacturer should be *prima facie* evidence of physician negligence. Instead of plaintiffs being forced to establish through expert testimony that their physicians did not follow the community standards of care, the physicians would bear the burden of demonstrating through expert testimony that deviations from the manufacturer's instructions were consistent with good medical practice. Elimination of the community standard of care defense would encourage physicians to be more conscientious in learning about the proper use of the drugs they prescribe.

A federal role in eliminating the community standard of care defense in drug-injury cases is somewhat problematic. State courts and legislatures determine the liability rules that apply in their jurisdictions. The federal government might draft a model liability rule and provide financial rewards to encourage its adoption. A more radical approach would be to allow plaintiffs to bring suit against physicians in drug-injury cases in federal courts. The constitutionality of federal jurisdiction could be based on the argument that the products involved are part of interstate commerce. However, rather than encroaching on the traditional jurisdiction of the state courts, the more reasonable approach might be to accept a less than totally successful educational effort by the federal government.

Follow-Up Studies

Although insufficient emphasis on postmarketing studies is provided under the current system, simply abolishing the FDA would very likely not prove effective in stimulating such studies. However, the need for these studies might be met by strengthening strict liability laws and prohibiting marketing of drugs unless manufacturers were insured against both design and manufacturing defects.

Mandatory insurance is an approach for guaranteeing manufacturer compliance with industry standards of testing and quality control that would also encourage greater investment in postmarketing studies. Before introducing drugs into interstate commerce, manufacturers would be required to show proof that they had secured insurance to cover liability, up to a specified amount per drug product, for injuries resulting from manufacturing defects. The registration of proof of insurance would provide a way of linking manufacturers to products found to be defective. The insurers would have an incentive to monitor the quality-control practices followed by the manufacturers. Additionally, the system would provide a source of compensation for those who are injured by the defective products of "fly-by-night" firms.[81] The mandatory-insurance requirement would replace the registration and inspection services provided by the FDA. Registration could be handled by the Department of Commerce and enforcement by the Department of Justice. Because insurance companies are licensed by the states, there would be no need for federal regulation of the insurers beyond specification of the minimum liability coverage that must be carried.

Under a system of strict liability in which manufacturers would be held liable for any harm caused by their products for which they did not adequately warn, extension of the mandatory-insurance requirement to cover design as well as manufacturing defects would lead to greater investment in postmarketing studies. Insurance providers, as well as manufacturers, would have an incentive to attempt to discover unanticipated adverse reactions as soon as possible so as to limit their ultimate liability. Insurers might even offer payments to physicians for adverse-reaction reports. Lower premium rates would be offered to manufacturers who conducted scientifically valid postmarketing studies.

Although insurers would undoubtedly be willing to offer coverage for liability resulting from manufacturing defects, insuring against design defects might be more problematic because of the greater difficulty of developing actuarial experiences for new and often unique products. However, if liability laws were strengthened and insurance were mandatory — that is, no drug could be marketed without defect insurance — insurers and manufacturers would have to find some way of resolving the dilemma at costs acceptable to both. Becasue of the lack of actuarial data and difficulties in proving the cause of harm, a system of no-fault insurance might emerge.

Two factors would encourage drug companies to accept a no-fault system. First, the mandatory-insurance requirement would necessitate their having some sort of design-defect insurance. Second, since the premiums might be exceedingly high without a no-fault system, it would be in the interest of drug firms to accept a no-fault system. Similarly, insurance companies would hesitate to enter a very risky business, even with high premiums. A no-fault system would provide a way of limiting their risks.

A no-fault system would circumvent, to a large extent, the need to resort to costly and sometimes inefficient court proceedings. Nonetheless, some means of adjudicating disputes would still be necessary. It is conceivable that insurance companies and drug manufacturers might devise a compensation program similar to current workers' compensation schemes.

At the turn of the century, a perception developed among the general public that liability laws did not provide an adequate means for workers to gain compensation for injuries suffered in the workplace. It was often difficult to prove that injuries resulted from employer negligence. The extended adjudication process left disabled workers without compensation for long periods. Additionally, juries often made widely different awards in factually similar cases. Beginning with New York in 1898, the states adopted workers' compensation programs to provide quicker and more uniform compensation to those injured in industrial accidents, without requiring proof of employer negligence. Workers' compensation programs generally involve mandatory insurance coverage for employers and administratively determined awards by a compensation board. Programs that allow insurers to base premiums on accident rates provide an incentive to employers to invest in accident prevention.

Workers' compensation provides a model that can be used to develop a program for compensating and reducing drug-related injuries. The program should be administered by a compensation board consisting of medical practitioners and researchers from various specialty areas. The compensation board would be served by a permanent staff, which would be responsible for maintaining an adverse-reaction reporting system. The program itself would consist of the following components: a partially refundable fee on each drug product, compensation awards for injuries for which the manufacturer did not warn, and payments to physicians for fully documented adverse-reaction reports.

Whenever a manufacturer began selling a new pharmaceutical product, an account for that product would be established. On a regular basis the manufacturer would be required to deposit in the account a fixed percentage (perhaps 10 percent) of the whole-sale revenue from the drug. At the end of 12-years, the amount accumulated in the account, less any payments made by the compensation board for injuries and reporting fees, would be returned to the manufacturer with interest. Also at the end of 12-years, the manufacturer would no longer be required to make payments for the drug unless compensation claims were still outstanding. The manufacturer would have the option of withdrawing money from the account prior to the end of the 12-year period for conducting postmarketing surveillance studies. Upon completion of postmarketing studies, the compensation board would be permitted to waive the fee for the remainder of the 12-year period and return the accumulated funds if it believed the studies demonstrated that the drug was safe and effective for the conditions for which it was being promoted. As is the case in the Federal Republic of Germany, manufacturers might have the option of moving drugs from prescription to over-the-counter status after 3 years of postmarketing surveillance.[82]

The compensation board would have authority to award payments out of the deposit account when it determined that the manufacturers failed to warn adequately of the possibility of adverse reaction. The board would be free to use its professional judgment in deciding whether or not apparent injury could be reasonably linked to inadequate drug labeling. Those who sought awards could simultaneously seek compensation in the courts. Any awards made by the board, however, would be subtracted from compensation payments ordered by the courts.

The compensation board would also have the authority to establish payments to be made to physicians who submitted fully documented adverse-reaction reports. The payments would be made from the account of the drug involved. Once the board judged that the rate of occurrence of a particular adverse reaction had been adequately determined, either through adverse-reaction reporting or postmarketing studies, it could discontinue payments for reports of that particular adverse reaction.

The compensation program would help to improve the incentives faced by manufacturers. Because awards would be made only when adequate warning was not given, manufacturers would have an incentive to provide full information in labeling about the adverse reactions they believe likely to occur. The possibility of early payback of the deposit-account funds should make manufacturers more willing to conduct postmarketing studies. The incentive to conduct postmarketing studies would be greatest for the most widely selling drugs because these drugs would accumulate the largest accounts. It is therefore likely that more information about safety and efficacy would be generated for the drugs reaching the most patients.

Another advantage of the program would be its capacity for providing compensation quickly. Viewing the payments made by the compensation board as discretionary grants rather than as entitlements, the board would be free to operate with a minimum of formal procedure. Speed and flexibility would be purchased at the cost of somewhat higher levels of error in decision making than would probably result from a more formal adjudicative process. The costs of error, however, would be limited because undercompensated patients could still seek higher awards from the courts, and the loss the manufacturers suffer when patients are overcompensated could not exceed the amount in the deposit accounts.

On balance, the desirability of the compensation-board approach depends on one's perception of the likely behavior of pharmaceutical and insurance firms under the system of strict liability that may already be evolving in the courts. It is reasonable to believe that strict liability would lead firms to invest a satisfactory level of resources in scientifically valid postmarketing studies. If one believes the inefficiencies and inequalities in tort law (transaction costs, delay, and the difficulty of establishing causality) are of minor consequence, the compensation board might be unnecessary and even undesirable. Alternatively, the more serious one believes the imperfections in tort law to be, the more likely it is that one will consider compensation boards desirable. In evaluating the compensation board, the trade-off is between the added costs to firms and consumers, which could be as high as the deposit-account fee, and the benefits of having available an alternative route to compensation, akin to small-claims court, that might contribute to more adequate levels of postmarketing surveillance.

Promotional Claims

In a free society, individuals engage voluntarily in a variety of risky behaviors. Hang gliding, elective surgery, and cigarette smoking, to name just a few, are activities that involve a risk of premature injury and death. Perception of consumers' ability to evaluate information and to choose rationally among courses of action generates public acceptance of risk in these activities. However, the consumers' ability to assess rationally the risks and benefits associated with pharmaceuticals is less accepted. Physicians are considered capable of advising patients adequately of the risks and benefits associated with surgery, but not of the risks and benefits associated with drug treatments.

Information about surgical procedures comes largely from experience and scientist-refereed journals. Information about drugs also comes from these sources but more often comes from manufacturers with an incentive for overpromotion. It would follow, therefore, that provision of the equivalent of scientific refereeing of promotional materials would reduce the distinction between the information available in surgical and pharmacological treatment. In other words, elimination of the overpromotion problem might be viewed as an important pharmacological concern of society.

In part, the problem of overpromotion could be alleviated by strengthening antifraud laws. Such laws might be supplemented by establishing a nonbureaucratic bounty system that would allow individuals and organizations to share in fines levied against manufacturers found guilty either of failing to warn of possible side effects that could have been reasonably known or of exaggerating claims of effectiveness beyond those that can reasonably be supported by scientific evidence. The size of the fine would be a function of the sales revenue of the product involved and the degree to which the court found the overpromotion to be therapeutically or economically important. A special court could be given jurisdiction over complaints filed under the law. It would be staffed with statisticians and pharmacologists, as well as law clerks, to assist the judges. The court would have the authority to consolidate cases to protect manufacturers from being sued by more than one party over claims made for a single product. Power to order corrective advertisements would also be vested in the court.

The bounty (share in fines) would motivate enforcement by private organizations. Perhaps pharmaceutical competitors, but more likely consumer organizations, would have a financial incentive to monitor drug promotion for gross inaccuracies that could lead to easy victories in court. Because the size of the fine would be a percentage of the sales revenue of the drug product involved, the consumer organizations would have an incentive to pay closest attention to widely used products. Of course, the prospect of being taken to court would discourage manufacturers from engaging in overpromotion.

The effectiveness of the bounty law would depend largely on the ability of the special court to evaluate scientific information. In addition to providing staff memebers with scientific training, it would probably be necessary to provide training for the judges selected to sit in the court. The required training and staffing would be costly but insignificant compared to the current budget of the FDA's Bureau of Drugs.

Given the potentially large threat to revenues posed by the bounty system, drug firms would very likely insure against it. Insurers might well set up one or more promotion-certification programs to systematize their evaluation of drug-firm performance in this regard. In addition, consumer groups might well set up their own evaluation and certification program, modeled after *The Medical Letter,* with funding derived partly from the bounties. The intent of such a certification program would be to provide physicians and patients with an independent scientific assessment of the accuracy and reliability of claims made in promotional materials. It would involve the creation of certification boards for each of the medical specialties. Each board would have a permanent staff of statisticians and pharmacologists. The boards would have authority to add evaluative statements to promotional materials.

Under the program, a manufacturer wishing to market a new drug would submit summaries of animal and clinical testing, other relevant scientific information, and proposed promotional materials to the appropriate certification board. After reviewing the submitted information, the board would specify the statements concerning safety and efficacy that the labeling, advertising, and other promotion for the drug must include. One of five possible general statements of safety would be made: insufficient evidence to evaluate safety; not safe; possibly safe; probably safe; and safe for use as directed. A similar general statement would be made for each of the major therapeutic claims that are made: insufficient evidence to evaluate effectiveness; not effective; possibly effective; probably effective; and effective for the indication. In addition, the board could order the inclusion of specific warnings in promotional material.

While the manufacturer was waiting for the initial review, the drug could be marketed with the warning that its safety and effectiveness had not yet been reviewed by the certification program. Any changes in promotional material would have to be reviewed by the board. The manufacturer could submit additional evidence to be considered by the board at any time. Failure by the manufacturer to submit information suggesting harmful effects would be a criminal offense (fraud) punishable by substantial fine and imprisonment. Similarly, falsification of reports submitted to the board would be a criminal offense. The categories of the general statements are similar to those used by the NAS-NCR review of pre-1962 drugs.[83] In fact, the NAS-NCR panels provide a model for implementation of the certification program.

It must be noted, however, that this certification scheme poses considerable problems. According to Dale Gieringer, "Drug safety and efficacy are strongly dependent on individual variables of the patient's situation, such as age, pregnancy, other health conditions, how the drug is used, what it is used for, and so on. To summarize these in just a few categories is impossible."[84] Devising categories that are sufficiently clear to be meaningful yet not cumbersome is a difficult task.

Effective operation of the certification program would help provide physicians and patients with unbiased assessments of the accuracy and reliability of promotional claims. Physicians and patients would then be free to decide whether or not the available information warranted use. Manufacturers would have an incentive to initiate testing and postmarketing studies so as to increase the safety and efficacy ratings of their products. At the same time, manufacturers convinced of the safety and efficacy of their products could begin marketing without delay, although widespread sales would be unlikely with low ratings by the certification boards.

Of the foregoing alternatives, strengthening strict liability laws, abolishing the community-standard provision, encouraging no-fault insurance, and promoting a bounty system would improve incentives for manufacturers and physicians to promote and develop effective and safe drugs without resorting to expensive and often innefficient centralized bureaucratic structures. The community-standards, insurance, and bounty combination is particularly desirable because it would improve the system of incentives without introducing centralized decision making. The improvement might not be enough, however, because the courts, as currently organized, are imperfect mechanisms for handling injury claims. Consequently, some form of compensation program might be a necessary complement for further improving the system of incentives. If the bounty system proved unworkable and the pharmaceutical industry failed to develop a certification program on its own, the promotion-certification program might supplement the other remedies.

The Benefits of Deregulation

Preventing unsafe and ineffective drugs from reaching the market is a laudable goal, but granting premarketing clearance authority to a regulatory agency is a blunt, expensive, and burdensome approach to achieving that goal. The political environment, in which therapeutic harm is deemed more serious than denied therapeutic benefit, leads to overly conservative decisions and inflexible procedures. In light of the criticisms of the current regulatory system, the marketplace can provide drug safety and efficacy if legal arrangements that protect consumers against fraud and make physicians and manufacturers fully liable for harms are strengthened. Such mechanisms could lead to greater aggregate health at lower costs, with no greater incidence of harmful side effects and without bureaucratic manipulation. Above all, the proposed market alternatives would protect individuals while simultaneously expanding the scope of individual choice and responsibility.

Several nonbureaucratic alternatives to regulation of drug development and promotion by the FDA have been suggested. (Similar approaches could be taken to replace the role played by the FDA in regulating food additives and cosmetics.) The analysis of the alternatives was, of necessity, speculative; in considering radical departures from current practice we must rely largely on theories of behavior. Nevertheless, several of the alternatives — mandatory insurance, the compensation program, and the certification program — have analogues in other areas or at least have some historical precedent. If the political climate becomes ripe for substantial reform of the regulation of health and safety, these alternatives deserve consideration.

NOTES

1. Even such a familiar and apparently safe drug as aspirin (acetylsalicylic acid) can cause gastrointestinal hemorrhage that sometimes leads to death. Dixon M. Woodbury and Edward Fingl, "Analgesic-Antipyretus, Anti-Inflammatory Agents, and Drugs Employed in the Therapy of Gout," in *The Pharmacological Basis of Therapeutics,* eds. Louis S. Goodman and Alfred Gilman (New York: Macmillan, 1975), pp. 325-358.

2. David Seidman, "The Politics of Policy Analysis: Protection or Overprotection in Drug Regulation?" *Regulation,* July-August 1977, pp. 22-37.

3. Between 1969 and 1979, the *Congressional Information Service Index* reported congressional hearings on FDA decisions concerning 38 specific drugs or drug classes. Of these hearings, only 2 questioned FDA decisions not to approve marketing of drugs. One of the latter hearings was on laetrile.

4. Stephen Wilson, *Food and Drug Regulation* (Washington, DC: American Council on Public Affairs, 1942), p. 22.

5. Oscar E. Anderson, Jr., *The Health of a Nation: Harvey W. Wiley and the Fight for Pure Food* (Chicago: University of Chicago Press, 1958), pp. 133-134.

6. U.S., *Statutes at Large,* vol. 34, pt. 1 (Washington, DC: Government Printing Office, 1907), pp. 768-772.

7. Arthur Kallet and F. J. Schlink, *100,000,000 Guinea Pigs: Dangers in Everyday Foods, Drugs, and Cosmetics* (New York: Vanguard Press, 1932).

8. Charles O. Jackson, *Food and Drug Legislation in the New Deal* (Princeton, NJ: Princeton University Press, 1970), p. 15.

9. For an account of the Elixir Sulfanilamide-Massengill disaster, see Jackson, *Food and Drug Legislation*, pp. 252-270.

10. U.S., *Statutes at Large*, vol. 52 (Washington, DC: Government Printing Office, 1938), pp. 1040-1059.

11. Alan Stone, *Economic Regulation and the Public Interest* (Ithaca, NY: Cornell University Press, 1977), pp. 153-164.

12. For a journalistic history of the 1962 amendments, see Richard Harris, *The Real Voice* (New York: Macmillan, 1964).

13. Bruce E. Thorp, "Washington Pressure — Drug Lobby Braces for Battles over Prescription Prices and Effectiveness," *National Journal*, 26 September 1970, p. 2093.

14. For a detailed history of the thalidomide tragedy, see the Insight Team of the Sunday *Times* of London, *Suffer the Children: The Story of Thalidomide* (New York: Viking Press, 1979), and Michael Pearson, *The Million-Dollar Bugs* (New York: G. P. Putnam, 1969), p. 209. For the birth defect figures in this paragraph, see *Suffer the Children*, p. 72.

15. As late as July 19, the general feeling in Washington was that Kefauver's Senate bill was dead for the session. See Harris, *The Real Voice*, p. 181.

16. U.S., *Statutes at Large*, vol. 76 (Washington, DC: Government Printing Office, 1963), pp. 791-792.

17. This provision was prompted by the charge that manufacturers deliberately selected unpronounceable generic names so that use of the brand names would be more attractive.

18. U.S., *Statutes at Large*, vol. 76, p. 781.

19. *Federal Register*, 10 August 1962, p. 7990.

20. For details, see U.S., Department of Health, Education and Welfare, "Clinical Testing: Synopsis of the New Drug Regulations," *FDA Papers*, March, 1967, pp. 21-25.

21. National Academy of Sciences, National Research Council, Division of Medical Sciences, "Final Report to the Commissioner of Food and Drugs," in *Drug Efficacy Study* (Washington, DC: National Academy of Sciences, 1969).

22. Milton Silverman and Philip R. Lee, *Pills, Profits, and Politics* (Berkeley and Los Angeles: University of California Press, 1974), pp. 121-133.

23. Charles C. Ames and Steven C. McCracken, "Framing Regulatory Standards to Avoid Formal Adjudication: The FDA as a Case Study," *California Law Review* 64 (January 1976): 14-73.

24. For a discussion of these regulations see William M. Wardell, "More Regulation or Better Therapies?" *Regulation*, September/October 1979, pp. 25-33. A recent review of regulations by the Bureau of Drugs suggests that the FDA has been incorrectly interpreting its own regulations on multiple studies. See U.S., Department of Health, Education and Welfare, FDA, Bureau of Drugs, *Investigational and New Drug Regulations-Revisions: Concept Document*, October 1979, p. 180.

25. Annabel Hecht, "New Standards for Clinical Research," *FDA Consumer*, November 1978, pp. 16-19.

26. However, manufacturers wishing to market new combinations or dosage forms of previously marketed drugs, to suggest new indications, or to use new manufacturing processes for previously marketed drugs are still required to submit full, or original, NDAs.

27. U.S., Department of Health, Education and Welfare, FDA, "Guidelines: Manufacturing and Controls for IND's and NDA's *FDA Papers,* June 1971, p. 4.

28. U.S., Department of Health, Education and Welfare, FDA, "Providing a Breakthrough for Drugs with Promise," *FDA Consumer,* July/August 1979, pp. 25-26. For a critique of the drug classification system, see William M. Wardell, Jean DiRaddo, and Michael Weintraub, "The Measurement of Therapeutic Value," *Journal of Clinical Pharmacology,* in press.

29. In the cases of methadone and L-dopa, the postmarketing requirements have substituted for portions of the normally required Phase III investigations. For this and other similar cases, see *Federal Register* 11680, 29 March 1974; Marion J. Finkel, "Phase IV Testing: FDA Viewpoint and Expectations," *Food Drug Cosmetic Law Journal* 33 (April 1978): 181-189.

30. FDA, "Providing a Breakthrough," p. 25.

31. Bureau of Drugs, *Investigational and New Drug Regulations-Revisions.*

32. Recent court cases have held drug companies liable for damages when their detail people have provided information nullifying otherwise adequate warnings provided in labeling. See Marsha Wertzberger Gardner, "Increasing Patient Awareness in Drug Therapy: Ramifications of a Patient Package Insert Requirement," *Georgetown Law Journal* 66 (February 1978): 837-867, pp. 104, 105.

33. United States v. Johnson, 221 U.S. 488 (1911).

34. Richard B. Ruge, "Regulation of Prescription Drug Advertising: Medical Progress and Private Enterprise," *Law and Contemporary Problems* 32 (Autumn 1967): 650-673.

35. U.S., Department of Health, Education and Welfare, Food and Drug Administration, *Annual Reports 1950-1974* (Washington, DC: Government Printing Office, 1977), p. 1073.

36. *Federal Register,* 25 June 1979, pp. 37434, 37467.

37. See Peter Temin, "The Origin of Compulsory Drug Prescriptions," *Journal of Law and Economics* 22 (19 April 1979): 91-105.

38. Although it is considered unethical, manufacturers sometimes plant stories in the press about new drug breakthroughs in the form of press releases or reports on scientific research.

39. *Federal Register,* 6 July 1979, pp. 40016, 40041.

40. Mashaw suggests a process whereby regulation begets regulation. Jerry L. Mashaw, "Regulation, Logic, and Ideology," *Regulation,* November/December 1979, pp. 44-51.

41. See, for example, William M. Wardell and Louis Lasagna, *Regulation and Drug Development* (Washington, DC: American Enterprise Institute, 1975).

42. William N. Hubbard, Jr., "Preclinical Problems of New Drug Development," in *Regulating New Drugs,* ed. Richard L. Landau (Chicago: University of Chicago Center for Policy Study, 1973), pp. 36-51.

43. The FDA requires statistically significant findings of efficacy. In the context of a placebo-controlled study, rejection of the null hypothesis that the treatment group had the same response as the control group in favor of the hypothesis that the treatment group had a more favorable response forms the basis for claims of statistical significance. In the context of an active-treatment-controlled study, the natural null hypothesis is that the active control and treatment groups gave the same response. The requirement for statistically significant findings in the active-control

case would require the new treatment to be not only effective but more effective than the existing treatment. Although many critics have argued for the greater-effectiveness standard, it is neither consistent with the law nor desirable, since two drugs with the same effectiveness may have different side effects for different patient groups.

44. William M. Wardell, Michael C. Tsianco, Sadanand N. Anavekar, and Henry T. Davis, "Postmarketing Surveillance of New Drugs: I. Review and Objectives and Methodology, *Journal of Clinical Pharmacology* 19 (February/March 1979): pp. 85-94.

45. U.S. Congress, House Committee on Government Operations, Subcommittee on Intergovernmental Relations and Human Resources, "The FDA's Regulation of the Drug 'Triazure,'" 27 October 1976.

46. Seymour Shubin, "Triazure and Public Drug Policies," *Perspectives in Biology and Medicine,* Winter 1979, pp. 185-204.

47. This discussion of cyanoacrylate is based on David A. Mathisen, "Whatever Happened to Human Body Glue?" *Reason,* May 1980, pp. 21-27.

48. This exchange took place during a question-and-answer period following Dr. Finkel's presentation at the Post Graduate Seminar in Clinical Pharmacology, Center for the Study of Drug Development, University of Rochester, November 1 1979.

49. Wardell, "More Regulation or Better Therapies?" pp. 25-33.

50. Those who criticize the pharmaceutical industry and the FDA for the existence of too many "me too" drugs may have an unrealistic view of the way pharmaceutical advances most often occur. For a review of the "me too" controversy, see Michael J. Hallerstan, "Too Many Drugs?" *Forum on Medicine,* March and April 1979, pp. 170-176, 284-291.

51. Such a change is advocated by Dr. Sidney Wolfe, director of the Citizen Health Research Group, a major consumer advocacy organization in the health and safety fields. See "Drugs: A Consumer Advocate's View," FDA Consumer 12 (December 1978 - January 1979): 10-15.

52. U.S. Senate, *Regulation of New Drug R&D by the Food and Drug Administration,* Hearings before the Committee on Labor and Public Welfare and the Committee on the Judiciary, 93rd Congress, 2nd Session, 25 September 1974, p. 207. This reference came to my attention through David Seidman, "The Politics of Policy Analysis."

53. William M. Wardell, "Introduction of New Therapeutic Drugs in the United States and Great Britain: An International Comparison," *Clinical Pharmacology and Therapeutics* 14 (September/October 1973): pp. 773-790.

54. William M. Wardell, "British Usage and American Awareness of Some New Therapeutic Drugs," *Clinical Pharmacology and Therapeutics* 14 (November/December 1973): pp. 1022-1034.

55. William M. Wardell, "Therapeutic Implications of the Drug Lag," *Clinical Pharmacology and Therapeutics* 15 (January 1974): pp. 73-96.

56. William M. Wardell, "A Close Inspection of the 'Calm Look': Rhetorical Amblyopia and Selective Amnesia at the Food and Drug Administration," *Journal of the American Medical Association* 239 (12 May 1978): pp. 2004-2011.

57. William M. Wardell, "The Drug Lag Revisited: A Comparison by Therapeutic Area of Patterns of Drugs Marketed in the United States and Great Britain from

1972 through 1976," *Clinical Pharmacology and Therapeutics* 24 (November 1978): pp. 499-524.

58. Martin M. Eisman and William M. Wardell, "Incremental Time Study: An Analysis of Time Spent in the Development and Approval of Drugs for the U.S. Market," Center for the Study of Drug Development, University of Rochester, 8 February 1980.

59. William M. Wardell, "Scientific Criteria and Methods of Drug Assessment: Requirements in the United States of America," in *Drug Assessment: Criteria and Methods,* ed. J. Z. Bowers and G. P. Velo (New York: Elsevier North Holland Bio-medical Press, 1979), pp. 91-100.

60. Lewis H. Sarett, "FDA Regulations and Their Influence on Future Research," *Research Management* 17 (March 1974): pp. 18-20.

61. Ronald W. Hansen, "The Pharmaceutical Development Process: Estimates of Development Costs and Times and the Effects of Proposed Regulatory Changes," in *Issues in Pharmaceutical Economics,* ed. Robert I. Chien (Lexington, MA: D.C. Heath, 1979), pp. 151-187.

62. Louis Lasagna, "Who Will Adopt the Orphan Drugs?" *Regulation,* November/December 1979, pp. 27-32.

63. For a review, see Henry G. Grabowski, *Drug Regulation and Innovation* (Washington, DC: American Enterprise Institute, 1976).

64. Sam Peltzman, "An Evaluation of Consumer Protection Legislation: The 1962 Drug Amendments," *Journal of Political Economy* 81 (September/October 1973): pp. 1049-1091.

65. Peltzman also provided a less convincing and conceptually flawed analysis of consumer behavior in support of this argument. For a critique, see Thomas McGuire, Richard Nelson, and Thomas Spavins, "An Evaluation of Consumer Protection Legislation: The 1962 Drug Amendments: A Comment," *Journal of Political Economy* 83 (June 1975): pp. 655-667.

66. Martin Neil Baily, "Research and Development Costs and Returns: The U.S. Pharmaceutical Industry," *Journal of Political Economy* 80 (January/February 1972): pp. 70-85.

67. Henry G. Grabowski, John M. Vernon, and Lacy Glenn Thomas, "Estimating the Effects of Regulation on Innovation: An International Comparative Analysis of the Pharmaceutical Industry," *Journal of Law and Economics* 21 (April 1978): pp. 133-163.

68. Michael Weintraub, "The United States: Hospital Formularies" in *Controlling the Use of Therapeutic Drugs: An International Comparison* ed. William M. Wardell (Washington, DC: American Enterprise Institute, 1978), pp. 31-55.

69. Ibid., pp. 32-33.

70. M.C. Meyer, H. Bates, Jr., and R.G. Swift, "The Role of State Formularies," *Journal of the American Pharmaceutical Association* 14 (December 1974): pp. 663-666.

71. This information was provided in a personal communication from Dale Gieringer (Menlo Park, 1981). See also John B. Blake, ed., *Safeguarding the Public* (Baltimore: Johns Hopkins University Press, 1970).

72. Telephone interview, 28 May 1980, with Dr. Mark Abramowicz, editor of *Medical Letter on Drugs and Therapeutics* (Medical Letter Incorporated, 56 Harrison Street, New Rochelle, New York, 10801).

73. William L. Prosser, *Handbook of the Law of Torts* (St. Paul, MN: West Publishing, 1971), pp. 646-649.

74. National Academy of Sciences, "Final Report," in *Drug Efficacy Study.*

75. U.S. Congress, Senate, Select Committee on Small Business, Subcommittee on Monopoly, *Hearing,* statement of J. Richard Crout, Director of the Bureau of Drugs of the Food and Drug Administration, 28 April 1976, pp. 14064-14104.

76. Silverman and Lee, *Pills, Profits, and Politics,* p. 73.

77. Dale Gieringer made this point in a personal communication (Menlo Park, 1981).

78. A major exception is Minnesota. In Mulder v. Parke Davis & Co., 288 Minn. 332, 181 N.W. 2d 882 (1970), the Minnesota Supreme Court ruled that failing to take account of information provided in the labeling is *prima facie* evidence of negligence. It appears that Illinois and South Dakota have adopted the *Mulder* approach. See Gardner, "Increasing Patient Awareness," n. 141.

79. Dale Gieringer noted these two problems in a personal communication (Menlo Park, 1981).

80. Merrill also suggests that manufacturers be held liable for any injury that is not the result of physician or patient negligence. Richard A. Merrill, "Compensation for Prescription Drug Injuries." *Virginia Law Review* 59 (January 1973): pp. 1-120.

81. To gain these advantages, firms would have to be prohibited from self-insuring.

82. Hermann Kampffmeyer, "West Germany," in *Controlling the Use of Therapeutic Drugs: An International Comparison,* ed. William M. Wardell (Washington DC: American Enterprise Institute, 1978), pp. 145-154.

83. The categories used by the NAS-NRC were effective, probably effective, possibly effective, effective but not for all recommended uses, ineffective as a fixed combination, and ineffective.

84. Quoted from a personal communication from Dale Gieringer (Menlo Park, 1981).

3

Interaction Effects

Toward an Automobile Industry Policy

WILLIAM A. NISKANEN

Problems

The U.S. auto industry is in serious trouble. U.S. firms lost over $4 billion in 1980, and at the end of 1980, nearly 200,000 auto workers were on indefinite layoff. American Motors managed to survive only by merging with Renault, a firm owned by the French government. Chrysler avoided bankruptcy only by divesting its European operations, by an infusion of U.S. government loan guarantees that total $1.2 billion to date, and by labor-contract concessions that may total over $1 billion during the 3-year contract. Ford Motor Company is in serious trouble, despite the success of its overseas operations. Even mighty General Motors, the world's largest industrial firm, lost nearly $1 billion in 1980.

These bleak conditions led each of the three smaller firms to seek different forms of assistance from the federal government. American Motors occasionally sought and received selective relief from regulatory standards. Chrysler sought and received a commitment of $1.5 billion in government loan guarantees, conditional on concessions

---

AUTHOR'S NOTE: This chapter was prepared when the author was a professor at the UCLA Graduate School of Management. The views expressed do not represent the position of the Council of Economic Advisers or the U.S. government.

from the banks, the auto workers, and the most affected states. Ford Motor Company and the United Auto Workers (UAW) asked the International Trade Commission (ITC) for severe import quotas. Although the ITC rejected this proposed quota, based on a finding that increased imports were not the primary cause of the industry problems, the government of Japan later imposed a "voluntary restraint agreement" on car exports to the United States, apparently in response to U.S. pressure.

Automobile manufacturing is one of the largest industries in the United States. Auto production generates about 4 percent of the gross national product (GNP) and employs about 3 percent of the labor force. The relative importance of this industry, of course, is much higher in such states as Michigan, Missouri, and Ohio. Thus, continuation of the distressed conditions in this industry undoubtedly will lead to even more such proposals for special government assistance.

Causes

An understanding of the several causes of the distressed condition of the auto manufacturers is necessary background to addressing the numerous proposals to assist the industry. The four primary causes are the recession, oil and gas price increases, industry errors, and state and federal regulations.

The Recession

The automobile industry, like housing and other durable goods industries, is unusually vulnerable to recessions. Auto sales and profits often decline even if the economy grows at a slower rate than in the previous year. Most of the recent decline in total vehicle sales and in U.S. production was clearly attributable to the recession that began in February 1980. Table 3.1 compares car sales and U.S. production from February through September of 1979 with the same months in 1980, illustrating the effect of the recession in the later period.

During this period, the sales of domestic cars declined less than total sales, because import sales also declined slightly. U.S. car production declined somewhat more only because of the excessive inventory level at the beginning of the recession. Based on these figures there is no plausible way to attribute the decline in U.S. car production during this period to the alleged surge of import sales.

TABLE 3.1 The Effect of the 1980 Recession on the U.S. Car Market

	*U.S. Retail Sales**			*U.S. Production**
	Total	*Import*	*Domestic*	
February-September				
1979	7.394	1.677	5.717	5.138
1980	5.973	1.647	4.326	3.621
Difference				
Units	−1.421	−.03	−1.391	−1.517
Percentage	−19.2	−1.8	−24.3	−29.3

*In millions.

The 1980 recession, like all recessions, was primarily caused by erratic monetary policy. A reduction in money growth in the winter was followed by a decline in the money supply in the spring, combined with a wholly perverse set of credit controls. Then the money supply increased at a very rapid rate during the summer, followed by a moderate growth in the fall. This policy also led to unusually wide swings in interest rates. The automobile industry is only the most visible and regionally concentrated victim of this erratic policy.

The Increase in Gasoline and Oil Prices

The large increases in real gasoline and oil prices in 1974 and 1979 substantially changed the composition of new vehicle demand in the United States and the relative competitiveness of the U.S. auto industry.

Some history is necessary to an understanding of the nature of these effects. Since the 1930s, the United States and Canada have been the only major markets for large cars, primarily because of a distinctive gasoline tax policy. Starting in the 1930s, most other nations levied high gasoline taxes to raise general revenues and to reduce the demand for imported oil. The United States and Canada levied much lower gasoline taxes, using these revenues primarily to finance the construction and maintenance of highways. Just prior to the first major oil price increase in 1974, as a consequence, the price of gasoline in Europe and Japan was roughly 4 times the U.S. price. The differences among the major automotive markets primarily reflected these tax-induced differences in gasoline prices. In Europe and Japan, most cars were small and fuel efficient. In the United States and

TABLE 3.2 The Effect of the 1979 Gasoline Price Increase on the U.S. Car Market

	*U.S. Retail Sales**			*U.S. Production**
	Total	*Import*	*Domestic*	
April-January				
1978-1979	9.541	1.655	7.886	7.657
1979-1980	8.649	1.989	6.660	6.541
Difference				
Units	−.892	.334	−1.226	−1.146
Percentage	−9.3	20.2	−15.5	−14.9

*In millions.

Canada, most cars were larger and not very fuel efficient. Several other conditions abroad — such as specific taxes on larger engines and vehicles, denser cities, less developed highway systems, and lower incomes — reinforced the gasoline price effect on the automotive market. The combination of the substantial differences in the characteristics of new vehicle demand and strong economies of scale created an effective import barrier around each major market. The price of small cars was based on costs in Europe and later Japan, and the price of large cars was based on costs in the United States and Canada. The effective protection of the North American market during this period permitted the United Auto Workers to bargain for a level of labor compensation that is around 60 percent higher than the average U.S. industrial compensation without any significant loss of sales or employment to foreign producers.

The large increases in real gasoline and oil prices in 1974 and 1979 substantially reduced this effective protection of the North American market, probably forever. In 1974, the price of oil quadrupled and the U.S. price of gasoline increased around 50 percent. From 1974 until the spring of 1979, the real price of gasoline declined gradually, reviving the demand for larger vehicles. In the spring of 1979, the price of oil doubled and the U.S. price of gasoline again increased around 50 percent. Table 3.2 compares car sales and U.S. production from April 1978 through January 1979 with the same months in 1979 and 1980, illustrating the effect of the gasoline price increase in the later period.

During this period, changes in U.S. car sales were dominated by the substantial shift from large to small cars, induced by the gasoline price increase. Overall sales of domestic cars declined less than overall sales of large cars. Although import sales increased substantially, the import share in the sales of small cars declined. In general, the sales changes during this period are characteristic of the longer period since 1973. The progressive increase in the import share of total sales has been entirely attributable to the progressive increase in the small-car share, with no apparent trend in the import share of small-car sales. In the absence of trade restrictions or fuel economy regulations, I would expect the import share to fall relative to its present level. I also would expect the small-car share to fall a bit relative to its present level, and, as a consequence, the import share as well, primarily because in any durables market the first-year effects of changes are larger than the long-term effects. Over a longer period of time, again in the absence of rapid increases in gasoline prices or trade restrictions, I would expect the small-car share to stabilize at around 50 percent of total sales and the import share to stabilize at about 22 percent.

Another major effect of the increase in oil prices is not generally recognized. The oil price increases have substantially weakened the exchange rates of oil-poor nations relative to the currencies of oil-rich nations and those in which the OPEC (Organization of Petroleum Exporting Countries) nations have invested their payments surplus. This has increased the competitiveness of manufactured products from Japan relative to the United States and, particularly, Britain. Each of 2 major oil price increases reduced the dollar price of the yen by around 10 percent. The increases in oil prices thus both increased the demand for small cars and reduced the dollar price of Japanese cars. The exchange-rate effects are primarily responsible for the increase in the Japanese share of total imports and the reduction in the profits on U.S. small cars. The combination of the exchange-rate effects and the UAW compensation premium relative to average U.S. industrial labor costs is the primary reason that the U.S. firms are not competitive in the production of small cars.

U.S. Industry Errors

Many commentators on the present distressed conditions of the U.S. auto industry have casually attributed these problems to an alleged persistent industry failure to provide the types of cars demanded by American consumers. However, these charges, with one possible exception, are not consistent with the facts. The record indicates that the U.S. industry has introduced a very wide range of vehicles and has continued to supply any vehicle that proves to be profitable.

Since World War II, the history of the U.S. auto industry includes the failure of 4 firms that introduced small cars too soon. The surviving firms continued to test the small-car market with both domestic and imported vehicles. The Vega and the Pinto were introduced in the early 1970s; although large numbers of these cars were sold, neither was apparently profitable. The U.S. industry overreacted to the 1974 gasoline price increase by overproducing small cars that had to be discounted the next winter. Each of the present companies started a major restructuring of its product lines in 1974 to provide the range of smaller cars introduced in 1979 and 1980. Sales of the Chevette, the first U.S.-produced "world car," were far below expectations until the 1979 oil price increase. Even in recent years, there has been a regular negative correlation between company profits and average fuel economy. Granted that the U.S. auto companies did not forecast the large increase in gasoline prices in 1974 and in 1979, but neither did anyone else. The government studies produced in 1977 to rationalize the 1981-1984 fuel-economy standards forecast an average gasoline price of $.65/gallon during the 1980s. The industry forecasts were often wrong, but there is no evidence of a persistent failure to underestimate the demand for fuel-efficient cars. The one consistent finding is that U.S.-produced small cars have not been very profitable.

The record is similar on most other product attributes. For example, in 1956 Ford introduced and promoted cars with improved safety features, but there was no significant market demand for these features. The U.S. companies, however, apparently did underestimate the demand for product reliability for some years. Japanese cars, for example, have a far lower repair rate during the warranty period than even the best U.S. cars, and this has undoubtedly contributed to their sales success. In a belated response, the U.S. companies initiated a major quality-improvement program in 1979. Some uncertainty remains concerning whether the U.S. companies can be competitive in supplying increased reliability, given their high labor costs.

The major persistent error by the U.S. auto firms has been the failure to discipline labor costs. A part of this problem is the asymmetry of the bargaining relation. Each three years, the general provisions of the labor contract are negotiated by one target firm and the UAW. Since the target firm bears all of the costs of a strike and only a proportion of the benefits of a favorable contract, the firm's short-run interests are served by making concessions to avoid a prolonged strike. Chrysler usually caves in within a few days, Ford takes a couple of weeks, and General Motors a little longer, just in proportion to the share in the benefits of a good contract that they realize. Some form of joint action by all of the firms, such as a lockout or a strike cost-sharing arrangement, would be necessary to correct this bias, but such action may be judged illegal under present labor law. This negotiation process, combined with the effective protection of the U.S. market from foreign competition until 1974, has led to labor costs that are now around $20.00 per hour, about 60 percent higher than average U.S. industrial labor costs. Prior to the rapid growth in the demand for small cars, these high labor costs increased U.S. vehicle prices but did not substantially reduce U.S. auto industry profits, production, or employment. In recent years, however, these high labor costs have made the U.S. firms uncompetitive in producing cars that now account for over half of total sales. (They never were competitive in the production of small cars, but now small cars are 60 percent of the market instead of 15 percent of the market.)

This problem cannot be resolved by producing better small cars or by retooling U.S. plants, because the Japanese firms can also use this technology; this problem can only be resolved by reducing the UAW labor cost premium relative to average U.S. industrial labor costs. In this regard, it is important to recognize that the relevant comparison is not between U.S. and Japanese wage rates; the relevant comparison is UAW wage rates relative to U.S. average industrial wages. The dollar/yen exchange rate will reflect the average wages and productivity on traded products.

U.S. Auto Regulations

The U.S. auto industry is subject to a unique, complex, and conflicting set of regulations:

- Federal fuel-economy standards increase domestic costs and reduce safety. An estimate has been made that auto deaths may increase by 2300 lives a year by 1984 as a consequence of the mandatory reduction in car size.
- Federal emissions standards increase prices and reduce fuel economy by roughly 7.5 percent.

- Federal safety and damageability standards increase prices and reduce fuel economy, at a cost in gasoline of about $25 a year per car.
- State insurance regulations reduce safety.
- State franchise regulations increase prices.
- Federal tariffs on steel and other materials and components increase domestic costs.
- Federal energy price controls and price guidelines have adversely affected the auto industry in the past.

This tangled web of auto regulations is only one of the several causes of the industry problems. In the absence of any industry-specific regulations, the industry would still have serious problems adapting to the changing auto market. Nevertheless, the problems attributable to these regulations should be the primary focus of any government actions to assist the auto industry, because these problems are of the government's own making. The Carter Administration's response to the industry conditions was to consider a new set of interventions developed by several government-industry task forces. This review was summarized in the Goldschmidt report, which encouraged a "socioeconomic compact" among government, industry, and labor to resolve the problems of this industry. A more attractive alternative would be to review the whole set of existing regulations to determine whether they serve the general interest.

The Fuel-Economy Standards

The Energy Policy and Conservation Act of 1975 established gasoline mileage standards of 20 mpg for model year 1980 and 27.5 mpg for model year 1985, with the secretary of the Department of Transportation authorized to set the standards for the interim years (1981-1985), to reduce the 1985 standard to 26 mpg, and to set the standards for light trucks. The current standards for cars and light trucks, presented in Table 3.3, are front-loaded.

This same act maintained the price controls of oil and gasoline, which prevented the U.S. price of gasoline from increasing to a level based on the world oil price. Thus Congress simultaneously reduced the market demand for fuel economy and mandated the production of more fuel-efficient new vehicles. This act also requires that 75 percent of the value added for each car and truck line be produced in the United States and Canada, thus preventing the domestic companies

TABLE 3.3 Fuel-Economy Standards

Model Year	*Miles per Gallon*	
	Cars	*Light Trucks*
1981	22	16.7
1982	24	18
1983	26	19
1984	27	20
1985	27.5	21

from counting imported vehicle lines against the fuel-economy average. This constraint forces domestic companies to produce their entire vehicle lines in North America, regardless of whether it may be more efficient to produce smaller vehicles abroad. This provision, for example, led Ford to withdraw its most fuel-efficient car, the Fiesta, from the American market because of a concern that it would displace sales from its new Escort, sales that count against the fuel-economy average.

The primary short-term problem caused by these standards is that the domestic companies must finance a more accelerated rate of product development than they would in response to market demands. The domestic companies are now expected to spend around $3.6 billion for each one-mile increase in the fuel-economy standards. The Department of Transportation has now acknowledged that the total product development costs and retooling costs for the U.S. auto industry will be about $70 billion in 1980 dollars. These huge fixed costs are the primary reasons that the company losses in 1980 were so great. In the more severe 1974-1975 recession, by comparison, both General Motors and Ford reported small profits.

Over a longer period, consumers will bear most of these costs in the form of higher prices for large cars and in reduced interior space, acceleration, ride quality, and safety. The domestic costs of producing all cars will be increased by the 75 percent constraint. The price of small cars will be less affected, because these prices will be based on Japanese production costs, where they have already achieved the higher fuel-economy levels.

The Emission Standards

New emission standards were imposed in model year 1981, reducing the allowed emissions of hydrocarbon, carbon monoxide, and nitrogen oxide. In order to meet these standards, all cars must incorporate catalytic converters and must use unleaded gasoline. These standards increased new car prices by around $200 and, just in terms of the difference between unleaded and leaded gasoline, will increase annual gasoline costs per car by around $25 per year. For a given automotive technology, the emission standards also reduce fuel economy. The 1981 standards are estimated to have increased the task of meeting the fuel economy standards by about 2 mpg, thus increasing the fixed costs of meeting these standards.

The Safety and Damageability Standards

The National Highway Traffic Safety Agency (NHTSA) earlier established a standard that passive restraints (either automatic belts or air bags) must be included in new large cars in model year 1984. The passive belts can be bypassed easily; around 20 percent of the passive belts that people have voluntarily purchased have been disconnected. The airbag will cost over $500, will probably reduce the use of seat belts, and will not be effective in side collisions. In addition, the high relative cost of airbags will probably restrict their use to luxury and large cars. The original timing of this standard would have increased the relative price of domestic cars during the next two model years, but this standard was repealed in late 1981.

Other Regulations

In most states, insurance regulations allocate high-risk policies among the insurance providers. This reduces insurance rates on high-risk drivers, increases rates on other drivers, and probably reduces highway safety.

State franchise regulations restrict the number and location of new auto dealers and the provisions of the franchise relations between the auto manufacturers and the dealers. A recent study by Richard Smith[1] estimates that these regulations increased average car prices by around $500 in 1972. These regulations also probably increase the relative price of small cars and thus reduce fuel economy.

President Carter reimposed the trigger prices on steel, potentially increasing steel prices by 12 percent. The tariffs on other materials and components range up to 15 percent. (For comparison, the tariff on an assembled car is 2.9 percent.) The trigger prices and tariffs increase the cost of domestic manufacture relative to the cost of importing an assembled vehicle.

Although most of the price controls established by President Nixon in August 1971 were removed in April 1974, price controls on oil and gasoline were retained. President Ford also removed the small fee on imported oil. These actions reduced the relative price of gasoline and reduced the demand for fuel economy. The gasoline price controls and allocations were also directly responsible for the gasoline shortages that developed when the price of oil increased sharply in the spring of 1970.

President Carter's overall price guidelines attempted to restrain the rate of increase. Although it is difficult to determine whether any of these guidelines were binding, there is reason to believe they were more restraining on prices than on wages and more restraining on larger companies than on smaller companies. Thus some part of the record losses of the domestic auto companies in 1980 may have been due to a differential effect of these guidelines on prices and costs. With the Reagan Administration some of this has been changed. President Reagan eliminated the gasoline and oil price controls as well as the Carter wage-price guidelines in the first few days he was in office.

General Effects

One general effect of many of these regulations has been to increase the economies of scale in the auto industry, because the costs are more a function of the range of a company's product lines than of total production. As a consequence, the U.S. market may not be able to support more than two full-line companies. Another general effect is that these regulations have substantially restricted the ability of U.S. companies to respond to the market forces and to correct the industry errors that are the dominant causes of the present problems.

Solutions

Many policies are now being considered to assist the U.S. auto industry. Most of these policies share two characteristics — they are unrelated to the major causes of the industry problems, and they would impose substantial costs on those consumers and taxpayers who do not work for the auto industry. The difficult and critical challenge is to choose an auto industry policy that merits broad support.

The Chrysler loan guarantee and the Ford-UAW proposal for import quotas illustrate the characteristics of most of the proposals now being considered. The expressed rationale for both of these policies is that the auto companies are experiencing a temporary cash-flow problem resulting from the recession and the high costs for product development and retooling of production facilities. However, these policies only delay the day of reckoning, because the U.S. companies, even with new products and new production facilities, cannot generate adequate profits on small cars under the present labor contract. The Chrysler loan guarantee will probably cost taxpayers $1.5 billion to defer bankruptcy for 1 or 2 years. Moreover, the price of government financing has included restrictions on Chrysler's opportunities to rationalize its production base. A government study estimated that import quotas would cost auto buyers several times the annual salary of auto workers for each job protected.

Any auto policy that will prove effective must address the basic causes of the industry's problems. Any auto policy that merits broad support must also generate benefits to the broader American community. The four basic policy proposals summarized in this section are designed to meet both of these criteria.

Stabilization of Monetary Growth

The auto industry has become increasingly vulnerable to recessions, given the high fixed costs and increasing debt necessary to finance accelerated product development and production retooling. Nevertheless, the government should avoid any specific assistance to the industry to compensate for the effects of the present period of weak demand and high interest rates. The primary way to avoid both future recessions and high interest rates is to maintain a slow, steady increase in the money supply. (Contrary to popular impression, high interest rates, with a short lag, are the result of rapid money growth.) This policy would substantially reduce the cash-flow problems of the auto industry, reduce the production capacity required to meet peak demands, and generate substantial benefits to the broader community.

Termination of Price Controls on Gasoline and Oil

The price controls on gasoline and oil have already been removed. One effect of this action has been to eliminate the rationale for the fuel-economy standards. Reimposition of a fee on imported oil, at least sufficient to finance the strategic petroleum reserve should also be considered. At the present time, these actions will not have a significant effect on prices; over time, however, their primary value to the auto industry would be to reduce the sort of gasoline shortages that developed in the spring of 1979 and to reduce the rationale for the fuel-economy standards.

There is no effective way to offset the increase in the competitiveness of Japanese manufacturers that resulted from the oil price increase. Any restraint on the import of Japanese vehicles would only further weaken the yen, increasing Japanese competitiveness in other product areas.

Reduction of the UAW Bargaining Advantage

Companies in any industry will make temporary errors; after the fact, it is easy to identify numerous errors by the U.S. auto industry. These errors, however, are not likely to persist unless reinforced by government policy. Thus it is especially important to avoid any specific government actions designed to offset temporary industry errors. The auto firms themselves have much better information and incentives to correct these errors than would any government agency.

The major persistent error by the U.S. auto companies has been to allow their labor costs to increase relative to those in other U.S. industries. This error has been reinforced by 5 government policies: (1) the Chrysler loan guarantee; (2) the 75 percent domestic content rule on each vehicle line; (3) broader eligibility for trade-adjustment assistance; (4) the high relative tariffs on materials and components; and (5) National Labor Relations Board (NLRB) restrictions on industry bargaining practices. A change in each of these policies would substantially reduce the UAW's bargaining advantage. The following 5 changes should be considered:

Do not extend the Chrysler loan guarantee. The potential bankruptcy of Chrysler has been the only event in recent years to reduce UAW labor costs. Chrysler has already gained concessions of over $1 per hour and is seeking more. A bankruptcy would permit Chrysler to break the labor contract and would strengthen the position of the other firms to offer jobs for contract concessions.

Broaden or eliminate the 75 percent rule. A change in legislation should be considered that would change the 75 percent domestic content rule from *each* vehicle line to the *whole* vehicle line, thus permitting the automobile companies to import the smallest vehicles and specialize in the domestic production of larger vehicles, an area in which they have a comparative advantage. A more drastic alternative would be to eliminate any domestic content rule, but there is probably no potential consensus for this alternative. A change in the present situation, however, would reduce the demand for U.S. auto labor and thus increase the potential for contract concessions.

Restrict the eligibility for trade-adjustment assistance. Most of the auto workers now receiving trade-adjustment assistance, at a cost to taxpayers of over $1 billion a year, were involved in the production of large cars. However, the decline in demand for large cars was primarily due to the recession and the increased gasoline prices, not to an increase in small-car imports. Restricting this assistance to workers who were directly displaced by imports would reduce both taxpayer costs and the UAW bargaining advantage.

Reduce the tariffs on materials and components. At present, the tariffs on automotive materials and components are substantially higher than that on assembled cars. Reducing these tariffs would reduce the demand for UAW labor that is now producing materials and components and reduce the cost of producing an assembled vehicle.

Change the NLRB rules affecting bargaining practices. At present, the industry response to UAW contract demands is restricted by National Labor Relations Board rulings. A strike cost-sharing fund would probably be allowed, but a joint lockout would not. Clarifying and relaxing these rules would facilitate a more symmetric bargaining relationship.

These five actions involve hard choices, but there is no apparent way to maintain the benefits of both free trade and a healthy U.S. auto industry unless the relative UAW labor costs are reduced.

Substantial Reduction of U.S. Auto Regulation

The United States is the only nation with a broad set of regulations on automobile product attributes. No other nation has similar fuel-economy and safety regulations. Only Japan has similarly restrictive emissions regulations. Most of these U.S. auto regulations generate no general benefits or the incremental benefits are less than the incremental costs. The following major changes in auto regulations should be considered:

Reduce or eliminate the fuel-economy standard. In the absence of price controls on gasoline and oil, auto drivers pay the full cost of their energy consumption plus the cost of building and maintaining highways. In this condition, auto use generates no external costs on the broader community, other than the costs of air pollution and congestion. The termination of price controls, thus, eliminated the basic rationale for the fuel-economy standards. If, for whatever reason, gasoline is considered to be more valuable than its market price, an oil import fee or a phased increase in the gasoline tax would be much more efficient than imposed standards, because it would both reduce driving by existing vehicles and increase the demand for more fuel-efficient vehicles.

Whatever the rationale for the fuel-economy standards, they do not meet a cost-benefit test. Table 3.4 summarizes the major benefits and costs of the present standards on cars. The gasoline savings per car year are based on an average mileage of 10,000 miles per year and a gasoline price of $1.25 per gallon. Total annual savings are based on an average production of 11 million domestic vehicles per year. Total benefits from reduced gasoline consumption are the present value of the annual benefits in perpetuity, discounted at a 10 percent rate. Total costs are based on the estimate that the domestic companies must spend around $3.6 billion per mile increase in the fuel-economy average. The net benefit column indicates that each of these standards would generate substantial net costs at the present price of gasoline. Since the future price of gasoline and oil is so uncertain, Table 3.4 also presents the implicit price of gasoline and oil at which the benefits would be equal to the costs; these prices are so much higher than the present prices that there seems to be no plausible set of prices for which these standards would generate net benefits. It is, I think, not irrelevant that the price of gasoline in Europe and Japan is now about $2.50 a gallon, and that the fuel economy of new vehicles in those countries is about 28-29 mpg, suggesting that these numbers are roughly consistent with the foreign experience in terms of long-term market response to higher gasoline prices.

This simple example is abstracted from a number of important considerations. The benefits due to gasoline savings are overestimated, because actual fuel economy has been only 75-85 percent of

TABLE 3.4 Benefits and Costs of the Current MPG Standards

Model Year	MPG	Annual Gasoline Savings per Vehicle (gallons)	Annual Gasoline Savings per Vehicle (dollars)	Total Annual Gasoline Savings* (dollars)	Total Costs* (dollars)	Net Benefits* (dollars)	Implicit Prices Gasoline (dollars)	Implicit Prices Oil (dollars)
1981	22	—	—	—	—	—	—	—
1982	24	38	47	5.208	7.2	−1.992	1.73	58
1983	26	32	40	4.407	7.2	−2.793	2.04	65
1984	27	14	18	1.959	3.6	−1.641	2.30	75
1985	27.5	7	8	.926	1.8	−.874	2.43	81

*In billions.

the test-stand fuel economy on which the standards are based. The costs are substantially underestimated, because they do not reflect any loss to the consumer caused by reduced interior space, ride quality, acceleration, and safety. Incorporation of these effects would increase the net costs of the present standards.

Without a change in the law, the new administration could reduce the 1985 standard to 26 mpg, requiring an increase of only 1 mpg per year for the next 4 years. This action would reduce the net costs of these standards by over $2.5 billion and should receive immediate attention. My preference would be to repeal the entire fuel-economy law, but there is probably no consensus for this alternative.

Reduce or change the emissions standards. Automotive emissions generate external costs on the broader community, so there is a clear basis for some form of emissions policy. The present standards, however, were established prior to any substantial evidence of the effects of automotive emissions on health and aesthetic conditions. The still rudimentary present evidence indicates that there are no significant effects on mortality from either hydrocarbons or carbon monoxide. Oxides of nitrogen at high concentration levels appear to have a significant effect on mortality, but these emissions are unusually costly to control. Most air pollution damage is due to oxides of sulphur and to particulates, neither of which (except the particulates from diesel exhaust) is a product of automotive emissions.

Moreover, the present standards do not meet a cost-benefit test. A study prepared by the National Academy of Science (NAS) estimated that the present standards would generate net costs of $3 billion a year in 1973 dollars. The real price of gasoline has doubled since 1973, so the annual net costs of these standards are now probably higher.

Given this information, my case against the emissions standards is not based on their conceptual rationale, but concerns their level, or form. The NAS study recommended that either the nitrogen oxide standard be relaxed or that 2 standards be maintained. The latter alternative would permit individual states to select standards based on their local conditions. The authors of the NAS study estimated that either approach would reduce the costs to a level more nearly equal to the estimated benefits. A more radical alternative would be to substitute a "smog tax" (such as several colleagues and I, then at Rand Corporation, proposed over 20 years ago[2]) for the entire standard-setting policy. A high gasoline tax, say 50 cents a gallon, would be levied in each affected airshed. After a voluntary vehicle inspection, auto owners would receive rebates in proportion to the efficiency with which their vehicles controlled the relevant pollutants. This policy would have several advantages to a policy of emissions standards. Automobile owners would be taxed in proportion to the amount of their cars' emissions, rather than as a function of new-car purchases. They would also have an incentive to maintain their engines and emissions control devices prior to vehicle inspections. The auto manufacturers, in turn, could then choose any engine and emissions technology to meet the market. For any level of emissions control, this policy would be more efficient than vehicle standards and would also generate substantial revenues for local governments.

The present auto emissions policy is very costly and is not working very well. Smog is a continuing problem in many areas. The federal government is now in a confrontation with the State of California over the frequency of vehicle inspections. A thorough review of federal auto emissions policy should be considered, both to increase its effectiveness and to reduce its costs.

Substantially reduce the safety and damageability standards. Auto safety is one of those issues that often seems to defy rational discourse. Since there is no way to value the life of a specific individual, some people dismiss the use of any form of calculation as a basis for evaluating safety issues. Several aggregate conditions, however, must be recognized as the basis for any discourse on these matters. For a half century prior to establishing the first federal auto safety regulations in the late 1960s, there was a progressive reduction in traffic fatalities per 100 million vehicle miles, with small variations due to economic and demographic conditions and the rate of alcohol consumption. Over this period, however, there was a remarkable stability in the traffic fatalities per 100 million persons, suggesting that the primary value of improved auto safety has been the value of increased driving, rather than the value of a reduced probability of death due to a traffic accident. During the last 15 years, the continued decline in traffic fatalities per 100 million vehicle miles is almost entirely explained by the same set of conditions that explains the earlier history. Although there has been a progressive increase in auto safety regulations in this later period, there is no evidence that these regulations have significantly improved the aggregate auto safety rate.

There are three conditions under which auto manufacturers may not provide vehicles with sufficient safety characteristics:

- Auto manufacturers may not have sufficient information about the market demand for safety characteristics. In this case the only obvious role for government to play is to inform the manufacturers about the results of auto safety research, because the manufacturers have sufficient incentive to provide any product attributes for which there is a market demand.
- Auto users may not have sufficient information about the relation between auto safety and vehicle characteristics. In those cases in which this information is easy to understand, the most efficient government action is to inform consumers, as with the "Buckle Up for Safety" campaign. In those extremely limited cases for which the cost of informing consumers is high, the variance of consumer demands is low, and the cost of the vehicle characteristics is low, some regulation of vehicle characteristics can be justified. Auto manufacturers probably have sufficient incentive to provide these characteristics without regulation, but are not likely to oppose regulations that standardize these characteristics.
- Auto purchasers may not have sufficient incentive to purchase safety characteristics because they do not bear the full expected costs of auto accidents. This condition provides the rationale for mandatory auto liability insurance and a concern that insurance rates reflect full actuarial costs. In addition, the general community may value safety more highly than do directly affected individuals. This paternalistic concern provides a rationale for some form of subsidy of safety conditions but does not by itself justify regulation that increases the cost to the affected parties. (I find it difficult to rationalize safety regulations on a benevolent ground by imposing costs on the party that you are presumably benevolent toward. I was intrigued that the Goldschmidt report suggests that there may be a basis for the federal government to both mandate air bags and pay part of the cost.)

The passive restraint standard will increase the safety of front-seat occupants of vehicles in a limited range of crash conditions, perhaps reducing auto fatalities by as much as 6000 per year. However, whatever the rationale for auto safety regulation or the value of improved auto safety, this standard does not meet a cost-effectiveness test. This standard would cost auto purchasers around $2 billion a year, about equal to the sum of all auto regulations to date. The cost per life saved is far higher than the cost of small increases in seat belt usage or of many potential investments in highway conditions. It is difficult to identify any public purpose that is served by protecting people who choose not to protect themselves by the use of seat belts. There is some evidence, moreover, that people drive faster when it is safer to do so; in this case, forcing new-car buyers to purchase safer vehicles may reduce the safety of others. This standard was recently repealed.

NHTSA also imposes several standards — such as a requirement that bumpers withstand a 5-mph collision — to reduce the physical damage to vehicles. These standards also increase price and weight, reduce fuel economy, and serve no public purpose; the auto manufacturers and auto buyers have sufficient incentive to provide vehicles that are not easily damaged, and no other party is affected. A review of the damageability standards should be considered.

Several other types of government actions are likely to be more effective in increasing auto safety than incremental regulations of vehicle characteristics. State insurance regulations could be changed to increase the insurance rates on high-risk drivers. Drunken driving, now responsible for around 40 percent of traffic fatalities, could be reduced by increased penalties. These actions would substantially reduce the external costs of automobile use, without imposing costs on all drivers. The government could also redirect a larger portion of highway funds to improving highway safety conditions. These actions are more consistent with our shared criteria for the appropriate role of government than the misdirected paternalism that has led to the extensive regulation of vehicle characteristics.

Redirect the Federal Trade Commission. At a time when the structure of the U.S. auto industry is changing so rapidly, the recent FTC investigation was particulary wasteful, and the threat of any actions based on this investigation increased planning uncertainty. This study was recently terminated.

The FTC could serve a much more useful role by investigating the two bodies of state regulations affecting, respectively, auto insurance rates and the franchise relations between retail dealers and the auto manufacturers. A change in the state insurance regulations could both increase highway safety and reduce average insurance rates. A change in the state franchise regulations could significantly reduce the retail price of new vehicles and thus increase the rate at which the more fuel-efficient, pollution-free, and safer new vehicles are phased into the existing fleet. In many cases, this form of indirect government action, operating on the general incentives to which people are subject, can be a more efficient means to achieve our shared concerns than the dominant reliance on direct government regulation.

Conclusion

The U.S. auto industry is in serious trouble. Many of its problems are attributable to the doubling of gasoline prices since 1973, a condition that neither the industry nor the government anticipated. Some of its problems, however, are clearly attributable to the unique, complex, and conflicting set of regulations affecting this industry. An auto industry policy that consists primarily of reducing these industry-specific regulations will resolve only those problems for which the government itself has been responsible. The recent course of events promises a continued proliferation of these regulations, combined with new tariffs, subsidies, and government-industry "cooperation," which will lead the auto companies to end up as wards of the state, an automobile version of Conrail. An alternative that merits the support of the American community is to review the whole set of existing regulations to determine whether there is a basis for a competitive industry consistent with those regulations that clearly serve the public interest.

NOTES

1. Richard L. Smith III, "Franchise Regulation: An Economic Analysis of State Restrictions on Automobile Distribution" (unpublished ms., Arizona State University).
2. D. Fort et al., *Proposal for a "Smog Tax"* (Santa Monica, CA: Rand Corporation, 1959). The notion has apparently been rediscovered by L. J. White, "Effluent Charges as a Faster Means of Achieving Pollution Control," *Public Policy,* Winter 1976, pp. 14-25; and Robert Crandall, "Regulations and Regulators: The Best Laid Plans," *Policy Commentary,* December 1978, pp. 1-52.

4

Passive Restraints and Auto Safety

Another Look

JOHN MENDELOFF

Although it has been called the single most studied of all federal regulatory decisions, the National Highway Traffic Safety Administration's (NHTSA) passive restraint standard (which requires air bags or automatic seat belts for front-seat passengers) remains extremely controversial. People still disagree about how much restraints will cost. And although much effort has been devoted to asking whether crash-test dummies respond like people, little has been devoted to asking whether people will respond like dummies. More precisely, experts disagree about whether people can rationally assess the merits of passive restraints and about how many will try to sabotage them.[1] Finally, an assessment of passive restraints depends on how much we value averting highway deaths and injuries. This chapter starts with a review of the rationale for regulatory intervention, retreats to an analysis of benefits and costs, and, finally, suggests a direction for policy.

AUTHOR'S NOTE: I would like to thank William A. Niskanen, Jr., Leon Robertson, Brian O'Neill, Carl E. Nash, William Haddon, Jr., Richard Arnould, and Henry Grabowski for discussions of these issues. None of them, however, are responsible for the views expressed here. Judy Lyman and Monica Paskvan helped with typing and editing.

Rationales for Government Intervention

If major externalities are absent, the rationale for government action on passive restraints depends largely upon consumers' abilities to make informed choices about safety.[2] Different assessments of these abilities lead to different policy implications, as the debate on seat belt usage demonstrates. In one view, seat belt use is a result of rational calculations about the protection of being belted versus the time costs and inconvenience of buckling. In other words, the reason most people do not wear seat belts is that they have calculated that it is not worth it. Because it reflects rational choice, this behavior should be respected by government.[3] Consistent with this view are several pieces of evidence: (1) calculations that show time and inconvenience do not have to be valued very highly to justify a rational decision to forgo belts;[4] (2) survey evidence that people are more likely to wear belts on longer trips,[5] that is, where the cost-benefit ratio is presumably higher: and (3) econometric findings that variables reflecting the benefits and costs of seat-belt use behave as expected in predicting whether people wear belts.[6]

The opposing perspective is that individual calculations are likely to be highly distorted. The problem is not simply that consumers lack information about the benefits of belts; if that were all, the remedy of providing this information would be clear-cut. But consumers cannot, it is argued, accurately process this information. Very small probabilities of harm are simply below the threshold that people consider.[7] Moreover, people are biased in their interpretations: Surveys find that most people say they are better drivers than most people;[8] therefore, providing information on aggregate risks will still lead to underestimates of individual risks and thus to underestimates of the benefits of belt use.

Arnould and Grabowski have recalculated the individual benefits of buckling up and conclude that time and inconvenience costs seem unlikely to outweigh them for many people, implying that belt disuse often is not economically rational.[9] Other data consistent with that interpretation include survey findings that individuals who perceive relatively high accident risks or feel less control over the occurrence of accidents are *not* more likely to wear belts.[10] Finally, Blomquist and Peltzman believe that seat belts have become more comfortable and convenient, which, under a rational-choice model, should have led to increased belt use. Under that assumption, the decline in belt use from about 25 percent in the early 1970s to 10.9 percent in 1979 would tend to contravene the rational model.

Perhaps after giving seat belts a try, some people have decided that since they have never had a bad accident, wearing the belts is not worthwhile. If past experience is a good predictor, this choice could be rational, but given the low frequency and unpredictability of serious accidents, it probably often is not. However, the assumption of increased convenience may simply be wrong. The proportion of cars with lap/shoulder belts increased through the 1970s, although as late as 1978 about 40 percent of all cars were still equipped with lab belts. Lap/shoulder belts undoubtedly caused added inconvenience for some people. In addition, some of the new single-retractor systems make the latch plate harder to reach than it was with the older dual retractors.[11]

Since both positions have some backing, it is not surprising that the truth about consumer behavior regarding seat belts is difficult to pinpoint. Many people do make calculations and others may try, but probably underestimate the risk they face in ways that information strategies may be hard pressed to alter; and still others may simply make the choice on some other — irrational — basis.

In addition to information problems, another possible rationale for government intervention is the presence of external costs that consumers do not necessarily consider in their purchases. The first type of externality is exemplified by medical expenses that are typically paid by insurance or by public funds. The ideal remedy here would be for insurance rates to be tailored so that each risk group pays the full costs it imposes. In the absence of mechanisms to fully accomplish that, it can be asked whether people who do not wear their seat belts or refuse to buy air bags would do so *if* they bore those costs. If the answer were yes, then a requirement could be justified on efficiency grounds.

The other externality arises because people care about each other; people's actions may not take account of others' concern for them. Niskanen feels that "this paternalistic concern provides a rationale for some form of subsidy of safety conditions but does not by itself justify regulation that increases the cost to the affected parties" (see Chapter 3). To rephrase the idea colloquially, if our friends make us worse off (by coercing us), then we indeed may not need enemies.

Limited market experience with the air bag has not revealed a strong demand, but surveys have elicited considerable support for an air bag requirement. This discrepancy undoubtedly arises, in part, from the usual factors: In surveys, costs are ignored or are not well perceived, and people exaggerate their willingness to do something toward fulfilling an approved goal such as safety. Nevertheless, the discrepancy may also reflect more fundamental differences between individual choice in the market and public choices, differences that are related to both types of externalities discussed above.

In states without no-fault insurance, drivers can reduce their expected liability cost if *other* drivers are wearing seat belts and thus avoid injury.[12] Indeed, this point can be generalized beyond financial liability. For most people, highway accidents represent the greatest risk they face of unintentionally maiming or killing another person. It seems plausible that significant reductions in this have more than trivial value.

The existence of external costs may be perceived by some people as an issue of fairness: "Why should I spend money on passive restraints and save other people money unless they do the same for me?" In addition, people who refuse to purchase air bags on their own may support an air bag requirement in order to protect particular people they care about: "I want to make sure my son and daughter aren't driving around unprotected."

The issues of liberty and benevolence both have a special character in the case of auto safety. Of the 50,000 people killed in traffic accidents in 1978, over 22,000 were under the age of 25. About 4,000 of these were children and the rest were 15-24 years old. Over one-third of all deaths in the latter age group are due to motor vehicles, and it remains the leading cause of death through the early 30s.[13]

A major explanation for the elevated crash rates for young drivers is their special willingness to take risks.[14] This willingness declines with age, of course, and leaves most of us with a mixture of amusement and amazement at how crazy we were when we were younger. This view that people's preferences change in predictable ways provides a basis for restricting the self-hazardous behavior of youth. The existing prohibition on driving by persons under 16 years old is intended to protect both young drivers and their possible victims.

Another important feature of the problem is that early death is arguably the most tragic. Some survey data report that most people picked death at age 25 as more tragic than deaths at age 7, 45, or 70.[15] Presumably the more tragic death is the one that people should be willing to spend more to prevent. Thus valuations based on risks to older workers may not reflect the value of preventing auto accident deaths. This argument is not based on the human capital approach of measuring forgone earnings, although that does favor the young adult. Instead, the tragic quality of early death is based on the more personal phenomena of missed experiences and shattered ties. The reason for emphasizing these features is that benefits due to the caring of third parties are likely to be especially important when it comes to preventing these deaths, yet are particularly unlikely to weigh heavily in the choices made by young people.

Even if all of the externalities cited here really exist, the crucial question involves their magnitude. For example, whether people are willing to support an air bag requirement in order to protect others will depend on such factors as the cost of the bag, estimates of its effectiveness, and the extent of people's benevolence. And, as is usually the case, the critical questions about consumers' information and rationality are difficult to answer clearly. In response we again fall back on attempts to see whether the social benefits of intervention exceed the costs.

Effectiveness

Passive restraints can be roughly as effective as current lap/shoulder belts, as the figures in Table 4.1 indicate.[16] The difference between the NHTSA estimates of effectiveness and those of researchers Huelke and O'Day reveal the extent of disagreement among experts. The latter estimate is lower for fatalites but higher for less severe injuries; thus for some plausible weighting schemes the two can give very similar overall results. Because the Huelke and O'Day figures are based on a disproportionately rural sample of accidents, which tend to be relatively severe (for example, at such high speeds that the driver's compartment is crushed), the NHTSA estimates seem more plausible as technical estimates of effectiveness.[17] These may have to be modified for two factors. First, people may drive less carefully when they feel safer.[18] This proposition often enrages safety advocates, but they probably should not get too excited. Although the argument that such "substitution" occurs is strong, the magnitude of the effect is probably small. Similarly, some

TABLE 4.1 Estimation of Annual Benefits to Society from Universal Installation of Passive Restraint Devices*

	Alternative Effectiveness Ratio Estimates							
	NHTSA				*Huelke-O'Day*			
Injury Category	*Lap Shoulder*	*Passive Belts*	*Air Cushions*	*Air Cushions and Lap Belts*	*Lap Shoulder*	*Passive Belts*	*Air Cushions*	*Air Cushions and Lap Belts*
AIS6 Fatal	60	50	40	66	32	28	25	34
AIS 4 and 5 Life threatening	60	50	40	66	64	58	58	58
AIS3 Severe (not life threatening)	59	45	30	46	64	58	58	58
AIS2 Moderate	57	40	22	33	—	—	—	—
AIS1 Minor	30	20	0	15	—	—	—	—

	Steady State Estimates of Annual Benefits to Society			
	*Estimated Lives Saved***		*Estimated Severe Injuries (AIS3-5) Prevented***	
	NHTSA	*Huelke-O'Day*	*NHTSA*	*Huelke-O'Day*
Passive Belts				
(I) 60% usage rate	8160	4570	19,578	24,684
(II) 70% usage rate	9520	5331	22,841	28,704
Air cushions with				
(I) 0% lap belt use	10,880	6800	22,840	41,006
(II) 20% lap belt use	12,294	7290	24,667	42,420
Manual lap shoulder belts				
(I) 20% usage rate	3264	1741	8375	9050
(II) 10% usage rate	1620	864	4186	4525

SOURCES: NHTSA data are taken from the *Federal Register.* Huelke and O'Day data are taken from "The National Highway Traffic Safety Administration's Passive Restraint Systems — A Scientist's Viewpoint" (Paper presented at the Brookings Institution Conference on the Scientific Basis of Safety and Health Regulations, November 8-9, 1979).

*Reprinted with permission from Richard J. Arnould and Henry Grabowski, "Auto Safety Regulation: An Analysis of Market Failure," *Bell Journal of Economics and Management,* Spring 1981, p. 37.

**These estimated steady state values are computed using NHTSA's distribution of injuries (without protection) for 1975.

adjustment, again probably small, is needed to reflect the reality that some of those saved will be drunk drivers who will live to cause a disproportionate number of future accidents.[19]

A more important question about passive restraints is whether people will use them. One model of the Volkswagen Rabbit comes equipped with passive belts connected to an interlock system — so that the engine will not start if the belts are not buckled — but about 22 percent of observed drivers have defeated the system.[20] NHTSA is prohibited from requiring an interlock, but cars must have emergency release devices so that passengers can free themselves even if the car doors will not open. As a result, usage is likely to depend crucially on engineering decisions about the ease of unbuckling and storing the unused belt.

Interestingly, the issue of passive belt evasion was totally ignored in Secretary Brock Adams's 1977 justification of the passive restraint standard; nor did NHTSA seriously pursue the issue after the decision. Yet, in the absence of clear regulatory language, the auto companies were beginning to compete to see who could produce the passive belt that was easiest to evade. For instance, the belt developed for the 1981 Cadillac, which General Motors intended to use to meet the 1982 NHTSA requirement, is less comfortable than an active belt, but disconnects in exactly the same manner and stores easily on the door panels.[21] This competition was spurred by the oil crisis because producers had planned to put air bags in large cars and passive belts in small ones. The near elimination of the former meant that consumers with a strong aversion to the belts (which are somewhat inconvenient and unsightly) would have no good alternative (that is, an alternative profitable to the companies). In one of the most dramatic turnabouts of the Reagan regulatory program, the new NHTSA announced that incremental belt use might increase as little as 5% or as much as 50% depending on the designs chosen.[22] Under both administrations, NHTSA leaders have treated the design issue as a factor outside their control. Attempts to amend the passive restraint regulation to influence the design of the emergency release system, while possible in theory, would have encountered legal and technical obstacles as well as political opposition. As a result, even under Joan Claybrook, a former Ralph Nader associate, NHTSA shied away from explicitly demanding measures that would increase effectiveness only by increasing inconvenience. NHTSA feared that such increases could trigger a political reaction that would destroy the standard.

As noted above, experience with the Volkswagen Rabbit has dubious relevance (except as an upper bound) because of its interlock feature. The Chevrolet Chevette provides added data because it was sold with a passive belt without an interlock in one 1980 model. Unfortunately, only survey data — not observations of actual use — on the Chevette are available. Of all automatic-belt 1980 Chevette owners 70 percent said that they wore a safety belt the last time they drove, compared to 31 percent of manual-belt 1980 Chevette owners. General Motors points out, however, that when not in use the automatic belt on the 1980 Chevette simply dangles in front of the seat, a design that causes annoyance and will be modified in favor of the Cadillac design.[23] Because of the dearth of experience with different designs and uncertainty about which will prevail, usage rates remain difficult to pinpoint. At the low end, General Motors contends that with its Cadillac belt model usage would not change significantly from rates with manual belts. At the high end, even with belts that do not store easily, incremental use of more than 30-40 percent is very improbable.

However, effectiveness in preventing injuries does not depend on overall belt use rates, but rather on belt use by people who get into accidents. Unfortunately, drivers who get into serious accidents are less likely to be wearing seat belts than the average driver. Thus, although observers report that about 78 percent of the drivers of automatic Rabbits wear their belts, only 57 percent of the occupants in tow-away crashes of those cars were wearing theirs. Similarly, when overall seatbelt use figures were 14 percent, the figure in tow-away crashes was 9 percent. An NHTSA study has emphasized that the former statistic applies only to drivers, while the latter applies to all passengers, who are less likely than the driver to be belted. Adjusting for this difference, however, still suggests that the increase in effective belt use will be 20-25 percent below whatever increase occurs in overall use, at least for the range of use being considered.[24] Thus a 24 percent increase in overall use would imply an 18 percent increase in effective use.

Another relevant unknown is whether a given driver is more likely to wear a seat belt under circumstances in which accidents are more likely. If such behavior is common, it would imply an even greater difference in seat belt use between drivers who do get involved in tow-away accidents and those who do not and thus smaller benefits from a given increase in overall belt use. The answer depends on whether and how much those circumstances differ from normal driving and on the responses of different drivers. Do they use seat belts, drive more cautiously, or both?[25]

The air bag effectiveness estimates in Table 4.1 appear less subject to amendment on behavioral grounds. The estimates already include the possibility of zero percent lap belt use (lap belt use is required for protection in other than frontal collisions). A small downward adjustment (0 to 5 percent) would be warranted if no one replaced the air bag after it detonated; however, as long as insurance pays the tab, most accident victims will probably be willing to purchase new bags. One troubling — but probably minor — uncertainty is that "busting the bag" could become a new teenage fad or spur an epidemic of automotive "chicken."

Valuing Health Effects

The problems of valuing health effects seem less difficult for injuries than for fatalities. It is easier to think about what would compensate us for a broken leg or crushed ribs than it is about how much we value reductions in the risk of death. An alternative proposed by Arnould and Grabowski seems especially plausible for valuing nonfatal injuries. In terms of the categories in Table 4.1, it would value minor injuries at $300, moderate injuries at $3,000; severe (but not life-threatening) injuries at $15,000; severe (life-threatening, but survival probable) injuries at $200,000; and critical injuries (survival uncertain) at $300,000.[26]

Studies aimed at identifying the willingness to pay for risk reduction have relied principally on measuring how much extra people get paid for taking risky jobs. One set of studies suggests values in the range of $240,000 to $1 million (in 1981 dollars) per fatality prevented. Others imply values of several million dollars per fatality. Martin Bailey has argued that the former are more believable. His illustration assumes a family of 4 with an annual income of around $20,000 faced by measures that would lower the annual risk of death to each of them from 0.0060 to 0.0055 annually, about a 10 percent reduction.[27] A valuation of $500,000 would imply that the family would be willing to pay a total of $1,000 for that benefit. In contrast, a valuation of $5 million would imply that the family would be willing to spend half of its total annual income.

Because highway accident victims are, on average, about 15 years younger than industrial accident victims, we might choose to value helping them more highly, for the reasons cited earlier. The issue of voluntariness also affects valuation, but its impact is more complex. Almost everyone has to drive, while workers have some choice about whether to enter risky occupations. Yet, once employed, workers cede some of their autonomy to management, while drivers are largely held reponsible for how safely they drive. Highway safety engineers report strong public demands for median barriers that can avert head-on collisions. But little outcry is heard for the removal of roadside obstacles, presumably because such accidents are thought to result more directly from victims' carelessness.[28] My view is that the value of preventing highway fatalities should be around $1 million, but the analysis below indicates how much you have to value them in order to make the benefits equal the costs.

One particular problem facing passive restraints is that people who value protection the most probably tend to be among current seat belt users. This fact surely weakens the demand for passive restraints, whether we measure it by willingness to pay or by willingness to take political action. In fact, some current users may feel that the requirement is unfair. Not only do they pay without gaining protection, but some passive belt models could actually leave them less safe than they would be with a lap/shoulder belt.

Costs of Passive Restraints

While lowering its estimates of passive belt use, NHTSA under Reagan has also raised its estimates of the costs of passive restraints. In 1977, the agency estimated that, compared to manual belts, passive belts would cost an extra $34 each and air bags an extra $154. In 1981, the comparable figures were over $100 for belts and at least $400 for air bags, rising to over $1000 for low volumes.[29] These increases obviously can not be explained just by inflation, and economist William Nordhaus has complained that NHTSA seems to have forgotten the rules of the regulatory game by accepting industry figures at face value. Since air bag suppliers, who have the opposite incentive, have estimated costs of about $270 for large-scale air bag production, that figure can probably be taken as a lower-bound estimate. Under manufacturers' current plans, no more than a small percentage of new cars will have air bags. The inability to realize economies of scale almost guarantees that costs will be in the $500 to $1000 range. For passive belts, Nordhaus has argued that an incremental cost of $60 seems more plausible than NHTSA's estimate.[30]

Passive belts are unlikely to impose added time costs; in fact, for drivers who would use belts anyway, they will reduce time costs, the inconvenience and discomfort costs may be substantial for some people; after all, over 20 percent of the Rabbit owners bothered to have the belts disconnected. Of course, to the extent that the belts can easily be stowed away, these costs — along with any protective effect — can be avoided. Thus at low levels of use these costs are unlikely to be large. Air bags may generate a lot of anxiety about whether they will pop inadvertently, but they may also calm many people's anxieties about getting killed. While the extent of these feelings and fears can be measured by surveys, attempts to value them have little credibility.

Comparing Costs and Benefits

In the following discussion, the capital costs of restraints have been annualized over ten years using a 10 percent discount rate (the rate mandated by the Office of Management and Budget), then added to the annual costs (extra gas consumption due to extra weight, replacement of deployed airbags, and so on) to construct a figure that can be compared to the annual health effects.[31]

Table 4.2 shows the net benefits from different levels of use of passive belts for 2 different cost estimates, assuming a value per fatality averted of $1 million. The figures in parentheses show the value per fatality that would be required to break even.[32] It is important to remember that these are calculations based on *effective incremental* use. Thus an increase in effective use of 10 percent would require an increase in overall use of about 13 percent. Estimates in that range would hardly justify much enthusiasm for the standard. With incremental use above 20 percent, the standard starts looking much better.

Benefits for the air bag were calculated assuming lap belt use of 5 percent. If the capital costs are around $400, the steady-state net benefits would be around $3.7 billion a year ($11.6 billion minus $7.9 billion), more than for passive belts with the lower cost estimate and a

TABLE 4.2 Net Benefits from Passive Belts Valuing Fatalities at $1 Million Effective Incremental Use*

Incremental Capital Cost	*10%*	*20%*	*30%*	*40%*	*50%*
$ 60	$290 M ($770,000)	$1.8 B ($290,000)	$3.3 B ($130,000)	$4.8 B ($50,000)	$6.4 B ($5,000)
$114	−$630 M ($1,500,000)	$890 M ($650,000)	$2.4 B ($370,000)	$3.9 B ($230,000)	$5.4 B ($150,000)

*Reprinted with permission from Richard J. Arnould and Henry Grabowski, "Auto Safety Regulation: An Analysis of Market Failure," *Bell Journal of Economics and Management*, Spring 1981, p. 42.

30 percent use rate. Yet the very existence of *any* net benefits for air bags is sensitive to fairly moderate changes in assumptions: for example, they would disappear if capital costs went over $600 or if the value placed on averting deaths went below $600,000. For the same reason, of course, somewhat lower costs or higher valuations would lead to very large gains in net benefits.

Conclusion

Many critics of passive restraints have suggested that even if they have net benefits, they should not be adopted because there are much more cost-effective methods to prevent highway injuries. Often they point to evaluations of safety construction projects, which often claim to be averting fatalities at costs from $100,000 to $300,000. Unfortunately, these evaluations are not credible indicators of the value of current spending and they are not helpful for predicting the impact of increased spending. The reported figures are based on comparisons of accident rates twelve months before and after the construction. Regression to the mean cannot be ruled out as an explanation, nor can biased selection, since not all projects are evaluated. Also, the effects found during the twelve-month period are extrapolated over the entire life of the period (often twenty years). Yet, although adjustments are made for expected increases in traffic volume, no adjustments are made for changes in the safety of vehicles. In any event, since no one has suggested other feasible methods for preventing an added 4,000 to 10,000 highway deaths, the resort to cost-effectiveness arguments cannot resolve the issue of what to do about passive restraints.

Most observers believe that the Reagan Administration will rescind the passive restraint standard, due to an aversion to paternalism and an avuncular solicitude for the health of the automobile industry. The data we have reviewed leave a good deal of leeway for judging whether this is the proper choice. What does seem clear is that the value (in real dollars) of preventing highway deaths will grow. In part, this growth simply reflects growing wealth and a willingness to spend some of it for this purpose. A more particular reason will be the continuing disparity in mortality-rate trends as most age groups continue to post declines because of progress against disease while the rate for the fifteen to twenty four age group remains constant. This result will be felt especially acutely as the "baby bust" generation takes to the road. The 25 percent downturn in births that began in the mid-1960s is just now showing up in the driving population. Its full brunt will be felt around 1990. This trend is important because most of the dip in the birthrate is a result of the fact that couples who have children are having fewer of them, rather than that more couples are having none.[33] Parents of an only child probably invest more in that child, both emotionally and economically, and the child's death is likely to be a greater loss. From the societal perspective, members of a small cohort are likely to make a relatively large economic contribution.

On the bright side, the drop in young drivers will work to offset the tendency for the increased number of miles driven to push up the overall number of auto deaths. But another factor pushing upward will be the shift to smaller cars. One study indicates that accidents involving 2 subcompact cars are almost 50 percent more likely to result in death or serious injury than accidents involving full-sized cars. Lester Lave has recently estimated that, compared with 1977, the expected growth in the small-car share of the fleet could increase deaths in 1984 by about 1400, an increase of a little over 5 percent. The benefits of passive restraints would rise in response, although probably by a somewhat smaller percentage.[34]

In cases such as that of automobile regulation — where technology requires lead times of several years or more — it seems predictable that, unless a solid consensus about policy emerges, the result can be no policy; or, more precisely, continual changes as policy conditions shift, all of them occurring before any one policy has a chance to be implemented fully. The current political distaste for passive restraints may be transient, but private research and development work is collapsing as the private market disappears. In retrospect, there is a certain irony about Transportation Secretary Brock Adams's decision — justified by desires to adopt restraints quickly — to cancel previous Secretary William Coleman's plan to conduct large-scale pilot programs with air bags, programs that Coleman thought could test (and perhaps build) public acceptance. In light of the discussion above, a resurrection of Coleman's plan would probably be a wise decision.

NOTES

1. For a review of several questions about the devices themselves (such as their effectiveness in test situations or the hazard from sodium azide), see "Passive Restraints for Automobile Occupants — A Closer Look," U.S. General Accounting Office Report CED-79-93, 27 July 1979. For a more fundamental criticism of safety devices (that they induce greater carelessness among drivers) see Sam Peltzman, "The Effects of Automobile Safety Regulations," *Journal of Political Economy* 83 (August 1975). For critiques of Peltzman, see note 21.

2. This section relies heavily on Richard J. Arnould and Henry Grabowski, "Auto Safety Regulation: An Analysis of Market Failure," *Bell Journal of Economics and Management,* Spring 1981. They cite all of the points except the decline in use of seat belts, the paradoxical pattern of usage found in the Teknekron study, the evidence on long trips, and the Blomquist seat belt study.

3. The clearest exposition of this view can be found in Glenn Blomquist and Sam Peltzman, "Mandatory Passive Restraint Systems and Social Welfare" (Paper presented at the Brookings Institution Conference on the Scientific Basis of Safety and Health Regulations, November 8-9, 1979).

4. Richard Thaler and Sherwin Rosen, "The Value of Saving a Life: Evidence from the Labor Market," in *Household Production and Consumption Studies in Wealth and Income, No. 40,* ed. N. E. Terleckyj (New York: Columbia University Press, 1975), p. 297.

5. See P. Marzoni, Jr., "Motivating Factors in the Use of Restraint Systems" (Philadelphia: National Analysts, Inc., September 1971). He found that in 1970 and 1971, 17 percent of drivers used belts for short trips, 39 percent for longer trips, and 44 percent for cross-country trips.

6. See Glenn Blomquist, "Economics of Safety and Seat Belt Use," *Journal of Safety Research,* December 1977.

7. See Howard Kunreuther, "Limited Knowledge and Insurance Protection," *Public Policy,* Spring 1976, pp. 229-261.

8. See O. Svenson, "Are We All Among the Better Drivers?" (unpublished ms., Department of Psychology, University of Stockholm). This is cited in Baruch Fischoff, Paul Slovic, and Sarah Lichtenstein, "Lay Foibles and Expert Fables About Risk," in *Progress in Resource Management and Environment Planning,* Vol. 3, eds. T. O'Riordan and R. K. Turner (Chichester: John Wiley, 1981).

9. Arnould and Grabowski, "Auto Safety Regulation," pp. 31-34.

10. Teknekron, Inc., "Final Report: 1978 Survey of Public Perceptions on Highway Safety" (Submitted to NHTSA, U.S. Department of Transportation, 10 November 1978), pp. 49-51.

11. See Blomquist and Peltzman, "Mandatory Passive Restraint Systems," pp. 7-8. For safety belt usage figures from 1973 to 1978 see NHTSA's *Highway Safety 1978* (DOT HS 803 372, January 1979), p. A-32. The same volume also has the 40 percent estimate for lap belt prevalence, p. 11. For belt use estimates through 1979, see the Opinion Research Corporation, *May 1980 Final Report* (DOT HS 805 398), p. 3. It also discusses usage in 1979 for different model years and the problems with single retractors, p. 5.

12. For a discussion of this issue, see Roger Noll in *Auto Safety Regulation: The Cure or the Problem,* eds. Henry G. Manne and Roger Leroy Miller (Glen Ridge, NJ: Thomas Horton and Daughters, 1976), pp. 117-118.

13. U.S. Department of Transportation, *Highway Safety 1978* (DOT HS 803 372, June 1979), Tables A-12, A-15.

14. The poor accident record of young males is attested to by the insurance premiums they must pay. While circumstantial evidence is abundant, I have not yet located any studies that try to establish how much of this record can be attributed to age-specific attitudes toward risk.

15. See Richard A. Kalish and David K. Reynolds, *Death and Ethnicity: A Psycho-Cultural Study* (Los Angeles: University of Southern California Press, 1976), pp. 32, 57-58. For a fuller discussion of this significance of early death see James W. Vaupel, "Early Death: An American Tragedy," *Law and Contemporary Problems,* Autumn 1976.

16. The steady-state estimates in Table 4.1 are based upon NHTSA's estimate that 27,000 fatalities would have occurred in 1975 if no protection had been available. The usage rates in Table 4.1 were assumptions made by Arnould and Grabowski, "Auto Safety Regulation."

17. D. Huelke and J. O'Day, "The National Highway Traffic Safety Administration's Passive Restraint Systems — A Scientist's Viewpoint" (Paper presented at the Brookings Institution Conference on the Scientific Basis of Safety and Health Regulations, November 8-9, 1979), p. 8.

18. See Peltzman, "Effects of Automobile Safety Regulations." Peltzman's conclusion that the use of seat belts and other safety devices had no *net* effect on deaths (because more careless driving has killed more pedestrians, offsetting the reduction in passenger deaths) has not been supported by other research.

For other studies of auto safety effectiveness, see Leon S. Robertson, "State and Federal New Car Safety Regulation: Effects on Fatality Rates," *Accident Analysis and Prevention* 9 (1977): 151-156; and U.S. General Accounting Office, "Effectiveness Benefits, Costs of Federal Safety Standards for Protection of Passenger Car Occupants" (CED-76-12, 1976). For criticisms of Peltzman's work, see Leon S. Robertson, "A Critical Review of Peltzman's 'The Effects of Automobile Safety Regulaton,' " *Journal of Economic Issues* 11 (September 1977): 587-600; and Hans C. Jorsch, "Critique of Sam Peltzman's Study," *Accident Analysis and Prevention* 8 (1976): 129-137. For criticisms by economists, see the comments by Richard Nelson and Paul MacAvoy in *Auto Safety Regulation: The Cure or the problem,* eds. Henry G. Manne and Roger Leroy Miller (Glen Ridge, NJ: Thomas Horton and Daughters, 1976).

It is hard to deny that some amount of substitution occurs. The psychological literature is replete with experiments showing that drivers seek to maintain a constant level of tension and arousal. (I am indebted to James Hendry for a review of that literature.) However, it is not clear how drivers perceive the effects of particular safety devices. Rumar studied the effect of studded tires and found that cars with them drove faster around curves; however, the sacrifice in traction from the higher speed did not erase the traction advantage of the studs. See Kare Rumar et al., "Driver Reaction to a Technical Safety Measure: Studded Tires," *Human Factors* 18 (1976): 433-454. Drivers go faster on the interstates than they did on the roads they replaced, but no one doubts that the net effect has been to save lives. Peltzman's assertions about the magnitude of the substitution seem particularly high if we judge that seat belt use (and not, for instance, padded dashboards) was the only major change likely to cause substitution. Since only 20-25 percent of the drivers wore belts, their accident rates would have had to roughly double to account for the 25 percent "unexplained" increase in pedestrian deaths that Peltzman calculates. Since his model was formulated to examine vehicular deaths, not pedestrian deaths in particular, we should not expect it to perform the latter task very well.

19. For a discussion of the impact of preventing the deaths of high-risk drivers, see Richard Zeckhauser and Donald Shepard, "Where Now for Saving Lives," *Law and Contemporary Problems,* Autumn 1976, pp. 28-30.

20. This is the rate estimate in field surveys, according to Arnould and Grabowski, "Auto Safety Regulation," p. 35.

21. This was my firsthand impression of the Cadillac system, an impression shared by most people with whom I have spoken.

22. See NHTSA's two notices announcing postponement of the standard and initiation of new rule making in the *Federal Register,* 9 April 1981, pp. 21207, 21176.

23. For reported usage rates for 1980 Chevettes, see the Opinion Research Corporation, *February 1981 Final Report* (DOT HS 805 797), p. ix. This report became the subject of controversy when auto safety advocates claimed that NHTSA hid its existence. The data in the report were used by William Nordhaus in his revised benefit-cost analysis submitted to NHTSA on behalf of the insurance industry. See "Comments of William Nordhaus on Notice of Proposed Rulemaking on Federal Motor Vehicle Safety Standards Occupant Crash Protection," Docket No. 74-14, Notice 22, 26 May 1981. Nordhaus believes that the Chevette survey gives the best guess about the incremental use with passive belts. Although his analysis is generally penetrating (especially on the impact on the auto industry), he is insensitive to the issue of engineering design impacts. Richard Humphrey of General Motors made the argument to me about the special feature of the 1980 Chevette in a June 1980 interview. The Supplement to the 1980 Chevette Owner's Manual attests that "if the Automatic Lap/Shoulder Belt has been unbuckled, it will not retract fully, and will dangle loosely, and will not provide any restraint" (p. 3).

24. On the 57 percent figure for Rabbits, see the *Federal Register,* 9 April 1981, p. 21176. For the disparity in overall rates, see Carl Nash, "The Science and Policy of Automatic Crash Protection" (Paper presented at the Brookings Institution Conference on the Scientific Basis of Health and Safety Regulation, November 8-9, 1979), p. 2. The NHTSA study alluded to is "Restraint Usage and Effectiveness on the National Crash Severity Study," by Susan Partyka (DOT HS 805 151, September 1979). Partyka goes on to argue that the difference between accident-involved and

uninvolved drivers is even less if we adjust for the model year of the car. Drivers of older cars (pre-1972) are relatively unlikely to be wearing seat belts, but old cars are relatively likely to get involved in tow-away accidents. She adjusts for this effect by factoring out the influence of model year. However, if we are interested in knowing whether people in accidents will be belted, this procedure overadjusts. I have also slightly increased the disparity she found (11.2 percent versus 14.1 percent) when she adjusted for passengers to account for the slightly earlier data collection for the lower figure (January 1977 through March 1978 versus November 1977 through June 1978), because usage rates were declining over time.

25. We do have evidence that belt use increases in bad weather. See G. Fahner and M. Hare, "Seat Belts: Factors Affecting Their Use," *Accident Analysis and Prevention* 5 (1973): 27-43.

26. In the calculation of benefits by Arnould and Grabowski, "Auto Safety Regulation," this alternative is the one in Column 6 of their Table 1 (p. 32) which is labeled "I" in Table 4.

27. Martin J. Bailey, *Reducing Risks to Life* (Washington, DC.: American Enterprise Institute, 1980), pp. 45-46. Bailey's figures for the former set range from $170,000 to $715,000 in 1978 dollars. The Consumer Price Index went up about 40 percent from 1978 to 1981, raising these figures to $240,000 to $1,000,000.

28. This point was made to me by several top officials in the California highway safety program in interviews in August 1980. It raises the key issue of whether they should try to focus on improving public health or on reducing perceived risks.

29. *Federal Register,* 9 April 1981, p. 21206.

30. William Nordhaus, "Comments," p. 5.

31. This annualizing procedure is comparable to finding the discounted present value of the stream of costs and benefits. It is true, however, that cars get heavier use when they are newer. Counteracting this is the fact that older cars are more likely to be involved in accidents. Overall, the assumption used here will probably underestimate the net benefits, although the magnitude of the bias is not readily apparent.

32. Using the weights described above, the value of nonfatal accidents that would be prevented by 100 percent use of passive belts would be $2.38 billion a year. For an increase in use of 10 percent, the added benefit is $238 million. For all of my calculations, I assume that the present effective level of belt use is 9 percent, that is, preventing 1,458 of the 27,000 deaths that would occur without any protection. Each added 10 percent belt use would prevent 1,277 deaths (27,000 minus 1,478 = 25,542; passive belts are 50 percent effective if used; thus 10 percent use would prevent 5 percent of 25,542 deaths, or 1,277).

For passive belts, the annualized capital cost ($10 or $19) were added to annual costs of $2 a year (for gasoline due to extra weight) and multiplied by the 102 million cars in the U.S. fleet. For air bags, the annual costs included about $2 a year per car for replacement of deployed bags and $10 a year for extra gas. (Air bags weigh about 60 pounds, which requires an extra 5 to 10 gallons of gas per 10,000 miles driven. Taking that as annual milleage at $1.50 per gallon adds up to $7.50 to $15 a year per car.)

33. Among ever-married women aged 15-44, 22.8 percent were childless in 1950; in 1976, 18.8 percent were childless. Comparing 1950 and 1975, the overall birthrate (for white women) declined from 33.3 per 1000 women 15-44 to 26.9 per 1000 *for first births,* from 32.3 to 20.5 for second births, from 17.9 to 8.9 for third births, and from

18.7 to 6.7 for higher order births. See *The U.S. Fact Book, 1978,* Tables 82, 78 (New York: Grosset and Dunlap, 1978).

34. Lester Lave, "Conflicting Objectives in Regulating the Automobile," *Science* 212 (22 May 1981): 897. The impact of passive restraints might not be proportional because as people shift to smaller cars, they would probably become slightly more likely to wear seat belts, reducing the benefit from passive restraints. NHTSA officials Barry Felrice and Carl Nash reported that they were unaware of any studies on the efficacy of restraints as a function of car size.

5

Regulating the Auto Industry

Problems and Pseudoproblems

MICHAEL E. LEVINE

William Niskanen's work has been directed toward clarifying problems or phenomena, such as bureaucratic behavior, that often have been treated rather carelessly. His chapter on the possible alternatives to current regulations affecting the automobile industry raises significant questions about the role and effects of government intervention in an important industry. The only way to avoid "cures" that are worse than the problems they address is to employ the kind of precise diagnosis that has characterized Niskanen's work. I hope in this commentary to contribute to that tradition by refining further the analysis of a number of the problems that Niskanen has isolated and addressed.

Let me first turn to some examples of situations in which I think further refinement would help focus skepticism about regulation on real problems of the auto industry while avoiding useless — or worse — regulatory reforms that address only pseudoproblems, both those that are claimed to be caused by market failures and those wrongly attributed to poor regulation.

First, the U.S. auto industry has obviously suffered from the recession, but I think the popular assumption of disproportionate recessionary impact on that industry (compared to other consumer durable goods industries) will not withstand analysis. At least until very recently, sales of imported cars held up and the recessionary decline in the auto market was almost entirely borne by the U.S.

industry. But how do we interpret those events? It is theoretically possible that the recession affected the U.S. auto industry disporportionately by creating a marked income effect on consumers, to which they responded by substituting inferior goods, namely, Japanese and European cars, for superior goods, namely, American cars. That hypothesis is hard to believe. More likely, a dramatic shift in factor prices (that is, rising gasoline prices) changed the efficient production function for producing private transportation by automobile. This was seen in the market as a change in consumer tastes and it happened to coincide with a recession, which may or may not itself have been partly caused by the rise in energy prices. But it was just a dramatic coincidence that there was a recession at the time when the product mix of the auto industry had been made "wrong" by changed oil prices. I do not mean "wrong" in some moral sense; the auto industry just did not have for sale the kinds of cars that rational consumers, trying to get themselves around in the face of newly higher energy prices, would have bought.

This suggests that preoccupation with the recession as a particular source of the auto industry's recent problems is mistaken. It is always a good idea to avoid recession where (and if) you can by manipulating monetary policy or doing anything else that will work. But doing so is of no special significance to the auto industry relative to other durable goods industries and would not have averted the industry's current problems. Of course the auto industry gets hurt when we have a recession: It is a big industry, and it is a large share of the gross national product. If the GNP does not grow, or if it declines, and consumers postpone purchases of durables, the auto industry obviously takes a beating. But I do not think the recession is a special source of the auto industry's current predicament, except in the accounting sense that the large losses that resulted from consumer-taste responses to changing oil prices showed up on the books in an accounting year already made awkward by recession.

In the same way, I think one could easily be seduced into reflexively exaggerating the significance of the corporate average fuel economy (CAFE) standards. There are very long reaction times in the auto industry. Producing cars takes a lot of tooling; tooling has long lead times; the tooling lasts a long time; and management has powerful incentives to hang on to tooling that has not worn out and to try to produce cars, even if the cars that are produced by the tools may not be very popular.

Given these long industry lead times, two possible CAFE influences on industry choices suggest themselves. The first is that the CAFE requirements simply prodded the industry into a slightly earlier response to something they would have done anyway. General Motors recent announcement that it expects to be ahead of the CAFE schedule from 1982 on and that in 1985 it expects to exceed the CAFE standard because that is what will sell cars suggests that, in fact, the CAFE standards probably are no longer a significant influence on the product mix in the sense of forcing production different from what the public might want. They might have had that influence at the beginning; if so, we can give credit to those standards for helping the industry anticipate the long lead time necessary to make a *commercially* necessary shift in product mix.

The second CAFE influence on industry choices is that those standards are still influential in that they may now make it hard to shift the product mix back if factor prices unexpectedly shift again. Only time will tell whether the CAFE standards will have the effect of rigidly preventing cars from being redesigned to suit the public if petroleum prices should fall, or if the scientist at the California Institute of Technology who has been working on making fuel out of water, sunlight, and a catalyst succeeds.

The standards should be abandoned anyway. At this point, they have obviously done whatever good they could have done. If they produced the acceleration in research and development (R&D) their proponents have claimed, fine, but from here on out they can have only ill effects, and we should get rid of them. But we should get rid of them now *not* because they are a current source of harm to the industry, but rather because there is a possibility that they may be harmful in the future.

The research and development that the CAFE standards imposed on the manufacturers was clearly not wasted, given that the standards required production of the kind of cars that the public appears to be buying at the moment. The R&D may have been incurred in slightly different years than might otherwise have been the case, and as a related but separate matter a substantial excise tax on R&D is imposed by the effort necessary to meet wasteful standards such as the passive restraint standards and the bumper standards. They require R&D resources, and if a certain amount of the resources of a research establishment is devoted to meeting useless standards, it is either harder to meet useful standards or the research establishment has to be enlarged to an uneconomic size to preserve useful research. This suggest only that we should focus on the harm caused by squandering R&D on wasteful objectives and the rigidities imposed by regulations no longer needed, rather than waste deregulatory credibility exaggerating the harm done by the CAFE standards in the recent past.

Similarly, energy price controls have fortunately now been eliminated but it is possible to exaggerate the impact they have had on the auto industry in the past. Obviously they reduced the incentives to fuel economy — although in that case it should probably be conceded that the CAFE standards represented at worst an offsetting inefficiency — but they also clearly made the old product and old tools salable for a longer period of time than would otherwise have been the case. The net effect was probably to produce a wealth transfer from the oil industry to auto manufacturers. That is, oil companies got less for their oil than they might have gotten, and automobile manufacturers got more for the cars they could build most advantageously. In short, they were able to sell full-sized Buicks and Chevrolets for longer than they would have been otherwise because customers paid artificially low prices for fuel. I do not know what the auto makers were doing with the money, but it seems to me it is hard to claim that those energy price controls, whatever idiocy they may have represented as energy policy, had a particularly damaging effect on the auto industry.

Having identified some problems that perhaps have been overemphasized in William Niskanen's chapter, let me suggest a few that perhaps need more emphasis. The first, it seems to me, is product quality. Niskanen seems to focus on lower repair rates through the warranty period as the principal quality variance between U.S. and foreign cars. The preoccupation may obscure what a look at the *Consumer Reports* data (which are the very best data available on frequency of repair) will show, namely, that especially for Japanese cars, lower repair rates continue well beyond the warranty period. Consumers seem to have figured this out. I have little patience for commentary that addresses this problem in moral terms, chiding General Motors or Ford for obstinately building "bad" cars. But in trying to see what factors were important in explaining the shifts in the auto market of the last several years, it is hard to ignore an apparent consumer taste for virtues possessed by imports and not by domestic cars.

The fact is that the early efforts at small cars by the Americans were really very crude. The Pinto was designed to the interior standards of a Volkswagen beetle. The VW beetle is a 1935 design by Ferdinand Porsche and did not represent, even during the era when it sold extremely well because it was very reliable, modern standards of space efficiency. The Vega developed early and sustained a reputation for mechanical unreliability that was fully warranted. The Chevette is a less crude car; it was General Motors's first "world car" and in some respects the *first* world car, and perhaps for that reason, it is not a very technologically advanced car. But that is not its problem.

The Chevette was the U.S. version of General Motors's "T-car." It was simple enough to be produced in Brazil and for other not very advanced markets and was not an overwhelming seller in those more advanced markets — the United Kingdom, Germany, and Japan — in which it was sold against cars that were either more technologically advanced or more refined. While it was and is not a bad car, it certainly never was the best available in its class in either respect in any market. Technologically, the Chevette should be compared with the Toyota Corolla, which has the same basic design and is the best-selling car model line in the world. The Corolla is simply a more refined way to do the same things a Chevette does: It drives better, it lasts longer, it is built better, and, not surprisingly, those consumers around the world who have been faced with the choice between the T-car and the Corolla have consistently, for a decade, bought the Corolla. The U.S. market is entirely typical in that respect.

Japanese cars in fact have often been as far behind Europeans in technical sophistication as American cars were, but unlike our small cars, Japanese cars are very high in quality of fit and finish and in reliability. A critic once said of Rolls Royces that they represented a triumph of craftsmanship over design. To some extent, Japanese cars have had that characteristic, and it has turned out that consumers do not care as much about design sophistication as about reliability and quality of construction. The Europeans have discovered this to their dismay as Japanese cars have penetrated their market, even though Japanese cars may not be as sophisticated as the European cars they replace. In their home markets, the Europeans are having some of the same difficulties competing against Japanese imports that the U.S. auto industry has had. The Corolla competes against various European cars, and it and other Japanese cars are doing very well there. The reason is mounting consumer preoccupation with the fit, finish, and durability aspects of product quality.

Quality is probably not simply a function of labor costs per car. This is an area that really should be investigated further, but one thing we know is that the Japanese have both lower labor costs per person hour and lower labor content per unit of output than the U.S. industry. This suggests that even if labor cost per hour were equal, their labor cost per unit would be lower. Yet Japanese quality of construction is better than has been typical of U.S. production. This clearly represents engineering choices and management skill, and while it may also reflect union manning rigidities in the United States (I am not really familiar enough with the United Auto Workers contract to know), there is clearly more at stake here than simply the wage paid per hour. It is also very difficult to compare labor costs because Japanese practices, such as long-term hiring, providing dormitories at very low rates for unmarried workers, providing company food on the premises at very low rates, and so on, need to be taken into acount. I suspect that Japanese labor costs *are* lower once all those adjustments are made, but I do not know how much lower they turn out to be. But I think that rather than focusing simply on unit labor costs, we need to understand better the production function for quality and what motivates both labor and management to produce quality.

Another of William Niskanen's observations on labor costs also merits an expanded examination. The high labor costs that we experience in the United States are not simply a reflection of failures of manufacturers to hold the line against the greedy UAW. More likely, the natural protection of our market that stemmed from the fact that U.S. manufacturers were building for a market that wanted large cars when no one else in the world was created the opportunity to take oligopoly rents. As in the protected airline industry, the rents were split between management and labor, but the split was uneven. Management's share was on a kind of "what's-left-over" basis, which varied day to day and month to month and year to year, like equity. Labor's share came as a fixed price in a contract, like debt. As market changes make rents shrink and disappear, management's "equity" share of the rents is very flexible and tends to disappear as rapidly as the rents disappear, but labor's "fixed" share of the rents is embodied in contracts, which are much less flexible. Thus labor behaves like a creditor, and continues to take rents past the point where rents are available to be taken. The recent Chrysler negotiations represented the beginning of a belated adjustment by both labor and other creditors to the fact that rents are no longer there to pay debts incurred on the assumption that rents could be taken. And before we leap to any conclusions about permanent U.S. labor cost disadvantages, we ought to wait to see the results of the adjustment process now taking place. This process is analogous to what is going on now between labor and management in the airline industry, whose rents are being squeezed out by deregulation; I think it merits further inquiry.

Still another very interesting area that deserves a further look is the notion, touched on by Niskanen, that franchise regulation appears to add $600 to $700 per car to the cost of distribution. If this is true, it represents an absolute scholar's gold mine for investigation. If these claims are true, this problem may really be one that has an impact on the auto industry especially. But unless franchises work differently for imports than they do for domestic cars, I am not sure that it represents an explanation for the special bind in which the *domestic* industry finds itself.

There are some other popular regulatory scapegoats that are supposed to have threatened the industry but that have probably had a mixed effect on it — perhaps unduly punitive to the domestic industry in some cases, and perhaps unduly favorable in others. Many of these regulatory scapegoats are justifiably punishable; that is, they ought to be eliminated. But we ought to be clear. Getting rid of these culls from the regulatory herd will not always affect our domestic industry in an unambiguously favorable way. In some cases, the changes may *hurt* the industry's ability to make money as much or more than they will help it.

For example, take emissions standards. They are a favorite target for regulatory reformers and they are certainly not cost effective as written. They are theoretically acceptable — that is, there are reasons to control externalities. But the fact that there are externalities does not justify *any* set of rules that attempts to control them. And the ones imposed on the auto industry do not make sense.

While they may have slightly reduced overall demand for cars by making the cars slightly worse than they really need to be, our emissions standards probably have favored the U.S. industry versus imports. If they have had any effect at all, they have functioned as a nontariff barrier to imports from other countries, particularly from those countries whose home markets do not have these controls. The Japanese have emissions regulations almost as strict as ours and Japanese cars have been very successful in our market recently relative to European cars. As far as emissions regulations are concerned, Japanese manufacturers can export to the United States virtually any of their cars. The Europeans do not face emissions regulations at home (more accurately, they face a few trivial ones) and they have not been able to adapt their full product lines for import into the United States. Their home-market cars drive better and pollute more than do cars sold in the United States. It is expensive per unit for the Europeans to do the R&D on emissions controls necessary to meet the U.S. standards on a small fraction of their output. The technologies they have adopted have in consequence been cruder or more expensive and European cars sold here have generally been worse in cost, performance, and fuel economy than their counterparts sold in Europe. In short, European cars sold in this country are less nearly as good as European cars sold in Europe than are Japanese cars sold in this country when compared with Japanese cars sold in Japan. This has certainly helped the Japanese, but it also must have helped the U.S. industry. The emissions standards we have may not have made sense, but one should not assume they are necessarily heavily damaging to the U.S. auto industry vis-a-vis their foreign competion. If the Europeans had home-market standards like the U.S. pollution standards, the U.S. domestic industry would be in much worse shape than it is now.

Pursuing the same sort of analysis, I would agree that the passive restraint and bumper standards are not cost effective — especially when compared with mandatory three-point belt use as in Australia and Ontario, Canada. But, if anything, this again *favors* U.S. manufacturers relative to imports, just as do the emission controls. It is relatively more expensive per car for the Europeans and Japanese to meet these standards on a small fraction of their output than for U.S. manufacturers to design cars around them. As with badly designed emissions standards, these standards may make cars less valuable and shift the industry demand curve a little bit to the left, but they favor U.S. manufacturers relative to foreign manufacturers simply because the expenditures necessary to design and meet those standards must be more burdensome to foreign manufacturers. Engineering and tooling costs for compliance are spread over fewer cars because in most cases cars are less salable in the home market with these added safety features than without them. Expenditures for compliance with U.S. standards are useful only on cars for the U.S. market and not necessary for the home market, which does not demand five-mile-per-hour bumpers and passive restraints.

The attempts at wage-price controls undertaken in the Carter Administration may also have been inefficient and unfair but, again, they had little effect on the domestic industry's struggle to remain viable. In fact, under the demand conditions of the past year or two they were irrelevant. There is no evidence at all that auto prices in 1979 and 1980 were below the revenue-maximizing level, given the state of the demand. Indeed, the rebate programs that were conducted during that period, as well as the rebate programs undertaken as recently as the first quarter of 1981, suggest the opposite. However idiotic they may be, wage-price controls (or noncontrols) consisting of a lot of appearances on television by the chairman of the Council on Wage-Price Stability and, one assumes, a few phone calls to Detroit, clearly could not have been a major contributor to the auto industry's problems. The auto industry's problems was that *within* the permitted ranges of prices, it could not sell cars.

Finally, concern has been expressed about the potential decline to two in the number of full-line U.S. producers. I do not understand what question is answered by a census of full-line producers. Certainly the concern cannot be about industry viability. The Japanese have the most successful auto industry in the world at the moment, but there are only two full-line producers in Japan, Nissan and Toyota. On the other hand, there are a number of very successful less-than-full-line producers in Japan selling a limited range of cars on world markets. Toyo Kogyo (Mazda), Honda, Mitsubishi, and Fuji Heavy Industries (Subaru) all make relatively narrow ranges of cars, yet seem to do very nicely. Not only do they do nicely on the world market, but they do well in the Japanese home market. The Japanese are not very nice to outsiders, but these five or six firms, only two of which are full-line producers, together participate in a healthy, very competitive market. If we had as successful an array of firms in the United States we would not be concerned with "problems in the auto industry." I am not really interested in how many full-line producers we will have. I think the first question for public policy is, "Will consumers get the cars they want at competitive prices?" And there may be as well a separate public policy question: "Should we have a strong U.S. domestic auto industry?" But neither of these questions can be answered by referring to the number of full-line manufacturers remaining in the United States.

The odd thing about this catalog of analytical complaints is that I do not really disagree with very many of William Niskanen's prescriptions and I certainly do not disagree with the general orientation of his chapter. I think that there are occasional overstatements of significance, as I have suggested, and that occasionally perhaps his enthusiasm has obscured a few facts. For example, the European Economic Community (EEC) does in fact have product-attribute regulation for its cars: The standards happen to be more sensible than the ones we impose, but they exist and in fact they have been described as a nontariff barrier for imports of cars from outside the EEC. For example, U.S. cars, which are "safer," do not happen to meet the EEC specifications, so we cannot simply take a U.S. car and ship it to Europe. We have to modify it for that market in just the same way that the Europeans have to modify their cars to ship them here. This illustrates my point that, carefully considered, a number of U.S. auto regulations, including some very bad ones, favor domestic producers. Getting rid of them, which may be a very good idea, may not necessarily help the U.S. industry. The standards relating to externalities or hidden attributes (such as certain safety features) are not without conceptual support, but clearly have been mishandled. Niskanen recognizes this and would fix it. So would I.

I have gone through a lot of detail here, but in a sense that is my general message: Those people who are concerned with regulatory reform ought to go through a lot of detail. It is very easy and very fashionable to be hostile to regulation now, and it is all right to be hostile to regulation — a great deal of it is difficult to justify, much of it is worse than useless, and besides, the targets are often so gross that it's great fun to attack them. And perhaps in the political real world, where fine distinctions do not matter and may not even be possible, the country is better served by a carelessly wielded meat axe of broad hostility to regulation than by the suffocating blanket of regulatory schemes run riot. But a lot of painful sorting and careful evaluation is necessary to isolate the regulatory evils that matter from those that do not, and from the flawed but beneficial correctives that make up at least some fraction of regulatory activity.

This kind of analysis does not often lead to easily salable alternatives. The answers, such as they are, tend to lose appeal for those ideologues on both sides whose energies seem to be crucial to political change. But in the end, we may accomplish at least two things: First, if we do our jobs carefully enough, we may be able to damp the swings of the regulatory pendulum so that we do not oscillate endlessly between heedless laissez-faire on the one hand and paternalist mercantilism verging on occasion toward fascism on the other. Second, in doing so we can focus attention on "do-able" deregulation, on deregulation that may be more radical or less radical — that is not the important attribute — but that will produce public results good enough to allow the *further* elimination of regulation, to allow momentum to build up and reform to continue to spread from industry to industry. This requires good and careful guesses in advance of the implications of particular deregulations: both the implications in terms of the actual contribution deregulation can make to efficiency and, perhaps just as important, the implications for the interest groups that will be affected by change.

PART II

Regulatory Reform
Some Alternative Strategies

6

Implementing Tradable Emissions Permits

ROBERT W. HAHN
ROGER G. NOLL

One of the reforms of environmental regulation that has received considerable attention in the past few years is the replacement of source-specific standards with a system of tradable emissions permits. The theoretical case for the proposal is strong; however, only recently have analysts devoted much attention to developing a strategy for implementing such a system. This chapter addresses some of the problems of setting up an efficient market in emissions permits. We first present the case for taking seriously a proposal to use tradable permits to solve environmental problems. Then we raise and attempt to answer some of the implementation questions that decision makers raise about the proposal. Because this is essentially a feasibility study, our answers to these implementation problems are presented in the context of a particular problem: the case of particulate sulfates in the Los Angeles airshed. Some of the results of the empirical work for this case study are also included.

AUTHORS' NOTE: The research reported in this chapter was financed in part by a grant from the California Air Resources Board. The authors alone are responsible for the views expressed herein.

Theoretical Advantages of Marketable Permits

Decentralized, market-oriented methods for abating pollution have several theoretical advantages. Before discussing these advantages, it is useful to separate the methods available for regulation of air pollution into four general categories. The first is *input standards:* Regulators tell polluters what kind of equipment or abatement strategies to adopt, such as requiring a utility to install stack gas scrubbers and/or burn low-sulfur fuel at a generation facility. A second is *output standards:* Each polluter is told the quantity of emissions allowed at each source. Here the polluting firm is allowed to select the method for achieving the emissions target as long as the result is in compliance with the standard. A third category is that of *tradable permits:* A target rate of emissions is set for a region and a market mechanism is relied upon to determine how these permits are allocated among emissions sources. A fourth approach is that of *monetary incentives:* Abatement subsidies and emissions taxes are included in this category. Under such schemes a polluter is charged some amount for each unit of emissions and/or subsidized for each unit of emissions reduction beyond a specified baseline. Subsequent discussion focuses on taxes. Emissions taxes seem more likely to be implemented than subsidies because the former do not have to confront the problems of seeming to reward pollution, encouraging entry of polluting industries, and raising revenues for subsidizing industrial abatement efforts.[1] Nevertheless, subsidies are now used in one case — grants for sewage treatment facilities — and might prove politically more attractive if coupled with an emissions tax as the source of revenue for the subsidies.

In all cases, the purpose of environmental regulation is to achieve some overall reduction in pollution; in the case of air pollution, the target is an *ambient air quality standard.* In each case, an emissions target is selected that is thought to be consistent with the overall objective in terms of pollution reduction, although the link between environmental quality and emissions is often subject to considerable uncertainty. But in principle, input standards, output standards, emissions taxes, and the number of tradable permits are all chosen to achieve the overall objective of some target level of environmental quality.

In practice, environmental regulation has become a hybrid of all four of the approaches described above. In the Los Angeles airshed, for example, both input standards and emissions limits are used, a relatively low emissions fee is charged, and emissions permits can be traded according to the "controlled trading methods" that were developed through the Environmental Protection Agency (EPA) in the late 1970s. Moreover, nationally there is relatively little difference in the way that input standards and output standards are adopted. An input standard is imposed upon a firm because regulators anticipate that it is the best feasible strategy for reducing emissions; an output standard is imposed on the basis of analysis of the technical abatement alternatives, and is normally set after a demonstration that a particular technical alternative can achieve the standards. In fact, standards are often really a combination of the two: An output target is set, and an acceptable technical approach is identified.

All standards must be adopted in a quasi-judicial process that is subject to judicial review on the basis of the procedures that were followed and the adequacy of the evidentiary basis for the decision. In the process of setting the standard, the regulatory authority bears the burden of proving that the regulations are reasonable with respect to cost and effectiveness; hence the tendency to deal with both inputs and outputs in setting standards for a particular source. Once a standard is adopted, if a polluting firm wishes to adopt another method of abating the emissions, it then bears the burden of proving that the other technical option will work at least as well. In both cases, the process of adopting a standard requires considerable time and expense, especially if regulated firms or environmentalists elect to challenge the standards in the courts. Thus a key feature of the system of source-specific standards is that they are costly — in both dollars and time — to establish and to change.

One factor influencing the choice of a standard is ease of enforcement. When the technology of choice is a specific piece of capital equipment, enforcement is the simple task of inspection to see whether the equipment is present and working. Emissions taxes, tradable emissions permits, and output standards require monitoring to determine compliance, and monitoring performance is usually more costly and technically more difficult than inspecting inputs. However, in the long run, all regulatory approaches will be evaluated in terms of their performance with respect to pollution, and experience to date suggests that input regulation is too crude a control on performance to make worthwhile its lower enforcement costs. In Los Angeles, performance monitoring is relatively sophisticated already, so that no special problems are associated with a possible switch to tradable permits.

The standard-setting approach to environmental regulation has several important shortcomings.[2] A regulatory system that deals with each specific source of emissions — sometimes several at a particular plant — requires that regulators must learn enough about the production process they are regulating and the abatement opportunities available to it to be able to determine the optimal emissions reduction for it. Because of the adversarial nature of the process, firms are likely to be reluctant to go to great lengths to provide accurate information to regulators. Moreover, some abatement strategies may involve changes in the production process that, if revealed in a public regulatory process, would give away economically significant trade secrets. Consequently, the standards that are adopted are not likely to be the best possible set of cost-minimizing steps to achieve the overall air quality objective. In addition, significant differences among firms in the costs of complying with regulation not only are inefficient, but also can upset competition among firms in the same industry.

Standards also provide blunted incentives for technological innovation in abatement. In the current regulatory system, industries that produce abatement equipment have a strong incentive to invent new equipment that reduces emissions; however, the firms that are the objects of regulation lack that incentive, and indeed can be expected to fight the adoption of better performing but more expensive abatement technologies. In addition, the case-by-case regulatory approach raises the cost of any technical change by requiring preimplementation approval by the regulators.

Finally, standards inhibit the entry of new firms into an area. Before a firm may enter any area, it must obtain approval of its emissions from the regulatory authority. And if the area is not in compliance with ambient air quality standards, entry can be foreclosed if the new or expanded facility generates *any* emissions at all. In general, emissions standards for new plants tend to be substantially more rigorous — and expensive — than are standards for established plants in the same industry using the same production technology.[3]

In sum, standards (1) do not lead to the most cost-effective abatement strategies, (2) are promulgated in a costly, time-consuming process, and (3) impede technological change and new business investments. Given these problems, the question naturally arises as to whether taxes and tradable permits are better ways of meeting a prescribed set of environmental policy objectives.

The purpose of a marketable permits system is to achieve the ambient air quality standard for a particular pollutant at minimum total cost, including both the direct abatement cost and the cost associated with the regulatory process. This is achieved by relying on decentralized decisions to rationalize abatement strategies at all sources. Each firm faces an abatement/cost function — that is, a relationship between the amount of emissions that it will produce and the costs it will face. If the tradable permits market works efficiently (an issue that is examined in the next section), the best strategy for each firm is to abate emissions to the point at which the price for additional emissions (either the actual price of buying more permits or the opportunity cost of keeping, rather than selling, the permits it already has) equals its marginal abatement cost. If this solution holds for all firms, then all firms will pay the same amount for the last unit of pollution that they abate, and all firms together will achieve at minimal total cost the air quality standard that is implicit in the number of permits that are issued.[4] Moreover, this cost-minimizing abatement strategy will emerge without the necessity of a regulatory review of the costs and performance of the abatement strategies available to the sources and a formal approval of the technical approaches that are selected.

Emissions taxes have many of the same theoretical virtues as tradable permits. If firms are cost minimizers, effluent taxes also can lead to the cost-minimizing solution.[5] Like tradable permits, emissions taxes provide a continuing incentive for cost reductions. Moreover, because taxes do not entail the introduction of a market, they avoid the implementation problems of permits, assuming that an efficient, competitive market will emerge.

While the theoretical case for taxes is strong, they have seldom been implemented. One reason is political — they confer benefits on the general public, but they force firms to pay both abatement costs and emissions taxes. The extent to which firms pay taxes out of profits depends on whether the increase in taxes can be passed along to consumers. Nevertheless, it is usually in industry's interest to oppose taxes in comparison with standards because the latter avoid the tax. Tradable permits also can avoid net payments to the government if licenses are initially given away rather than auctioned.

Emissions taxes also present some difficulties in dealing with the entry of new sources of pollution. Unless taxes are adjusted upward, they will lead to ever-worsening environmental quality; however, if taxes are to be adjusted when entry occurs, something like a regulatory process must be used to examine the implications of each new entry and set an appropriate new tax. By contrast, entry under a permits regime requires only the acquisition of the necessary permits from other sources, neither posing a threat to environmental standards nor requiring a formal review of the entrant's likely emissions and abatement opportunities.

As mentioned above, all performance-related regulatory approaches raise questions of enforcement costs because of the difficulty of monitoring pollution. Emissions fees, however, are somewhat more difficult to enforce because they require continuous monitoring to estimate total emissions for the purpose of determining tax liabilitites. An emissions fee is normally some price per unit of emissions; hence total emissions during a tax period need to be estimated. Moreover, for the tax to be collectable, the monitoring process must be accurate enough to withstand legal challenges.

Performance standards and emissions permits can be enforced by intermittent monitoring. The key issue in either case is whether or not a firm is in compliance with its emissions ceiling, whether the ceiling is established by a regulatory process or by acquisition of permits through a market. Noncompliance fines need not be based upon the extent to which the firm is out of compliance (such as on total measured emissions), although the fines must be high enough and the probability of detection great enough so that a firm prefers to emit within its ceiling rather than run the risk of being caught with excess emissions.

Another characteristic of taxes that has caused opposition to them is that the consequence of uncertainties over the cost effectiveness of abatement techniques emerges in an emissions tax system as unpredictability in the quantity of emissions. By contrast, both output standards and a permits scheme would specify the overall quantity of emissions in advance, and the uncertainties in the system are with respect to cost. Input standards suffer from both uncertainties, because the use of a technology, not its effectiveness in reducing emissions, is the measure of compliance.

The reforms of environmental regulation pursued by EPA since the enactment of the Clean Air Act Amendments of 1977 foresee a limited role for emissions fees in the context of traditional standard-setting methods. This role entails the use of "noncompliance fines" for firms that fail to meet the standards, with the fees designed to be high enough to provide incentives to comply before all legal avenues for fighting compliance are exhausted. This, of course, avoids some of the political and technical problems of emissions taxes, but it also sacrifices their principal advantages in terms of minimizing abatement costs and providing an incentive to beat the standards.

The theoretical advantages of a tradable permits system make them worthy of further serious investigation. Indeed, both federal and state regulators have expressed considerable interest in this method. As mentioned above, EPA has developed several limited variants of a tradable permit system that are being applied experimentally around the nation. These so-called controlled trading methods are:

(1) *Bubbles:* A single plant that has several emissions sources may be permitted to increase emissions beyond the current standard at one location if it makes a greater reduction in emissions somewhere else at the same facility.[6]

(2) *Offsets:* A firm may add new emissions in a geographic area if it pays for a greater reduction in emissions somewhere else in the same area.

(3) *Banks:* A firm that reduces its emissions below the applicable standard may deposit as a credit some fraction of its excess emissions reductions in an emissions bank. These banked emissions credits can then be sold to other firms seeking emissions permits.

All of these policies are designed to introduce some flexibility into the means by which firms comply with environmental regulations by introducing the possibility of trading emissions at one place for emissions somewhere else. In this sense they are conceptually similar to tradable permits. But all retain important elements of the standard-setting approach as well. Each trade requires regulatory approval, and the source using the traded permit assumes a burden of proof that the trade is consistent with overall environmental policy.

Current distinctions in the stringency of regulations between new and old sources are retained in all of these policies. Thus firms seeking to locate an environmentally significant new source of emissions by acquiring tradable permits must still operate at the lowest attainable emissions rates. For new sources, the trading policies are regarded as a means for providing the possibility for entry when compliance with new source standards would still not be sufficient to comply with ambient air quality standards.

As of early 1981, the new policies did not yet have well-defined rules and procedures governing transactions, nor in most cases a convenient institutional arrangement for facilitating them. The offset policy has no formal process for informing prospective participants in an offset about the identity of potential partners, the likely cost of reducing their emissions, or the expected price of their emissions permits. Each offset transaction is the result of bilateral negotiations outside of any formal institutional structure established by the government. Emissions banks do have a formal record-keeping method for tracking the amount and source of marketable emissions credits, but at present the formal rules and procedures regarding trades are still being worked out. For both offsets and banks, trades must be approved by local regulatory authorities, although formal approval from the EPA can now be avoided if the trading system is established according to EPA guidelines.

A final problem with all three methods is that the long-term status of traded permits is not clear in any program. If environmental quality in any area falls short of the policy target, all permits — traded or not — are subject to revision; however, traded permits and banked credits from sources that reduced emissions below standards appear more likely to be confiscated or severely reduced in value than other permits do. For example, in listing the options available to a local air pollution control authority should a revision be necessary in the amount of emissions that is allowed, the EPA manual for setting up an emissions bank cites four alternatives:

(1) a moratorium on the use of permits obtained from the emissions reduction credit bank;

(2) on a source-by-source basis, a revision in the number of permits from the bank that are necessary to produce a unit of emissions at that source;

(3) an across-the-board reduction in the amount of emissions allowed for a permit acquired through the bank; or

(4) a forfeiture of all traded permits.[7]

Thus a traded emissions permit may have secondary regulatory status in comparison with an untraded permit, making the former less valuable. The possibility that traded permits will be treated this way will make firms reluctant to reduce emissions beyond current requirements in order to create marketable permits out of concern that their additional emissions reductions will be confiscated rather than made available to others. Potential trading partners will be equally reluctant to make long-term capital investments on the basis of emissions permits that have such an uncertain status.

The tradable permits system examined here is a more radical institutional change than has thus far been contemplated by regulatory authorities. It would eliminate distinctions among sources because of age, ownership, industry, or method of acquiring permits. It would simply establish a ceiling on total emissions within a geographic area, and it would allow the allocation of emissions among sources in the area to be determined solely by the market. No regulatory review of the methods used by any source nor of the distribution of emissions permits among the sources would be undertaken. Policy issues relating to the differential air quality effects of different geographical distributions of emissions permits would be dealt with by the way in which trading regions were defined, and by the rules for trading across regional boundaries, as will be discussed below. The role of the government would be reduced to the following activities: (1) establishment of ambient air quality standards; (2) determination of the total amount of emissions that is consistent with the air quality standard; (3) issuance of permits and maintenance of records of their ownership and markets for them; and (4) enforcement of the emissions limits by ascertainment of whether each source is producing no more emissions than the quantity of permits it holds and by imposition of noncompliance penalties.

Regulators also may wish to use direct regulation, rather than a tradable permits system, to deal with air pollution "episodes." Meteorological conditions have an important effect on the relationship between emissions and air quality. One approach to this problem is to have several different permit systems, each of which pertains to a particular weather pattern. The separate permits systems would correspond to the multiple-stage "alert" systems. Alternatively, the tradable permits system could apply only to normal conditions, and direct regulation could be used to deal with emergency conditions. Our study has assumed the latter approach for the present simply to avoid unnecessary complexity. Later, if and when the feasibility of tradable permits is demonstrated for the normal case, attention can be turned to whether a special permit system for emergency conditions would be more effective and less costly than the present episode policy.

Implementation Problems

Before we can be certain that tradable permits will be an efficient way to deal with any particular pollution problem, several questions must be answered. These questions all relate to whether a competitive market in enforceable permits can be constructed.

(1) Will the market have enough participants and frequent enough transactions to work efficiently?

(2) Because pollution has a geographic and temporal component, over what geographic area and which time periods will a particular permit be in force, and who will be allowed to buy a particular type of permit?

(3) In light of the fact that pollution is often the result of chemical processes and transportation of emissions, how can the number of permits be related to environmental quality standards for particular locations?

(4) What should be the lifetime of an emissions permit, and how can mechanisms be established that would enable regulators to change the number of permits as pollution policy changes without undermining the rationality of the choice by firms between strategies that involve long-term capital expenditures versus methods that primarily involve higher operating cost?

(5) What special provisions, if any, need to be made to assure ease of entry in polluting industries without sacrificing environmental policy objectives so that environmental policy creates minimum feasible problems in terms of inducing local monopolies in some polluting industries?

(6) What effects will a cost-minimizing abatement strategy have on the structure of the local economy? That is, are some industries likely to relocate elsewhere because combined expenditures on abatement and emissions permits erode their competitive positions relative to firms in other localities, and will the process by which the price of a permit adjusts to the long-run equilibrium be so slow that, temporarily, prices give false signals that cause inappropriate long-run decisions to be made about location and investment?

The object of the process of designing a market in permits should be to come as close as possible to a situation in which a large number of buyers and sellers will actively trade permits, will quickly establish a market price for permits that is close to the long-run equilibrium, and will take actions that minimize abatement costs and distribute emissions geographically and temporally such that ambient air quality standards are met. This may require that certain trade-offs be made in terms of the design features of the system.

For example, a fairly fine-tuned definition of the times and places at which a permit can be used may produce too few participants in each market to guarantee an efficient outcome. A broader geographic and temporal definition of a permit may be consistent with numerous substantially different patterns of pollution from the same amount of total emissions, some of which cause local "hot spots" at which pollution substantially exceeds environmental goals, even though the rest of the region is in compliance. Consequently, in defining the boundaries within which a permit will be valid, it is useful to have both a good model of the relationships between emissions and environmental quality, and a good approximation of how the market is likely to distribute permits among sources. This enables one to predict the environmental quality results that are likely to come about from alternative ways of organizing the permits market.

In order to predict how permits — and, therefore, emissions — are likely to be distributed, one needs to know the demand for permits by each source for the full range of possible market prices for permits. This requires being able to make a reasonable estimate of the abatement/cost function faced by each major source, because each firm will attempt to minimize the sum of permit purchases and abatement expenditures. From the abatement/cost functions, one can derive the cost-minimizing combination of permits and abatement that would result from different long-run prices for permits. This yields a demand curve for permits for the cost-minimizing firm.

Similar types of calculations are needed to answer questions about the market structure issues. In order to determine whether the market will be sufficiently competitive to produce an efficient result, one needs to be able to forecast the final distribution of permits. Whether the market for permits has monopolistic features that undermine its efficiency depends on whether one or two firms account for a large share of either sales or purchases.[8] To predict the concentration in permits transactions also requires solving the cost-minimizing problem for participants in the market. From this, one can predict the equilibrium price of a permit. Knowing the price, one can then use the abatement/cost functions to predict a final distribution of the permits. This can be compared to the initial distribution to generate an estimate of net sales (or purchases) by each firm, which can then be used to calculate expected market shares.

In similar fashion, cost data are essential for determining whether cost-minimizing abatement will alter the industrial structure of an area. They are also needed to figure out whether a short-run disequilibrium in the permits market could force relocation or bankruptcy of some firms that would continue to operate locally if the equilibrium price were established quickly.

Is Implementation Feasible?

In order to demonstrate the viability of marketable permits without actually implementing the alternative one must select a specific pollutant, identify the key implementation problems, and then design a market that will address these issues. We have selected the problem of controlling particulate sulfates in the atmosphere in the Los Angeles region as an example.[9] This problem was chosen because it appeared to be a likely candidate for marketable permits. The scientific aspects of the problem are well understood. Data on sulfur oxides abatement costs are available or can be constructed for most of the key sources, and monitoring and enforcement problems appear tractable. Finally, the present regulatory method is not regarded as working very well.

The current approach toward controlling sulfur oxides emissions in Los Angeles relies on standards, an offset policy, and a small emissions tax. New or expanded sources of pollution must adopt the best available technology, and must trade off the uncontrolled portion of their emissions by effecting further reductions at existing sources in the Los Angeles Basin. The owner of an existing source is thus vested with a valuable property right, which can be sold in whole or in part to new sources. The owner also has the option of retaining the opportunity for further abatement to facilitate subsequent expansion.

The offset policy is one limited form of a market in transferable permits to emit air pollutants. Its principal drawbacks are that the costs of negotiation are excessive and the number of trades that can be made by new sources is limited. Negotiation costs are high because new entrants must first identify existing sources of pollution where emissions reductions are feasible, then try to estimate a reasonable charge for the offset, and, finally, perhaps have to purchase the entire business operations of some polluter to obtain its emissions rights. Purchases of offsets by new firms are limited by the requirement that new firms must reduce emissions to the lowest achievable level before being allowed to enter the offset market.

Demonstration of the superiority of a permits market requires a good technical understanding of the problem. Fortunately, this is the case for the particulate sulfate problem in Los Angeles. Particulate sulfates are caused primarily by the combustion of sulfur-bearing energy sources, and are a regulatory concern because they reduce visibility, acidify rainwater, and may have harmful health effects.

Virtually all of the sulfur emitted in the Los Angeles area is embodied in crude oil. When oil products are refined or burned without controls, some of the sulfur contained in them is converted to SO_2 and SO_3 and released to the atmosphere. These SO_x compounds react to form sulfates through a series of atmospheric chemical processes.

Cass has succeeded in constructing an emissions/air quality model for particulate sulfates in Los Angeles.[10] An important finding from Cass's model is that mobile sources can be regarded as stationary sources by converting them to traffic densities over the airshed. Because the most likely strategy for reducing sulfur emissions from mobile sources is to reduce the sulfur content of fuels, regulation of mobile sources can be done indirectly by placing the responsibility on refiners. A tradable permits system could then be vastly simplified by counting both refinery emissions and sulfur emissions from mobile sources to determine the number of permits refiners must hold.

A major task of the project was to estimate abatement/cost functions for the primary sources of sulfur emissions in Los Angeles. A total of 30 source categories were identified, and abatement costs estimated for each. The published literature, regulatory proceedings, and interviews with representatives of local industry and state and local regulatory personnel were relied upon to generate preliminary cost estimates. The normal information obtained from a particular source was a point estimate: the cost at some historical date of using a particular method to obtain a specific rate of emissions from a particular kind of facility. These were combined to produce an abatement/cost function for representative facilities in each source category, based on 1977 regulatory conditions, and expressed in 1977 dollars.[11] The results of these analyses were submitted as industry studies to the relevant firms operating in Los Angeles, with requests for comments. The additional data received in this manner were used to produce a final cost study, including indications of the amount of disagreement about costs among the sources of information.

A number of factors make these cost estimates upwardly biased as estimators of the costs that would be experienced if a system of tradable permits were instituted. First, for source categories for which no control cost estimates could be found, emissions were assumed to be uncontrollable. Second, production and energy use at emitting facilities were assumed to be independent of the amount of control. In reality, firms with especially high emissions and stiff abatement costs are likely to reduce output or to make more efficient use of energy. Third, although several process changes are available to many firms, they are reluctant to reveal them because they are trade secrets that may confer significant competitive advantages upon these firms in a more stringent regulatory environment. No allowance for these process changes is made in the study, although an effort is now being made to model the possibility of changes in refinery mix in the oil industry as one means of changing emissions from refineries and refined products. The effect of all these sources of bias in estimated abatement cost is to understate the benefits of a tradable permits system because these lower-cost opportunities could only be taken advantage of if an incentive-based system replaced current regulations.

Because SO_x emissions in Los Angeles result largely from the combustion of petroleum products, the availability of natural gas, which has negligible amounts of sulfur, can significantly affect SO_x emissions. This, in turn, will affect the demand for permits and, hence, their price. For this reason, three separate cases were analyzed: one assumes a low level of natural gas availability, reflecting the fears, if not expectations, of regulators and the energy industry in the late 1970s about future gas production; a second corresponds to the supply in 1973, when supplies were somewhat curtailed (an intermediate supply assumption); and a third assumes a high supply of natural gas. In all cases, natural gas used is based upon allocation priorities established by regulators, rather than the market. This has an important effect on the results because allocation priorities are not related to the value of natural gas in terms of either its direct use or its effects on air quality.

With these caveats in mind, the cost data were used to estimate the demand for emissions permits and the distribution of permits under various types of market arrangements. Several specific design features of the market system are potentially important in determining the performance of the market.[12] One is the method for initializing the market. Each firm can simply be allocated a share of permits, with firms then being allowed to develop a market on their own by making buy and sell offers, much as buyers and sellers interact in a stock market. Another method is to use an auction, whereby the allocation of permits is based upon bids submitted to the regulators.

A second design issue is the duration of the permits. Here regulators face a trade-off between two conflicting objectives. One is the desire for introducing stability into abatement planning by firms through guaranteeing that permits will be respected for a period comparable to the investment planning horizon of business. The conflicting objective is the desire to maintain flexibility in the regulatory system in the face of new information about abatement costs, the effects of pollution, or even the dominating political values about the desirability of rigorous environmental quality standards. The latter objective is best served by giving regulators the ability to alter the number of emissions permits frequently and easily.

The importance of different design features depends to some extent on the particular application under study. The subsequent analysis illustrates how data from this case study can be used to help develop solutions to market design problems.

Market Structure Problems

One issue to be attacked is the possibility of an imperfectly competitive market structure. The first step in addressing this issue is to simulate the competitive allocation of permits. This is achieved by finding the minimum-cost allocation of abatement reponsibilities among the sources that achieves a target level of total emissions.

Although numerous market simulations have been made under varying assumptions about ambient air quality standards and the

TABLE 6.1 Fraction of Total Emissions Accounted for by Largest Permit Holder in Los Angeles

	(A) Competition %	*(B) Monopsony* %
(1) Make existing permits tradable with historical gas supplies	48	33
(2) Violate standard two weeks/year with historical gas supplies	43	40
(3) Satisfy standard all of the time with historical gas supplies	32	32

SOURCE: R.W. Hahn, "An Assessment of the Viability of Marketable Permits" (Ph.D. dissertation, California Institute of Technology, 1981).

availability of substitutes for petroleum fuels, three examples will be presented here:[13] The first assumes that the state's ambient air quality standards will be satisfied all of the time, the second assumes that the standards will be violated approximately 2 weeks per year, and the third assumes that the emissions allowed under regulations now in place become freely tradable. All cases assume an intermediate availability of natural gas. Under this assumption, the controls on sulfur oxides emissions that were established in 1977 would produce emissions of about 300 tons of SO_2 equivalent per day in Los Angeles; to meet the standard all the time requires that emissions be cut in half, but to meet it all but 2 weeks per year, on average, requires a further reduction of only about 50 tons per day. Thus the cases represent a major change, a minor reduction, and no change in currently enacted (but not yet fully in place) source-specific standards.

The single largest source of emissions is an electric utility. In 1973, prior to controls, this source accounted for approximately 28 percent of emissions in Los Angeles. Table 6.1 shows the share of permits that this firm would be expected to hold under 2 simulated market structures for the cases described above. The shares reported in Table 6.1 should not be taken too literally. Among the major source categories in Los Angeles, abatement costs are best known — and least likely to be overestimated — for electric utilities. This means that even greater efficiency gains may be possible by substituting abatement elsewhere for the emissions reductions at utilities that are calculated from the existing cost data.

With this caveat in mind, the results in Table 6.1 illustrate the possibility of serious market imperfections, depending upon the selection of an emissions target and an initial allocation of the permits. Column A shows the cost-minimizing allocation of permits under the 3 emissions targets described above. This allocation is the competitive equilibrium. If the initial allocation process is an auction so that all firms are buyers, the share of the largest source is the share shown in Column A. Other initial allocations can raise this figure substantially. For example, suppose all sources are allocated a proportion of their precontrol emissions that is calculated to retain present total emissions. In this case the largest source, assuming the market were competitive, would seek to increase its share of holdings by 20 percent of the total number of permits (the difference between 48 percent on Line 1, Column A, and the 28 percent share of baseline emissions). This would make this source an almost complete monopsonist, that is, the only source of demand for permits at the competitive equilibrium price (almost all other firms would be sellers). The potential inefficiency of a monopsonist is that it will systematically understate its demand in order to force the price of permits down. This is achieved by engaging in excessive abatement, the extra costs of which are made up in the effects of pushing down permit prices.

Column B of Table 6.1 shows the results from the most extreme degree of monopsony possible for each of the three cases. Here it is assumed that the largest source has an initial allocation of no permits, and that all other firms are given permits in a manner that causes them to seek to be sellers at any price equal to or above the monopsony equilibrium. The pattern of the results shows a greater divergence between competitive and monopsony shares for higher total limits on emissions. The reason is that, in the range of the competitive equilibrium for emissions limits around the most stringent standard, the supply of permits from other firms to the largest source is very sensitive to price changes. This undermines the opportunity of the monopsonist to take advantage of its high market share: Overabatement will not force much of a drop in permit prices, and hence the gains from the latter will not generate much of an offset against the higher abatement costs necessary to allow the firm to reduce its demand for permits.

The tentative conclusion from this analysis is that, for the particular case at hand, monopsony appears to be a serious design concern only if regulators do not conform to the existing ambient air quality standards. The actual allocation rule is certain to be less likely to cause monopsony than the extreme case analyzed here; yet, even under this extreme assumption, imperfections in the permit market appear relatively unimportant if the emissions limit is low. On the other hand, market imperfections could be important if existing permits were simply made tradable unless the initial allocation were designed to guard against it.

Multiple Permits Markets

Another important implementation issue is the degree of geographical resolution in the definition of an emissions permit. In the case of sulfates in Los Angeles, a permit could be defined as a right to emit a given amount of sulfur oxides anywhere in the airshed. Or, permits could have a variable value that depends on the geographic location of the source holding them, with the relationship based upon estimates of the damage created by emissions from different sources. Finally, permits could be defined in terms of the resulting pollution at each of several monitoring sites at which air quality is measured (in this case there are seventeen such sites). An air quality model could then be used to calculate the number of permits a given source must hold at each receptor site for each unit of emissions that it releases. The last alternative is the most complicated to implement, for it requires that sources participate in seventeen markets and that the state be continuously available to run air quality simulations whenever any firm seeks to change its emissions. While such a system is difficult — perhaps impossible — to operate in the real world, its results can nevertheless be simulated. The differences between the first system (all emissions are treated equally) and the last system (each receptor is associated with a separate market) thus provides a measure of the potential gross gains from a fine-tuned method of defining the permits.

Table 6.2 presents some of the results of these simulations.[14] The case analyzed here is one in which natural gas availability is low. This case is likely to produce the greatest differences in abatement costs among various methods for organizing the permits market. If gas supplies are available in intermediate quantities, abatement costs tend to be about 60 percent of the costs if natural gas supplies are low. Column A shows the annualized expenditures on abatement costs in

TABLE 6.2 Comparison of Universal and Receptor-Specific Permits (costs in millions of dollars)

Baseline Emissions Target in Tons/Day SO_2 Equivalent	*Annualized Costs of Competitive Equilibrium Abatement for:*		
		Receptor-Specific Permits that Produce:	
	(A) Universal Permits	*(B) Same Air Quality for Each Receptor*	*(C) Uniform Air Quality Equal to Worst Receptor*
150	682	682	682
250	565	557	545
300	515	513	505

SOURCE: R. W. Hahn, "An Assessment of the Viability of Marketable Permits" (Ph.D. dissertation, California Institute of Technology, 1981).

the Los Angeles area under the competitive equilibrium distribution of permits if there is no geographical resolution in the permit system. Column B shows the costs if firms are required to buy pollution permits for each of the seventeen measuring stations in the airshed, subject to the conditions that the air quality results at each station will be the same as the outcome from the system reported in Column A. Thus, the difference between A and B is the gain, if any, arising solely from geographical relocation of permits in a system that takes account of the specific polluting effects of emissions from each location in the region. Column C further relaxes the system, allowing pollution at all measuring stations to be constrained only by the air quality achieved at the most polluted station under the allocation corresponding to Column A. Thus emissions can be reallocated and total emissions increased as long as pollution does not increase at the location that is most polluted under the Column A allocation.

The general result from the analysis is that there is little to be gained from fine tuning the definition of permits. The reasons are twofold: The simple market allocates emissions relatively evenly over the region, and leaves relatively small differences among measuring stations in terms of the air quality results. Hence there is little opportunity for improving the efficiency of the allocation through adopting a more complicated market system.

While these results may not be generalizable to other pollutants in other areas, they nevertheless suggest an important lesson. In order for a tradable permits system to be able to capture significant gains from a fine-tuned, complicated definition of permits and their markets, it is *not* sufficient that different sources have a significantly different pattern of effects. It must also be the case that the equilibrium allocation of permits in a crude, simplified market be such that emissions would be concentrated in a particular location.

If the comparison is to be made between a simple tradable permits system and the existing regulatory arrangement, the issue is whether a tradable permits system increases or reduces the geographic concentration of emissions compared to the present pattern. Because the present source-specific standards system tends to force some activities to overabate (for example, electric utilities), while leaving other sources virtually unregulated, it should not be surprising to find that a tradable permits system evens out the pattern of emissions in comparison to the present system, and therefore makes more even the geographical distribution of measured pollution within a region. Moreover, if most sources face relatively low abatement costs for a substantial fraction of their emissions, a market system will lead to substantial abatement from all sources. In such a case, it should not be surprising to find situations in which there is relatively little additional gain associated with moving from a simple system to a complex system.

Thin Markets

The final major potential source of a failure in the permits market is that transactions will be too infrequent to convey meaningful price signals to polluting firms, to make relatively easy the acquisition of permits for entry and expansion of polluting facilities, and to allow a firm to avoid the expense of organizing the market and engaging in extensive bilateral negotiation every time it desires to make a trade. This is an especially difficult design problem to get a firm grip on in advance of operating the market, for the indicators of the extent of market transactions are so crude. One measure is the number of firms accounting for existing and expected emissions. In Los Angeles 10 companies account for approximately 85 percent of the sulfur oxides emissions under current standards, assuming mobile sources are assigned to the oil refiners operating in the airshed. Most major industrial polluters emit relatively small amounts of sulfur, so that the market for small quantities of permits is likely to be reasonably well functioning; however, a major expansion or entry of an oil refinery, an offshore oil terminal, or an electric utility generation facility would be especially difficult to accommodate because so few sources have sufficient numbers of permits to be potentially significant sellers to the new source.

A second problem in anticipating the extent of a problem of market thinness is that there is likely to be a systematic tendency to underestimate the possibilities for transactions. A substantial source of demand and supply in the market for permits will be factors that are not measurable in advance. Examples are innovations in abatement technology, entry, exit, contraction and expansion of polluting entities, and opportunities for more efficient abatement methods that may be known to existing sources but that have not yet appeared in the public domain (for example, process changes).

In Los Angeles, the problem is even more difficult because the local air pollution control authority has explicity adopted the policy of attempting to write standards in inverse order of their costs per unit of abatement. Thus, with few exceptions, the standards in place are the least expensive remaining possibilities. Of course, regulators are not prescient, and they have missed some possibilities for cost minimization, but the overall performance in Los Angeles is quite good. Consequently, most of the demand for trades, and the gains from a permits market, are unlikely to be measured using existing cost information since present standards tend to be based upon the same cost data. Therefore, the extent to which the thinness of the market is a potential problem is likely to be overstated. For example, given historical natural gas supplies and no abatement methods other than those whose costs are known publicly, the annual cost savings from a competitive reallocation of the emissions permits that are currently in place is estimated to save only about $20 million per year in abatement costs, which is about 7 percent of the total.[15] This indicates a strong possibility of a thin market, indeed; however, it is sure to be an underestimate of the potential savings, and hence the desire to trade.

Whether the market is thin, initially and in the future, again depends on the design of the system. A few examples illustrate this point: (1) If existing emissions (or some proportion of them) are simply made tradable, a thin market is a more likely prospect than if an auction process is used for the initial allocation; (2) fine-tuned, multiple-market systems are more likely to face a problem of thinness than single markets defined over a broad geographic area; and (3) if permits are perpetual, with no periodic reallocation process, a decision to make a major purchase or sale would then require that the firm wishing to make a market undertake the time and expense of organizing and negotiating a trade. At the other extreme, if permits have a fixed life and are reallocated by auction, a convenient time and place is established for facilitating major redistributions of permits should changes in underlying economic and technological conditions warrant it.

Selecting a Design: Conclusions

The preceding discussion should make clear that selecting a design for a system of marketable emissions permits is not a purely technical, scientific matter. Working out the details requires considerable judgment, including an assessment of which risks a political entity would prefer to run.

In Los Angeles market imperfections apparently are a far more important design issue than is the selection of appropriate definitions for the geographical extent of a permits market. Fine tuning the system in terms of multiple markets for sulfur emissions promises little gains, yet there may be formidable problems of transactions costs and market structure. Consequently, a system in which permits are simply stated in terms of allowable quantities of SO_2 equivalent emissions anywhere in the region appears to be the most desirable.

The Los Angeles airshed has a relatively large number of sources producing a small quantity of emissions, but only 10 firms account for about 85 percent of the total. Consequently, imperfectly competitive and thin markets are a potential problem for large transactions. The implication is that the method selected for initializing and maintaining the system should encourage an active, competitive market.

The most attractive method for the initial allocation is an auction mechanism. This provides a thick market (all permits are transacted in the initial distribution) and, because all polluters are placed on the same side of the market, it minimizes the likelihood of monopolistic imperfections. The mechanics of the proposed auction are as follows. Each source would be asked to write down the number of permits it would seek to purchase at each of several prices. The firm would be free to choose as many price gradations as it wanted. It could write down one price-quantity pair (for example, X tons per day at any price up to $Y per ton). It could provide a step function of several jumps, such as X tons per day for prices between $Y and $Z ($Y being larger), and X + W tons for prices below $Z. Permits would then be allocated to the highest bidders at the quantities requested, descending down the price bids until the permits were completely allocated. Among the bids not receiving any permit allocations, the one with the highest bid price determines the price of all permits (the allocation mechanism is a second-price auction). This process is the most likely theoretically to produce a competitive allocation of the permits.

A separable equity issue accompanying the auction is the allocation of the net costs of the permits. Whereas the permit price determined above could actually be paid to the state, an alternative is to pay the revenues according to a previously arranged provisional permit allocation. As a political matter, the chances of implementing a tradable permits system are probably greater if the revenues do not accrue to the governmental treasury, and if the provisional allocation of the rights to receive the revenues from the permit auction does not reward firms who have been most resistant to current environmental regulations. For example, one possible alternative is to base allocations on an amended list of existing emissions, with the few remaining uncontrolled sources being put through an emissions standard process before the initial allocation of tradable permits is made.[16]

In any case, the provisional allocation would be used solely for allocating auction revenues. Each polluting firm would make bids on permits, and thereby receive a final allocation of emission permits according to its bids at the price of the highest excluded bid. The firm would pay for these permits at the established price, and receive revenues at the same price for the permits it held provisionally. The net payment for a particular source would be the product of the auction price and the difference between its final allocation based upon the bidding procedure and its provisional allocation based upon its emissions baseline. For all firms taken together, the net payment would be zero.

It is worth noting that in a competitive auction, if a firm reports its true cost-minimizing demand for permits, any difference between the final and provisional allocations is a net financial gain. A firm will end up buying permits only if the permits allow an even greater savings in abatement costs, and will sell permits only if the revenues from the sale exceed the costs of the additional abatement that the sale will require. Hence, participation in an auction that reallocates all auction revenues in this way can harm a firm only if it is not truthful in stating its demand for permits.

To provide a continuing opportunity for entry and expansion, the initial permits could be separated into vintages according to useful life and periodically reissued by the same process. A predesignated portion of the permits would expire each year — for example, permits could be valid for nine years, with one-third expiring every three years. Prior to the expiration date, the regulators would determine how many permits would be issued to replace the expired ones, based upon considerations of cost and air quality. The new permits could be allocated by the same auction procedure as was used for the initial allocation. Provisional allocations for purposes of distributing auction revenues would be based upon holdings of the expiring permits, but the final allocation would be based upon an auction.

The system of permits with sequenced expiration introduces flexibility into the regulatory process while still retaining a substantial amount of stability. More risk-averse firms, or firms seeking to pursue abatement strategies involving long-term capital investments, could adjust their portfolios to hold permits with late expiration dates. Each three-year regulatory review would introduce the opportunity for altering total emissions in response to new information or political changes.

The system described above addresses the major questions about a tradable permits approach. In particular, the following answers can be provided to each of them.

(1) An auction process for sequentially expiring permits provides regularized transactions, involving all sources in the airshed; in addition, such a process appears capable of producing a stable, competitive price for permits.

(2) There is no significant loss in efficiency or air quality if the entire region is treated as a single, homogeneous market.

(3) The Cass model of the relationship between emissions and air quality provides a good basis for establishing an initial quantity of total emissions, and the sequential expiration of permits easily accommodates further adjustments to account for whatever errors might be present in the model's predictions.

(4) Sequenced expiration of permits can also provide the possibility for long-term stability for firms that desire it, facilitating capital investments in abatement methods for firms that want to use them, while still letting the regulatory system adjust to changes in information or political values.

(5) The sequenced expiration dates for permits and the auction method for allocating them facilitate easy entry and expansion of emissions sources without altering environmental quality.

(6) Even using the abatement/cost information available, which is likely to overstate abatement costs, implementation of tradable permits will cause no dislocations in the local economy, in part because the cost-minimizing abatement strategy does not impose costs on any industry that would cause a significant reduction in output, and in part because the auction mechanism avoids the problems of temporary, distorted prices that create false incentives to industry.

Thus, tradable emissions permits are an attractive alternative to command-and-control regulation for the specific case of particulate sulfates in the Los Angeles area. We also believe that the analysis contained in this chapter has wider applicability. First, the most important questions about the feasibility of tradable permits are likely to be pretty much the same for all pollutants in all regions. Second, the design concepts that have been developed for this particular problem do not appear to be idiosyncratic. This chapter, then, provides a methodological guide for examining the prospects for this approach in other areas, for other pollution problems.

NOTES

1. For an analysis of how taxes and subsidies affect entry, see R. Talbot Page, "Failure of Bribes and Standards for Pollution Abatement," *Natural Resources Journal* 13 (1976): 677-704.

2. For a more detailed discussion, see R. G. Noll, "The Feasibility of Marketable Emissions Permits in the United States," California Institute of Technology, Social Science Working Paper 397, (Pasadena, 1981).

3. See, for example, B. A. Ackerman and W. T. Hassler, *Clean Coal/Dirty Air* (New Haven, CT: Yale University Press, 1981).

4. A formal proof of this result for the case in which licenses are defined in terms of the ultimate pollutant to be regulated is contained in W. D. Montgomery, "Markets in Licenses and Efficient Pollution Control Programs," *Journal of Economic Theory*, 5 December 1972, pp. 395-418. If licenses are defined in terms of emissions, then the solution may not be the cost-minimizing strategy for achieving a given air quality target. The reason is that the same amount of emissions may have a different effect on ambient air quality if emitted at different locations. If so, charging firms the same price for a "unit" of emissions will typically imply that the marginal cost of improving the level of air quality will differ across firms. This result holds because firms are

being charged a uniform price for emissions and not for pollution. An estimate of the difference in costs between the two pricing approaches for the case of particulates in the St. Louis Air Quality Control Region has been developed in S. E. Atkinson and D. H. Lewis, "A Cost-Effectiveness Analysis of Alternative Air Quality Control Strategies," *Journal of Environmental Economics and Management,* 1 November 1974, pp. 237-250.

5. For a rigorous proof of this assertion, see W. J. Baumol and W. E. Oates, *The Theory of Environmental Policy* (Englewood Cliffs, NJ: Prentice-Hall, 1975), pp. 140-144.

6. Recently, the U.S. Environmental Protection Agency has extended this concept to include multiplant bubbles, which are conceptually similar to the offset method.

7. ICF, Incorporated, *Emission Reduction Banking Manual,* Environmental Protection Agency, Emission Reduction Banking and Trading Publication BG200 (Washington, D.C., 1980), p. 26.

8. For a thorough analysis of the problem of the structure of permits markets, see R. W. Hahn, "An Assessment of the Viability of Marketable Permits" (Ph. D. Dissertation, California Institute of Technology, 1981).

9. The "Los Angeles region" refers to the South Coast Air Basin and a part of Ventura County. The current definition of the South Coast Air Basin includes all of Orange County, the majority of Los Angeles County, and parts of San Bernardino and Riverside Counties. For a more precise definition, see *Air Report,* July/August 1980 (Pomona College, Claremont, California).

10. G. R. Cass, "Methods for Sulfate Air Quality Management with Application to Los Angeles" (Ph. D. Dissertations, California Institute of Technology, 1978).

11. For details on these cost estimates, see R. W. Hahn, "Data Base and Programming Methodology for Marketable Permits Study," California Institute of Technology, Environmental Quality Laboratory, Open File Report 80-8 (Pasadena: 1980).

12. For a more complete discussion of the range of design issues, see Noll, "Feasibility of Marketable Permits."

13. For more details about the choice of emissions limits and the various simulations, see R. W. Hahn and R. Noll, "Designing a Market for Tradable Emissions Permits," California Institute of Technology, Social Science Working Paper 398 (Pasadena, 1981).

14. For a more complete analysis, see Hahn and Noll, "Designing a Market."

15. Calculations are in Hahn, "An Assessment of Viability."

16. For a more thorough discussion of alternative ways to construct a baseline for provisionally distributing permits, see Noll, "Feasibility of Marketable Permits."

7

Marketlike Approaches

Their Past, Present, and Probable Future

JAMES E. KRIER

I should begin with a disclaimer. The project discussed by Robert Hahn and Roger Noll in their chapter on tradable emissions permits (see Chapter 6) is not one in which I am disinterested. To the contrary, I am a consultant on the project regarding some of its legal aspects. Therefore, even if I were critical of their undertaking (which I am not), I would probably be guarded about saying as much, and even if I had great admiration for the project (which I do), it would be somewhat self-serving for me to mention that. Accordingly, I have chosen the safe alternative of presenting no pointed remarks at all about the Hahn and Noll chapter, favorable or otherwise; instead, I will simply offer some brief views about the larger history of their project, about several of the legal barriers it might confront, and about the significance of the undertaking.

Some Intellectual History

By the "larger history" of the project on tradable emissions permits, I mean its intellectual background. While market approaches to control of environmental problems and related social ills are often talked about today as though they were quite new and different, the fact is that they have been a favorite of economists for many years. This happens particularly to be the case with respect to air pollution. According to common attribution, the English economist Arthur Cecil Pigou envisioned an emissions tax on factory smoke — the classic example of a marketlike approach to control — as long ago as the first third of this century, in various editions of his *Economics of Welfare*.[1]

That the smoke tax is attributed to Pigou is actually quite amusing, if not perverse. A fair reading of the pertinent parts of his book, which are murky to say the least, suggests that he regarded pollution *control* as an example of what he called an "incidental service," that is, an external benefit or economy. The overrunning of a neighbor's land by raising too many rabbits was Pigou's chief example of an "incidental disservice," an external cost or diseconomy. It is reasonably clear elsewhere in Pigou's treatment that he recommended bounties to deal with external benefits and taxes to deal with external costs. Thus it was not air pollution that Pigou proposed taxing, but rather the unduly fecund rabbit warren. The implicit remedy for pollution was a subsidy — the very alternative almost uniformly rejected by economists today!

Nevertheless, it is now taken virtually for granted that Pigou along with Alfred Marshall[2] brought the important idea of externalities to the forefront, showed how they could — through the failure of normal pricing mechanisms — lead to the overproduction of ills such as air pollution, and suggested how a governmentally imposed charge or tax could correct for the market failure. These "Pigovian taxes," as they came to be called, generated a substantial body of economic literature that continues to grow and mature.

While this is not the place to examine the corpus carefully, I do want to note several of its features.[3] First, and with regard to most but not all pollution problems, the theoretical advantages of emissions taxes and related approaches as compared to any practicable program of command-and-control regulation are regularly mentioned in the literature and now generally are considered to be beyond dispute. This of itself is hardly surprising, since the advantages in principle of anything usually outweigh the advantages in practice of anything else. Still, the relative strengths of emissions taxes, some of them suggested by Hahn and Noll, are noteworthy: (1) Taxes promise to be cost effective because they would induce high degrees of pollution control by sources with low control costs, and vice versa, thus minimizing total outlays on abatement; (2) taxes, levied on every unit of pollution output, would provide continuous incentives to control further and to find efficient new ways by which to do so; and finally, (3) taxes are claimed to entail lower administrative costs than command-and-control regulations (though this last is a contentious assertion).

A second point about the literature on Pigovian taxes concerns the introduction of an alternative approach that was popularized, if not conceived, by Canadian economist J. H. Dales in his book *Pollution, Property and Prices,* published in 1968.[4] Dales proposed, although in the context of water pollution, the very sort of marketable rights that make up the core of the project discussed by Hahn and Noll. Some of the reasons that one might favor marketable rights over emissions taxes (not to mention command-and-control regulations) are suggested both by Dales and by Hahn and Noll. Marketable (or tradable) rights (or permits, or licenses) have most if not all of the theoretical advantages of emissions taxes, but at least two practical advantages as well: They are more certain (it is easier to determine the "correct" number of rights than it is the "correct" emissions tax); the number of rights need not be adjusted, as emissions taxes would have to be, with fluctuations in the number of sources or in general price levels. Rights appear, in short, to be more manageable.

A third and final point to be made about the literature on Pigovian taxes and the related technique of marketable rights concerns the remarkable confidence (or is it hubris, or is it laziness?) that most of it reflects. Generations of economists have damned regulation as an approach to the control of environmental externalities and praised marketlike approaches without giving much thought or effort to the problems of implementing workable programs. It is as though it were all a question of religion — which, I suppose, in some respects it is. To the great credit of Hahn and Noll, and a few others who have undertaken similar studies that try to translate theory into practice, they are willing actually to test what most economists have known for years to be true, and actually to confront the problems of design and implementation that most economists have left, at least implicitly, to others. Those same economists, by the way, have been very critical of others for not picking up and running with the economists' ideas.

Legal Problems

For reasons that I will speculate about shortly, marketlike alternatives to the traditional regulatory approach are being taken very seriously today, by which I mean that they are not just talked about by economists but actually cast into the form of specific proposals or even, in several noteworthy instances, put into actual operation. Regarding environmental problems, the project discussed in the Hahn and Noll chapter is a modest case in point; other, more concrete illustrations are bubbles, offsets, and noncompliance penalties. On a broader front, one can point to well-known current examples of deregulation — with regard to airlines, for instance.

From a legal standpoint, it is important to understand that these new approaches stand in stark contrast to the familiar methods of regulation that have been used in many instances for well over a century. The new approaches, in short, are pretty much unprecedented, and for lawyers this is always troubling (or promising, depending on your viewpoint). By definition, the new approaches alter the status quo and thus promise to be challenged. (Notice, for example, the potential of tradable emissions permits to redistribute enormous amounts of wealth, and to introduce an unfamiliar governmental regime that is bound to make regulated sources and environmental groups alike very uneasy.) And, by definition, challenges cannot be answered with the simple explanation that this is the way things have always been done, because it is not. With particular regard to marketable rights, then, I would anticipate a number of challenges on a number of grounds from a number of fronts.

Despite this, I am optimistic that programs such as that being investigated by Hahn and Noll can quite easily be designed to survive virtually any legal attack. This does not mean that there are no legal constraints. For example, the model that underlies the definition and distribution of rights must be capable of rational justification, but it need not be shown to be perfect. The monitoring technology that lies behind enforcement of the program must be sufficiently precise that we can establish with reasonable confidence the existence and degree of alleged violations of program requirements. And enforcement itself might have to rely on traditional judicial sanctions rather than on the more modern and smooth approach of administratively imposed civil penalties — this, at least, may well be the case in California. By and large, though, I think that while it might not be possible to implement the ideal design, it should prove fairly simple to implement an acceptable one. In the realm of economic regulation, and that is what we are talking about here, concepts of due process and equal protection have become so elastic as to accommodate virtually any program that has some arguable basis.

But this is constitutional talk, and constitutions (state and federal) are not the only sources of legal constraints that bear on tradable emissions permits. Far more pressing, in fact, is legislation — particularly the federal Clean Air Act. For several reasons, the Clean Air Act in its present form forecloses anything close to full-scale reliance on tradable permits for air pollution control. To put the matter succinctly, several provisions of the Clean Air Act that apply to new and modified stationary sources establish individual source-by-source minimum requirements that are fundamentally inconsistent with the idea of marketable rights — the latter requiring as they do wide variation in degrees of source abatement if cost effectiveness is to be realized. To put the situation even more succinctly, let me express it in terms that demonstrate that the language of the New Deal lives: New and modified sources must achieve, on an individual, source-by-source basis, minimum levels of control consistent with NSPS or, in the case of PSD areas, BACT as set out in regulations of the EPA. These requirements significantly limit reliance on marketable rights. QED.

In saying this, I do not mean to suggest that the Clean Air Act could not, in its next round of amendments, be changed to accommodate marketable rights. The necessary changes will probably take time and trouble to obtain, though; worse, congressional politics might well suggest that all sorts of baggage will be attached to the amendments, with the effect that a marketable rights experiment might be weighed down to such a degree as to promise failure. Perhaps any region will be permitted to try the approach if it likes, even though it lacks the data needed to conduct a reliable experiment. Then subsequent failures can be used to show that a good idea was a bad idea. Or perhaps Congress will attach so much familiar regulatory junk to marketable rights that the approach will lose major advantages. Or Congress might take the idea too far, asking it to accomplish what at present it cannot. All of these, of course, are little horror stories, but if you do not believe such stories, you have not been following the congressional record in the environmental area over the last ten years.

One aspect of that record can serve to close this brief discussion of legal problems. Beginning in about 1970, Congress departed from its long history of passivism about the environment and embarked on a course of frenzied federalization. In consequence of this, environmental management today is unduly centralized; Congress has left insufficient authority and initiative to the states. That the Clean Air

Act at present forecloses a marketable rights experiment is one little piece of evidence of this — a symbol of the vices of substituting federalization for federalism.

Currents of Change

Still, things are changing. I expect, for example, that Congress will in the near future take action reflecting a greater sensitivity to variations among the states regarding what they want and are able to do about the environment. I expect even more that there will be considerable reliance on market-like approaches to control of environmental problems. Congressional tolerance of, or blessings on, bubbles, offsets, and noncompliance penalties point in that direction, as does the ideology of the Reagan Administration.

What explains the new interest in alternatives to regulation, such that now Hahn and Noll can discuss in a serious way an idea that would have been — I am sure actually was — dismissed as poppycock fifteen years ago, or such that they can actually anticipate implementing the idea of marketable rights, or such that we already have modest forms of the idea (bubbles and offsets again) already in operation? The explanation, I am confident, is *not* ideology, because the ideology that would support the idea has been around for a long time, yet nothing happened before now. Nor, I think, should the new current of interest be attributed to a larger enthusiasm for deregulation generally; the theory underlying deregulation of the airlines, for example — that competition works — simply does not apply to environmental problems — where competition does not work. (One could say it works backwards, encouraging rather than discouraging socially undesirable actions.) Finally, I do not think one can explain the new interest in alternatives to regulation by reference to theories of regulatory failure, because the regulatory approach is probably not failing any more or less than it has for many decades.

Its failings *are,* however, becoming more expensive — a point I, and probably many others, regard as crucially important in accounting for the recent interest in new approaches to pollution control. At least when one is talking about very high and very expensive levels of abatement, regulatory techniques, it is plausible to think, become wasteful — either they fail to differentiate among sources in ways that would, as explained earlier, be cost effective, or by trying to differentiate they give rise to great administrative expense. Marketlike approaches show much promise of reducing both or at least one of these kinds of waste. Given that pollution abatement today involves costs that are many times those of even ten years ago, it should hardly be surprising that accompanying the sharply rising cost curve is a sharply rising interest in techniques of control, virtually untried, that hold the potential of significant savings. Congress should be interested, regulated firms should be interested, environmentalists should be interested, and the EPA should be interested. And, the evidence suggests, they are.

The interests of these groups are not entirely aligned, however. Some environmental groups have become interested in emissions taxes, for example, but I doubt that many pollution sources ever will be. Existing sources no doubt tend to favor offsets, because as currently administered offsets have the effect of enriching those firms, as would some versions of tradable permits Hahn and Noll have talked about; new entrants, though, can be expected to be unenthusiastic. Many firms, I understand, endorse the bubble — at least if it can be freed of some of its present red tape — but environmentalists generally dislike the approach because it does not improve environmental quality but only holds it constant. And the EPA, I think, would not be in favor of utter deregulation, for many obvious reasons. Still, in the face of steeply rising costs it is in the uniform interest of all these groups to think about alternatives to regulation that share, if nothing else, a common promise of improving or maintaining environmental quality at less cost than under the present dominant regime. What we would anticipate, then, is a number of ideas that are very different from each other but are nevertheless tied together by that thread of efficiency. And that is exactly what we are seeing.

We are also seeing something else. Over the last ten years or so, economists have finally taken on the burden of reducing the abstract to the concrete. Why this is so I do not know; given the nature of economists, I suspect that they think that somehow it will make them better off. Whatever the reason, and whether their efforts fail or succeed, I am confident that we have begun a period of experimentation that will yield significant improvements in the means by which we control environmental problems.

NOTES

1. A. C. Pigou, *The Economics of Welfare* 4th ed. (London: Macmillan, 1962).

2. A. Marshall, *Principles of Economics* (London: Macmillan, 1920).

3. An insightful survey of the literature from the time of Pigou and Marshall up to the early 1970s can be found in T. Page, *Economics of Involuntary Transfers: A Unified Approach to Pollution and Congestion Externalities,* Vol. 85, Lecture Notes in Economics and Mathematical Systems (New York: Springer-Verlag, 1973).

4. J. H. Dales, *Pollution, Property, and Prices* (Toronto: University of Toronto Press, 1968).

8

Economic Incentives

Can They Replace or Supplement Direct Regulation?

ROY N. GAMSE

In the past, economists have proposed economic incentives for use in the field of environmental regulation, then stood back and criticized the regulators and the politicians for not implementing what they knew to be good ideas. I think that Roger Noll's work, plus some that I will describe in this chapter, indicates that the implementation of regulatory reforms is not that simple and that the political world is not going to accept these innovations until more people go through the kind of hard work that Noll and his associates have been doing with their design of a practical system for tradable emissions permits. Rather than focusing completely on Noll's work, however, I will also describe some other examples that relate to it, to try to amplify my message.

The sulfur tax was my first experience with the idea of economic incentives as substitutes for regulation. Back in 1972 and 1973 I had the dubious pleasure of working for EPA on the Nixon Administration's sulfur-tax proposal. It was a straightforward idea and a lot of economists have wondered for a decade now why it has not been accepted. The basic problem we encountered then was *not* that the sulfur tax was not a good idea, but that nobody had worked out exactly how it would be implemented. At that time the Clean Air Act had been in effect for several years. As a result, there were state implementation plans that required states to set emissions limits. Consequently, a number of companies had begun to invest in air pollution controls. Then the idea of taxing sulfur emissions was introduced — a proposal that the economists said would lead to a more effective, more efficient, and more equitable approach to controlling emissions. However, little research had been done forecasting exactly what would happen if these sulfur taxes were added on top of the existing regulatory approach, which already required specified emissions limits to be implemented. What kind of economic incentives would result? With sulfur taxes alone, the efficiency gains would come because firms that had very high emissions control costs would be able to avoid installing controls and pay the tax if it were lower than the abatement costs. To balance off this reduced control, firms that had low costs of control would control more than they might under an emissions limit system. However, if the emissions control laws remain in force as well as the tax, a company cannot simply avoid control by paying the tax, because it will still be under the threat of having the state EPA take it to court for not complying with the emissions limits.

The Nixon Administration attempted to resolve this problem. The Office of Management and Budget (OMB), which was in charge of coordinating development of this particular policy, was committed to the idea of sulfur taxes. Rather than go through countless debates, they limited discussion of the proposal to EPA, the Council on Environmental Quality, the Treasury Department, and OMB — in other words, just the agencies that were in favor of the tax. Nevertheless, we worked on it for six months and still could not agree on the right way to link up the existing regulatory program and the economic incentive. By the time we converged on a solution, the energy crisis was fully upon us, people were nervous about anything that would increase costs of delivered energy, and the power of the interest groups against this type of approach was very strong. Thus, the proposal was tabled.

I learned some principles from that experience that I have carried forward with me in looking at other approaches. One is that when we talk about economic incentives in lieu of regulation, the economic approaches require just as much analysis as do the regulatory approaches. I think a lot has been learned over the past ten years about what kinds of analysis and justification are necessary in the design and support of a regulation. Economic incentive approaches have to be held to just as high a standard because there is significant resistance to overcome from the regulated groups, the public interest groups, and especially the lawmakers — most of whom are not economists, but lawyers, who tend to think in more traditional ways. A second principle is that if economic approaches in the social regulatory areas are going to gain full acceptance, there must be some successes that demonstrate their feasibility. To gain these successes, I think we should begin by applying the new economic incentive approaches as pure economic incentives in areas where there is not a traditional regulation approach partially or fully implemented, so that there will not be conflicts between the incentives provided by the new approach and the incentives from the rules already on the books. If economic incentives are overlaid on existing regulations, then I would prefer to begin with approaches that support the regulations and are consistent with them, unless it is clear that it is a better idea to discard the existing rules and start over. Hence, in areas where there is already regulation, I prefer approaches such as the bubble policy, which starts with the regulations as a base and lets firms propose more cost-effective alternatives that accomplish the same purpose, or non-compliance penalties, which are really just an economic incentive-based approach to enforcement of existing regulations.

At the present time I think we at EPA are moving in the direction that is suggested by Roger Noll's work. In fact, I think we are moving in that direction faster than Hahn and Noll's chapter (Chapter 6) would suggest. First of all, in the area of controlled trading — which is the general term to describe the bubbles policy, offset trading, and banking — it was necessary to start with an approach that was based upon the existing legislation and existing regulations and that implied a lot of restrictions in the kinds of trades between emissions sources, because of both the legislative restraints and the political restraints of getting such a policy through a regulatory agency such as EPA. One by one, those restrictions are dropping, and it is possible that in the forthcoming Clean Air Amendments some of the remaining statutory restrictions might be dropped. Regarding case-by-case federal approval of bubble policy trades, EPA has, in recent months, approved a New Jersey proposal that allows the state to adopt an approach that does not require federal approval of hydrocarbon trades on a case-by-case basis. EPA will also broaden its approach in the future to allow states to approve trades without federal review among particulate and sulfur oxide sources that are close enough and similar enough that they do not require air quality modeling, and trades among small sources of pollution. Variations in approaches from pollutant to pollutant occur because there is variation among the pollutants in how closely ambient effects are related to emissions effects.

In their chapter Hahn and Noll identified an important difference between controlled trading and their approach: The long-term status of the permits is not clear under controlled trading. I agree that this is a valid criticism, and it is one that EPA is attempting to remedy. A banking policy is being developed that provides guidelines to the states on how to do that. There is a problem, however, in that the federal government cannot assert too specifically what the states can and cannot do, but our guidance to the states very clearly indicates that they must clarify what the future status of those permits will be. The greater certainty the states provide, the more likely it is that they will create a real market rather than just the illusion of one.

Another point that is focused on in the Hahn and Noll chapter is the importance of a smoothly functioning market and the fact that there is no such market for offsets. That is true, but not as true as it used to be. Recently there have been advertisements in the *Wall Street Journal* for buyers or sellers of offsets, and this is a good sign. Imagine what it would be like if there were no stock market — when you wanted to sell shares of your IBM stock, you would have to find the individuals who wanted to buy the shares. That is the situation that exists now with offsets.

EPA is trying to create the institutions, or to encourage the creation of the institutions, to run a market. The agency held a conference in January 1981 for potential brokers for these markets, and there were a number of interested parties. I think that over the next few years these markets will be established. However, I think that there is a danger in any inference that we ought to structure our approach to encourage as many trades as possible. That poses a problem of political acceptance. Right now these approaches may work better if a relatively small number of entities are involved in the regulation. There have been proposals for Clean Air Act regulatory schemes that suggest reducing emissions by a uniform percentage for everyone and then allowing trades to take place to lead to a minimal-cost solution. In theory this is fine, but if it requires an order of magnitude of more participants than would have been involved in a traditional regulatory approach, I think there will be a reaction by the many firms that were not involved before, but that will now have to be involved in such a market. It may be that such a system is theoretically ideal, from an efficiency standpoint, but politically unworkable.

The example that EPA is working on now that comes closest to Roger Noll's approach is in the area of controlling chlorofluorocarbons (CFCs). The government has banned most uses of CFCs for aerosol sprays, and there may be a need to go further than that. There is still a great deal of scientific debate on the issue, but EPA is looking into what it should do if it is to control CFCs further. The traditional approach that a regulatory agency would take to accomplish this would be to compile a list of the various uses of CFCs, conduct an economic analysis of what the costs are of banning each one, rank the uses in increasing order of cost, and then impose more bans by choosing items from the top of the list until the marginal costs equal the marginal benefits. For CFCs, I think, this is not as good an approach as using marketable permits would be. A marketable permits approach fits very well for CFCs, particularly because of their physical nature; that is, the geographic locations of the emissions of CFCs are not very important, so there could be a nationwide or worldwide market, without any restrictions.

The analysis that EPA has done on CFCs supports what Roger Noll's analysis has shown in the sulfates area, and demonstrates very clearly the need to do this kind of detailed analysis and detailed design work. The direct costs of dealing with the CFC problem would be cut roughly in half by using a marketable permits scheme as opposed to banning the uses of CFC that analysis suggests would be the cheapest and least painful to ban. This is a definite sign that the approach is a very efficient one. On the other hand, by constraining the market, by limiting the production or the sale of CFCs, in a few years a situation might occur in which the transfer payments would be an order of magnitude larger. So a regulatory reform that can cut the direct costs of regulation for the nation in half can also, if it is not carefully designed and implemented, create a situation in which the producers or users of CFCs — the permits could be granted either to the producers or the users — would end up paying an order of magnitude more for their product than they would have to under the direct-cost approach.

Additionally, if the auction approach to the distribution of permits were used, it would result in the unusual situation of having a cost-cutting regulatory reform that the regulated industry would fight to the death. I think the chances of getting that approach implemented are extremely small. The other approach, that of having the government distribute the permits without an auction, has various alternative forms, each of which has advantages and disadvantages. From a political standpoint, it may be that we ought to chose the approach that least visibly transfers large amounts of wealth to individual entities. This implies that permits should be given to the users of CFCs rather than to the producers. DuPont produces more than half of the CFCs in the country now, so if permits were distributed on the historical basis of production, DuPont would receive permits worth more than a billion dollars right at the start. Such problems as these illustrate the importance of going through a detailed analysis and design process before accepting either of these approaches.

Indeed, detailed analysis and planning is needed in many areas in which reforms are proposed. We must begin simply. We must have economic approaches that people can understand — the regulated public, the regulators, and especially the legislators. We need to get a foot in the door and show through analysis and especially through demonstrations that these things *can* work. For example, right now EPA is implementing a bubble policy, and we have about 70 applications for trades within or between plants that would average about $2 million in savings each in the systems. As people see that kind of potential, and as they see the kinds of potential there are for approaches that currently are blocked by restrictions, we will see those restrictions coming off one by one and it will be easier to gain acceptance for economic incentives. If during the hearings on the 1981 Clean Air Amendments industry representatives are able to say, "I saved 60 percent of my control costs with this application of the bubble concept," or "I saved $5 million on this one," there will be a real chance of the Congress being willing to accept some broader approaches.

On the other hand, I think if we propose a complete revamping of the system immediately, dismantling the whole regulatory framework that exists, the nations's lawmakers will be very reticent to give that kind of authority. A compromise may result that seems to embody acceptance of these ideas, but that attaches so many regulatory restrictions that the implementation and the achievement of potential efficiencies will be seriously hampered. But the outlook seems promising. At EPA we are implementing some reforms, and we are analyzing a number of others; the success of these attempts will undoubtedly lead to many more.

9

Some Caveats on Tradable Emissions Permits

W. R. Z. WILLEY

The project described in Chapter 6 by Robert Hahn and Roger Noll is an important experiment based on what has become a politically fashionable strategy for policy reform. But in describing in some detail the "radical" institutional change of creating new and different government mechanisms to implement a market for tradable emissions permits, the authors have also identified a number of possible difficulties with such a change. These problems, and many more, are likely to come under heretofore unseen levels of scrutiny in the future, particularly during the first few years of the Reagan Administration. The following comments are an attempt to address some of these problem areas and to determine whether the authors' faith in the feasibility of a market in tradable emissions permits is justified.

While the virtues of the competitive market system in allocating resources emerge unscathed from Hahn and Noll's discussion, their position that markets for tradable emissions permits can be created and administered with a net increase in social well-being is not convincingly proved. Indeed, the strongest point made in the chapter is one that is already widely accepted — that the burning of natural gas is one of the best abatement strategies for controlling SO_x emissions. Hence, another endorsement of the deregulation of natural gas pricing is implied. Beyond that, the notion that creating a tradable emissions market will somehow reduce the bureaucratic burden of regulation becomes a somewhat more, not less, tenuous proposition. One conclusion is certain: Implementing tradable emissions permits will create a new regulatory bureaucracy, in which a substitution of economists for lawyers and engineers will occur on a broad scale.

Relative Merits of Tradable Permits, Standards, and Taxes

Hahn and Noll note that output standards, emissions taxes, and tradable emissions permits all require costly monitoring to assure compliance, but claim that standards are especially cumbersome as well because regulators do not have sufficient information on abatement strategies and costs to meet environmental objectives in a cost-effective manner. Yet extensive information also would be required in order to construct a step function for the costs of abatement, an analysis that would be necessary for predicting the demands for a market in permits. Indeed, unless it can be assumed in the construction of this function that all firms utilize the same abatement technologies, information on each individual firm's abatement technologies and costs would have to be collected in order to allow the crucial derived-demand curve for the market in tradable emissions permits to be estimated. It may be possible that this kind of collection would not need to be repeated over time, that the information could be collected once and the analysis done as a feasibility study, letting the market take care of itself once it was initiated. However, I think that is a Pollyannish view. There are many complications that will arise — involving such factors as market power and restriction of new entry — that will require that such an analysis be redone and updated over time. We should not delude ourselves with the expectation that there is going to be a one-time analysis, and then some permits will be issued, and the system will be self-sufficient after that. The administrative costs of a tradable emissions approach are undoubtedly going to be high.

It is also asserted in Hahn and Noll's chapter that standards provide little incentive for firms to innovate in abatement technology. This seems true for input standards, but not for output standards. The essence of output standards is to comply with an emission constraint by whatever means possible. Even for input standards, which have dominated many of our pollution regulations, innovation on the supply side in abatement technologies has occurred as a result of the competition for best-available and best-achievable technology status. It seems incorrect to assert that little incentive for innovation has existed in the midst of the growth and competition among the abatement-technologies industries.

Substantial differences in abatement costs among industries and between old and new plants are noted as a result of standards. Yet a similar result may prove to be true for the tradable emissions case as well, with the primary difference being that some money would probably be spent on permits instead of on abatement equipment by some industries and older plants.

With respect to emissions taxes, one political impediment to their use is that they force firms to pay both abatement costs *and* emissions taxes. But this necessity for a double payment would hold true of tradable emissions permits as well, with the key difference being that, rather than emissions tax revenues flowing to the government, tradable emissions permit expenditures would flow to those private interests that were selling permits. The distribution of the benefits of these expenditures would depend very much on the initial distribution of permits by the government. The most likely method of distribution would be allocation permits according to historical use, which leads to the implication that the emitters, and not the public treasury, should benefit. While this is probably acceptable to industry, it is probably not readily acceptable to the public, which incurs economic costs as a result of emissions. In either case, the tax or the permit cost would be passed along to consumers and/or would reduce profits, depending upon the price elasticity of demand for the firm's product.

Industry is believed to usually favor standards over taxes becuase with standards at least payment of the tax can be avoided. This argument makes sense only if the costs of abatement with standards alone are less than those with a tax and without standards. There is no inherent reason why this should be so, given that both the setting of tax levels and the setting of standards are functions of environmental quality objectvies.

Unpredictability in the quantity of emissions is claimed to be another drawback to taxes, while the uncertainties in output standards and permits reside in costs. Another uncertainty of potentially great significance in permits (and output standards) is the problem of monitoring and enforcement.

The implementation of a market in tradable emissions permits has the potential for creating several new regulatory morasses. For example, the differences in geographical distribution of air quality effects would have to be compensated for by the way in which trading regions were defined, and by the formulation of rules for trading across regional boundaries. This appears to be a substantial task, since such a definition would require, among other things, an estimate of how the market is likely to distribute permits among sources, that is, an apparatus for evaluating the demand for permits by each source. Essentially, the derived demand for permits must be analyzed for each emitting firm or source as a prelude to setting rules for trading across regional boundaries. Once that is done, of course, if everything else works perfectly, then repeated analysis might not be needed. But if the world is somehow more complicated than that — say, with respect to market power or differential entry into new industries across regions (and it seems clear that it would be) — then more than a one-time analysis would be necessary to sustain that market.

Another part of the required role for government in the implementation of a marketable permits system would be the responsibility for enforcing the emissions limits to which each source's stock of permits entitles it. This would necessitate an individual source-by-source review, a process that appears to be tantamount to issuing individual permits.

Finally, an additional two-tiered regulatory apparatus is suggested to deal with air pollution "episodes." Some combination of a different permit system or a permit system plus direct regulation would be involved according to the weather. Again, this appears to hold the potential of becoming another regulatory entanglement.

Implementation Feasibility

Estimation of Derived-Demand Functions

Part of the Hahn and Noll discussion focuses on the specific case study of controlling particulate sulfates in the Los Angeles region. The analysis is based on the estimation of derived-demand functions for permits for a number of source categories, a result made possible by the estimation of abatement costs for each source category. These estimates turn out to have huge wealth-transfer implications if they are used to determine the initial distribution of permits and to evaluate policies to deal with market power. In order for this approach to be conceptually correct, the derived-demand functions must be a result of optimizing behavior on the part of the representative facilities in each source category from which the data base is drawn. The authors do not indicate why this should be so, and there is no apparent reason that it is. In fact, unless the market for abatement facilities is *already* working efficiently, such optimization has not occurred.

Another problem with these functions arises from the fact that they are based on representative facilities within each source category. This amounts to an assumption that the same abatement technology is used by all firms within each source category, an assumption that is probably incorrect. In lieu of making this assumption, the authors would have had to estimate the function of each firm within each source category.

Finally, point estimates from each source were used to estimate costs for representative facilities. The question of how much variance is associated with these estimates was not addressed, yet it also has tremendous implications for the magnitude of wealth transfers that would be possible.

Given these caveats, the derived-demand curves suffer both from conceptual problems and from estimation uncertainties. At this point they appear to be inadequate as a basis for implementing a tradable emissions permits market, particularly in light of the associated wealth transfers.

Impediments to Implementation

The Hahn and Noll chapter also includes models of competition and market power, and a discussion of the issue of the initial distribution of permits by the government. The discussion of market power explains what might happen in the case in which the only buyer of permits is the utility. Beyond that, the authors reach no conclusions about whether market power would undermine the efficiency of the permit market, and the methodology underlying the market-share numbers is not presented.

The political feasibility of the possible wealth transfers resulting from permit distribution is a serious problem. However, Hahn and Noll apparently believe that control over the distribution of permits somehow makes a politically acceptable solution more likely. This may be true, but it has not been shown why the permit scheme, which distributes the revenues from permit sales among emitters, is more politically feasible than emissions taxes, which benefit the public treasury, or output standards, which do not involve these kinds of transfers.

The issue of equity in the initial distribution of permits is dealt with by discussing several options for using emissions based either on prior history or on the estimated equilibrium market. Problems have already been mentioned with respect to the derived-demand functions underlying this estimated equilibrium. Again, it may be politically naive to propose that the emitters receive the direct economic benefit of this initial distribution.

With respect to the initiation of transactions of these initial stocks of permits, several approaches are proposed. One can only speculate, as the authors do, as to whether or not various types of market power would inhibit these transactions. The authors' anticipation of frequent conflicts between efficiency and the political perception of equity is well-founded.

Despite their identification of possible difficulties, Hahn and Noll believe that the institutional problems of a marketable permits system are tractable. However, it seems politically unlikely that this approach will not be attacked before it can even be implemented if some of these questions are not answered first. For consumer groups, the wealth-transfer question is the key one. A way will have to be found to avoid windfall redistributions to industry, otherwise the consumer groups will oppose the marketable permits approach in Washington.

In conclusion, I see many difficult problems with this economic incentive approach to reforming environmental regulation. I am less optimistic than Hahn and Noll, and I think that at this point there is a necessity to conduct experiments, not just in tradable emissions permits, but also in taxes and other innovations, with respect to standards. We have to experiment in a systematic way and evaluate the results so that we can decrease some of the uncertainties. Because of the political constraints, I do not think we can make a major change, at least in the near term, into such a scheme as tradable emissions permits until its benefits and drawbacks have been analyzed in more detail.

10

Mixing Public and Private Regulation

EUGENE BARDACH
ROBERT A. KAGAN

The rule of law was invented to restrain the willfulness of kings and nobles. It aimed to substitute consistency, fairness, and reasoned authority for impulsiveness, favoritism, and arbitrary despotism. The beneficiaries of this new principle were, at first, the new propertied classes of an emerging commercial society and, in later generations, all the subjects of the realm. In modern times, and in republican states, it is citizens, not subjects, who enjoy its blessings and who themselves call upon the law to restrain institutions and practices, public and private, that threaten their sense of security and justice.

It is ironic, therefore, that the rule of law, an idea intended to harness power in the interests of justice, has come to propel the growth of legal rules and controls applicable to citizens as well as to government officials. For legal rules, even if constrained by general principles of fair and uniform application, are still rules; and rules are blunt and unyielding instruments for attempting to shape human behavior in all its diversity and complexity. Thus in the modern regulatory state a considerable proportion of the citizenry resents the

---

AUTHORS' NOTE: This chapter is reprinted with permission of the publisher from Eugene Bardach and Robert A. Kagan, *Going by the Book: The Problem of Regulatory Unreasonableness,* A Twentieth Century Fund Report (Philadelphia: Temple University Press, 1982), Copyright 1982 by The Twentieth Century Fund, Inc.

restrictions imposed by law. The restrictions, to be sure, are felt to be merely vexatious rather than oppressive or confiscatory. But the domain of the contemporary regulatory state is broad and its attentiveness to detail fastidious. Even when the intentions of the law's framers are benign, the law's capacity for unintended restrictiveness and injustice is still great.

In the last fifteen years, for example, we have experienced a dramatic outpouring of new regulation. The impulse behind this regulatory outpouring has been protective. It has covered a broad range of social harms, perhaps too long neglected, including occupational injuries and diseases, environmental pollution, product-related injuries, highway accidents, discrimination in employment and education, and consumer fraud. The basic technique of these regulatory programs has been the elaboration of written rules of law setting forth in great detail the protective measures that must be instituted by regulated enterprises, and the enforcement of those rules by government inspectors and investigators, carefully instructed to decide all issues in accordance with the terms of the regulations, and not on the basis of their own potentially arbitrary judgment. But uniform regulations, even if justifiable in the generality of cases, inevitably appear to be unreasonable in a considerable proportion of particular situations. Consider, for instance, the experience of Al Schaefer (as we will call him), director of worker safety for a major aluminum manufacturing company, with the Occupational Safety and Health Administration (OSHA), and what its impact might be were it multiplied by thousands of similar encounters:

> By all accounts, Schaefer's company seems to have a positive attitude toward worker safety and an aggressive safety program. Still, the corporation's numerous plants have been visited by OSHA inspectors a total of 30 to 50 times a year; the company has received an average of 225 citations each year, and paid a total of $25,000 in fines over the last 7 years.
>
> Nevertheless, Schaefer argues that OSHA inspections have made little positive contribution to safety in his company. "The major problem with OSHA," he says, "is that they mandate safety standards even where they are not the highest priority risk in a particular plant. The standard may be important in 50 percent of the workplaces in the country, but the investment to come into compliance may be a complete waste in other places. They have forced us to spend money without regard to the risk level of the problem. We've

spent millions to comply with standards without contributing to the reduction of risk."

Schaefer gave several examples. One involved a requirement for a double safety brake on all hot-metal cranes, which his company used for moving molten aluminum, "even though no accidents have occurred with the single brake in the entire industry over the last thirty years."

Another example involved an OSHA regulation (adopted from a National Fire Protection Association voluntary standard, according to Schaefer) that called for "alternative means of egress" from public gathering places, such as restaurants. An OSHA inspector applied this rule to the lunchrooms in an aluminum-smelting plant. The heart of the smelter consists of long rows of furnaces (or "pots") in which molten aluminum is formed from alumina (refined bauxite). Crucibles of molten aluminum are transported along these rows by motorized vehicles. Small, air-conditioned lunchrooms are adjacent to the "potline," but separated from it by a cinder-block wall; the doors to the lunchrooms do not open directly into the potline, but open off side corridors. The lunchrooms have no rear exits.

OSHA said rear exits were required. The only justification OSHA could offer (other than the text of the regulation) was that if the molten aluminum spilled and went into the side corridors and a fire started, workers in the lunchroom would be trapped.

"Now that citation does not represent a rational assessment of risk," Schaefer said. "Of course, it *could* happen. Almost anything *could* happen. Never mind that it's more likely that an earthquake could happen. Never mind that in the 15 years the plant has been operating nothing like that has happened, or even any incidents that suggest it might happen."

Besides, he pointed out, because the lunchrooms are of cinder-block construction, the only thing that could burn is the wooden door. To cut through the other side and install a door, he said, would cost $6,000 per lunchroom, times 10 lunchrooms. "This is a total misapplication of resources. I could use that money for real risk reduction in plenty of other places."

To Al Schaefer OSHA appeared unreasonable. But *was* OSHA unreasonable? Although we did not investigate the details of the particular instances described by Al Schaefer, we did interview many regulatory officials from a variety of agencies, including OSHA, and a rebuttal to Schaefer might have sounded like this:

> Either directly or through state agencies that enforce the Occupational Safety and Health Act for us, we regulate worker safety and health in almost five million workplaces. They are extremely varied. If we had rules that were exactly suited to each hazard and each situation in every one of those workplaces, the inspector's manual would have to be transported in a truck. So we have to simplify and standardize, and obviously some cases of overinclusive rules and regulations are going to result. Remember, Al Schaefer or people like him can always file for a variance, because the law does give us latitude to waive compliance in cases where equivalent protection is provided by other means.
>
> True, we don't let the inspector at the field level have the discretion to waive compliance. But that is because he would then be susceptible to manipulation, bribery, and perhaps intimidation. Besides, not all 3000 occupational safety and health inspectors are sufficiently trained or clever or morally upright to be entrusted with discretionary power. It may be somewhat inconvenient for Al Schaefer and others in his position to seek waivers through the proper channels, and in some cases they just might choose to comply with regulatory rules rather than do it, but remember that workers' lives and well-being are at issue. If the system has to make errors, which of course, it does, it is better to err on the side of safety. We at OSHA think that, our statutory mandate indicates that Congress thinks that, and public opinion polls suggest that the public overwhelmingly thinks so too.

Was it Al Schaefer, then, who was unreasonable?

A famous old Jewish story tells of a litigant who comes before a rabbi and pleads his case with great passion. When he is done, the rabbi pronounces, "You are right!" Thereupon the second litigant hastens to tell his side of the story with even greater passion; and when he is done, the rabbi also pronounces, "You are right!" Dismayed, a bystander who has heard the entire proceeding leaps forward to observe that the two litigants' stories had been utterly incompatible and that it could not logically be the case that both were right. To which the rabbi responds, "You too are right!"

Al Schaefer has what we think of as a "civilian" perspective on his experience with regulation; and our hypothetical spokesman for OSHA is voicing what we call, by way of contrast, an "official" perspective. Unlike the litigants' mutually incompatible tales in the above story, both perspectives really *are* right. Even the best efforts at regulation — efforts that might produce, on the whole, quite laudable results — are bound to produce many unreasonable and even deplorable results as well. The official perspective that emphasizes the positive results is legitimate and defensible; but so too is the civilian perspective that is tinged with anger and resentment at regulatory departures from "common sense" in particular cases. The fact that regulatory unreasonableness is unintended and incidental to the accomplishment of a larger purpose does not make it less unreasonable to the individuals who are asked to absorb the force of it.

The Inevitability of Regulatory Unreasonableness

We have been living with what Thomas Schelling and, later, Charles Schultze have dubbed "command-and-control" regulation, whereby rules and standards are promulgated, a schedule of penalties is drawn up to be applied to parties who violate them, and a cadre of inspectors is deployed to monitor the field of potential violations and, as a result of their surveillance efforts, to deter actual violations. For legal, political, and bureaucratic reasons, which we shall explain below, this sort of regulation cannot help but be "unreasonable." Our purpose in this chapter is to explore a modification of the basic command-and-control strategy that might be less unreasonable while at the same time being equally effective, if not more so. The basic idea is to rely more heavily on the existing institutions of "private regulation" — industrial hygienists, quality-control engineers, in-house attorneys, and so on — than we currently do, albeit within the context of public regulators looking critically over their shoulders. Before turning to our own reformist suggestions, however, let us briefly survey the main difficulties of the command-and-control approach, putting a special emphasis on the problems posed by the political environment and its unceasing demands for bureaucratic accountability to external critics in the legislature, in the various pro-protection interest groups, and in the media.

Legal commentators have long recognized that legal rules are inevitably overinclusive. The rules are written and applied by mere human beings, whose ability to perceive, comprehend, and master the true diversity inherent in the objects covered by the rules is very limited indeed. As we implied in the anecdote about Al Schaefer and OSHA, it could be very costly for administrators to customize the rules and their associated enforcement to match the enormous variety of circumstances and motivations in the real world of affairs. In many cases, indeed, it is preferable, from the point of view of maximizing overall economic efficiency, to impose convenient oversimplification on the world even if the price is excessive regulation in a limited number of specific circumstances.

Of course, if field-level enforcement officials could underenforce the rules in these specific circumstances, the problem would be solved. But discretionary underenforcement, despite its prevalence, is very rarely adopted as a solution to the problem of rule-level overinclusiveness. That is to say, it is rarely the authoritative *policy* of a regulatory agency. This is so for a number of reasons. First, it makes inspectors more corruptible and necessitates special defenses against this increased risk. Second, it makes the supervisory tasks of middle- and upper-level agency managers much more difficult than they would be if all enforcement personnel had to "go by the book" and make no exceptions. Third, regulated enterprises themselves like the consistency and uniformity that comes from agency rule-boundedness, partly because they are protected against the possibility of governmental high-handedness and partly because they may have confidence that their business competitors are not receiving more favorable treatment than themselves. Finally, a policy of discretionary underenforcement creates the *appearance,* if not necessarily the reality, of regulatory laxity, lukewarm attachment to statutorily mandated goals, and possible corruption. Sticking by the rules is a safe harbor for regulators who wish to avoid a storm of criticism for "giving in" or "selling out." Even when cutting back on a particular enforcement target simply reflects a rational reallocation of resources away from less productive and toward more productive inspection targets, agencies might still be vulnerable to criticism, as the following three examples suggest:

> When the Food and Drug Administration (FDA) announced it would redirect food industry inspections from a primary emphasis on sanitation toward microbiological and chemical health hazards (on the theory that contamination due to poor sanitation is a relatively minor health hazard in most modern food-processing plants), a series of *Consumer Reports* articles attacked the agency for having "casually dismissed" the problem of "filth." The FDA continues to list sanitation at the top of its published list of enforcement priorities.[1]

Civil rights groups, notes Jeremy Rabkin, "protested vehemently on several occasions when the Office of Civil Rights (OCR) in HEW sought to restrict its enforcement responsibilities, as when it suggested in 1975 that it would no longer accept responsibility for investigating each individual discrimination complaint it received." The Secretary of HEW withdrew the plan, pledging the agency would investigate all discrimination complaints, perhaps because the agency had already experienced court cases, brought by civil rights groups, ordering the agency to conduct other kinds of compliance reviews within a time certain. Yet, says Rabkin, Office of Civil Rights officials believe that "the investigation of individual complaints is a far less productive use of investigative resources" than agency-initiated compliance reviews (individual complaints accounted for almost 90 percent of OCR's investigative efforts in 1977 and 1978), and that "fear of antagonizing constituent groups has made headquarters reluctant to clarify for regional offices the appropriate scope of individual investigations or the sorts of issues that are not worth pursuing in practice, whatever their status in official regulations."[2]

Bay Area Air Pollution Control District (BAAPCD) inspectors regularly are assigned to inspect each of the scores of huge gasoline storage tanks at the three major refineries in the area. To do so, they must climb atop the "floating roofs" of the tanks and measure emissions that may be escaping from the seals installed around the edges of the tanks. The company must provide technicians and safety people to go up there with them. A BAAPCD enforcement official told us that inspectors had never found a violation of the governing standard when a company had told the inspector in advance that the seals were working properly. We then asked why the BAAPCD persisted in checking each tank, if that were so. Why not get the companies to do it and certify their findings to the agency, and limit inspectors to spot checks of a random sample of tanks? That is a fine idea, the BAAPCD official told us, but they could not do it that way. "The state agency [the California Air Resources Board] and the feds [EPA] would say, 'What? You're trusting the industry?' " And because the state board provides much of the funding for the BAAPCD, "We have little choice but to enforce the regulations they give us the way they say."

If a regulatory agency adopts a policy of discretionary underenforcement for reasons unrelated to improving enforcement productivity but rather for reasons connected with sparing firms (or whole industries, or "society") excessive compliance costs, it is even more vulnerable to criticism as corrupt, "captured," or "in bed with business." Since agencies with field-enforcement responsibilities are always and inescapably subject to the temptation of bribery or more subtle psychological blandishments, an obvious strategy for countering such suspicions is to avoid discretion altogether, to stick close to the formal requirements as specified in official publications and manuals, and to document the fact that the formalities have indeed been observed. In bureaucratic argot this general strategy is known as "covering your ass" or "CYA." Indeed, from our interviews, CYA emerges as more than a mere strategy; it is a master principle, for most lower-level officials at any rate, that rivals Freud's pleasure principle or Bentham's felicific calculus.

This is not surprising, for the CYA principle speaks to the problem of survival, which is more basic than the experience of mere pleasure or pain. Moreover, the external political environment abounds in dangerous potential predators. Journalists are one important such predator species, for instance. Any journalist in need of a story can be sure to find one if he or she only looks long enough into the inner life of a regulatory agency. In journalistic argot, such subjects are "evergreens," because whenever a story is needed the subject is sure to be alive and ready to go. Of course, some regulatory agencies are consistently greener than others: building code inspection in Chicago, restaurant inspection in New York, and slum-housing inspection almost anywhere.

The effect of such news stories, or the prospect of them, is suggested by Bruce Vladeck's analysis of quality-of-care regulation of nursing homes in several states:

> The scandals of the early and mid-1970's changed . . . the political balance, from one in which rigorous inspection was more trouble than it was worth to one where the greatest fear was of revelations by a newspaper or legislative investigator of shocking conditions in a nursing home that had been found adequate by the survey process. Consultants became policemen overnight.[3]

In the nursing home example, as in most others, there rarely is evidence of direct corruption. The "scandal" arises from the disclosure that bad conditions still exist, together with hints that the owners are reaping unconscionable profits thereby. When that disclosure is combined with revelations that there are uncorrected regulatory violations or that inspectors had not been at the facility for six months, the implication is that the bad conditions are due to lax enforcement, and that lax enforcement is due to some undocumented but "obvious" link between the unconscionable profiteer and the regulatory agency.

Private Regulation as an Alternative

If the political environment, with all its demands on regulators for the appearance of toughness, fairness, and incorruptibility, is the main cause of regulatory inflexibility, then perhaps regulators should be shielded more than they are from such an environment. One way of doing this might be to create a basis of regulatory authority that is more independent of public norms of accountability and performance, and to endow regulators who are the agents of this authority with some financial independence from public regulatory agencies.

In fact, there is no need actually to create such regulatory institutions from scratch, for they already exist in great abundance in the private sector. The interesting problem for policy design is not so much to create public regulatory institutions that can exercise power and authority in a more private fashion, but to harness the existing institutions of private regulation more tightly to public purpose.

Although the main attraction of such a strategy is that it could make regulation more reasonable, another important attraction is the possibility of making regulation more effective as well by taking advantage of the fact that most of the regulation that takes place in the United States is in the hands not of government officials but of myriad individuals employed by private or not-for-profit organizations. These individuals create and administer a regulatory regime only indirectly responsive to governmental regulation. Corporations employ hundreds of auditors, assembly-line inspectors, quality-control engineers, weighers, and samplers to police their coworkers' adherence to company standards of quality and performance. Holiday Inns of America, like other franchising corporations, sends inspectors to check on individual Holiday Inns, incognito, to see that corporate standards are maintained. Department store buyers inspect their suppliers' products and sometimes their factories, as do utilities company foremen who purchase electric cable. Architects inspect the contractors' work at construction sites. The Consumers Union inspects and evaluates hundreds of products. A thousand independent laboratories specialize in product and materials testing, not to mention those that function as subunits in larger manufacturing organizations.

Consider further the vast number of rules, regulations, and standards invented and administered by the private sector. Every medium- or large-sized firm has its own policies and procedures, the expressions of which range from an informal oral tradition to a multivolume offset looseleaf manual. The professions, both old and new, have their codes of ethics, as do many trade associations, from advertisers to publishers of comic books. Product standards, formulated by engineers who serve a broad array of private committees, cover some 20,000 items, from the width of railroad track to specifications for stainless steel wire used in surgical implants, and the number increases to 55,000 if one includes the specification standards promulgated by large industrial purchasers and government agencies.[4] The United States Pharmacopoeia, prepared by pharmacists and pharmaceutical engineers, publishes manufacturing, testing, and sterilizing standards for thousands of products. The American Association of Blood Banks publishes and enforces rules for operating blood banks and handling blood products. Every corporate industrial hygienist we interviewed had at his or her desk *The Registry of the Toxic Effects of Chemical Substances,* containing "threshold limit values" for safe exposure levels in the workplace for hundreds of chemicals, together with designated measurement techniques; it is prepared by conferences of governmental and private experts, and covers far more than OSHA has dealt with by regulation.

There is also a multiplicity of institutions wielding sanctions for inadequate performance. For example, although we tend to think of the state board of medical licensure as the ultimate quality enforcer on the medical profession, in fact it is only one of about a dozen quality-control institutions that sits atop the medical profession (though not over each practitioner). Within hospital settings quality control is exercised during the process of staff appointment and reappointment; it is carried on by numerous peer review committees (such as emergency department, tissue, mortality-morbidity review); it is diagnosed during patient-care evaluation studies; it is improved by hosptial-based continuing medical education; and it is assessed during utilization reviews instigated by the Joint Commission on Accreditation of Hospitals. County medical societies have committees to review fee grievances, malpractice allegations, and allegations of incompetence, to name just a few. Insurance carriers are on the lookout for excessive surgical and other procedures. In product safety, too, the Underwriters Laboratory can effectively ban an unsafe electrical product from the market simply by refusing or withdrawing its seal of approval.

Finally, apart from these more or less voluntary private regulatory systems, as we suggested above, there has been enormous growth of private inspectorates in direct response to aggressive direct governmental regulation. Corporations have increased their staffs of industrial safety experts, toxicologists, industrial hygienists, affirmative action specialists, auditors, product safety experts, environmental engineers, technicians for maintaining pollution-control equipment, and so on. The regulatory compliance staff in one manufacturer of biologics that we interviewed included a research chemist and a former FDA compliance officer, and the members of this "response bureaucracy," as Barry Mitnick calls it,

> specialize in the regulatory area and center their personal plans on work in this area. They may have put in years of labor to gain expertise. . . . Such individuals may support regulation because it is in their self-interest to do so, as well as because of . . . genuine belief in the purposes of the regulation.[5]

These internal "regulators," in turn, formulate standards, lobby to have them promulgated as corporate policy, and organize and oversee in-house inspection staffs.

The Question of Comparable Effectiveness

There are many reasons to think that private, internal regulators can be more reasonable than their public counterparts. They are more specialized and more knowledgeable about the risks generated by their companys' operations. They are more likely to have the trust of the people they regulate and thus to have access to finer-grained and more relevant information. They can be seen, sometimes, as contributing to the overall goals of the organizations in which they operate. They are freer to use discretion in the application of general standards.

There are fewer reasons, however, to think that private regulation would be as effective as public regulation — at least at first blush. To be sure, many of the above-noted conditions that facilitate reasonableness also facilitate effectiveness. Furthermore, when the private regulatory system is reinforced by the pressures of the marketplace and the liability system and/or originates in a very strong tradition of professional ethics, private self-regulation can accomplish a great deal. Few people would advocate replacing hospital tissue committees with OSHA-like rules and inspectors to prevent unnecessary or incompetent operations, or to substitute governmental regulation for the private systems that attempt to ensure that pumps and valves and electrical meters are well made and safe. On the other hand, market conditions and the liability law often do not generate strong pressures for private standard setting and enforcement. Firms may not be induced to hire professional specialists in quality control, safety, or environmental protection, or, if they do, to give them any intracorporate "clout." Like the public inspectorate, the private inspectorate tends to occupy an "outsider" or even a pariah status in its relevant social niches. It is the formal superego of an organization. It specializes in repressing, blaming, criticizing, and admonishing. As one quality-control manager put it, "In most industries . . . I feel that quality control is looked upon as a scourge because QC personnel have a tendency to want to act as floodgates closing down production."[6]

Yet the advantages of private regulation, shielded as it is from excessive demands for political accountability and potentially able, therefore, to provide greater reasonableness than public regulation, make it worthwhile to explore ways to improve its effectiveness to the point that citizen expectations for ever-higher levels of protection can be met. Government regulation might be able to help in this regard. It can repair, strengthen, reinforce, improve, modify, and enlarge private regulatory mechanisms — or even help to create them anew. We will now review governmental efforts to do such things and will consider arguments for doing even more. We will organize our discussion according to the type of failure or weakness in the private regulatory system that government has sought to remedy. It should be emphasized that the types of failure are not in fact so neatly distinguishable, nor can any governmental policy be fitted so neatly into one type rather than another.

Stimulating Private Standards Development

Private quality or performance standards, formulated by committees of the American National Standards Institute, the American

Society for Testing Materials, and other organizations, exist for a large minority of goods and processes furnished in the marketplace, but not for all the activities for which they theoretically could be designed. Professional and industrial associations have formulated advisory standards for some emissions of chemicals into the environment or the air of factories but not for most of them. Product standards apply mostly to products furnished to industrial buyers; relatively few apply to consumer goods.

One reason for the substantial gaps is the absence of pressure from the marketplace and liability law. Consumers, whether individual or corporate, do not have sufficient knowledge or incentives to boycott the products of polluters. With respect to product standards, large-scale industrial purchasers are relatively few in number, purchase in volume, and want standardized parts and materials in order to facilitate switching from supplier to supplier; hence they push suppliers to establish and meet standards of quality and uniformity. Consumers, on the other hand, buy in small volume, make their choices via visual inspection, and usually like the variety of products that the ungoverned marketplace provides. The main areas in which there *is* a good deal of industry regulation of consumer products concern wiring, insulation, and standardized connectors for electrical products developed by Underwriters Laboratories, and building and plumbing standards developed by a variety of code-writing organizations. In these fields, as in many industrial-level product standards, the invisible hand of the market punishes sellers who would circumvent the private standards, and the private regulatory scheme is generally effective.

Still, there undoubtedly are many cases in which standardization would probably be happily received were it to occur. Why, then, does it not occur? The main answer is that the invisible hand, though skilled in encouraging competition, is unskilled at explicit consensus building. But it is through consensus that producers — competitors, indeed — write standards. Typically, firms throughout an industry — and especially the largest firms — send technical representatives to a standards-writing committee organized under the auspices of a professional association. Finding agreement on standards, however, is a political as much as an engineering or economic process, and there is nothing in the structure of the marketplace as such that guarantees that the processs will have a happy result, and little in the nature of politics — especially where power is not tightly concentrated — to guarantee consensus. The result is as likely to be anarchy, as some participants argue for a slightly higher emphasis on safety, some for economy, some for uniformity, some for flexibility. Government can play a role in tipping the scales toward consensus, however, by providing either the inducement or the coercive power to stimulate and validate private agreement on standards.

As in many anarchies, the threat of an ouside enemy is sometimes enough of a stimulus to bring self-regulating institutions into being. Government, in the eyes of many, is just such an enemy. Fearing a revitalized Federal Trade Commission (FTC) and the growing strength of "Naderism," the advertising industry in 1972 established a National Advertising Review Board, which has served to strengthen the preexisting National Advertising Division of the Council of Better Business Bureaus. There have also been attempts to copy this self-regulatory mechanism at the local level.[7] The Association of American Home Appliance Manufacturers (AHAM) came into being in 1967 and by 1971 was effectively pursuing a wide range of self-regulatory activities, including the preparation of safety standards, product standards, certification, and consumer complaint handling. By the account of the AHAM technical director, deflection of government regulation was an explicit primary motive for self-regulation.[8]

One could imagine regulatory agencies using those typical industry reactions systematically, employing the threat of direct regulation explicitly to prod trade and professional associations to prepare self-regulatory standards and procedures as an alternative to government prescription or authorizing them to "fill in the details" of broadly worded governmental regulations, subject to some governmental participation, review, and veto power. The Consumer Product Safety Commission (CPSC), for example, has "forced" various industries to formulate and adopt voluntary standards for dozens of consumer products simply by publicizing injury rates and threatening to promulgate a mandatory regulation. In one instance, to reduce the flammability of upholstered furniture the CPSC proposed a regulation that manufacturers thought unduly stringent, complex, and expensive to comply with in view of the level of risk involved. The industry responded by developing a voluntary standard that they argued was a reasonable and more practical substitute. The commission agreed to suspend its own proceedings for a year while the voluntary standard was implemented and evaluated.[9]

The U.S. Administrative Conference has urged federal agencies charged with the task of formulating complicated health and safety regulations to try to get private standard-setting bodies to do the job, while providing them with government-collected information, sending government representatives to participate, and monitoring final standards for fairness.[10] The FDA announced that it will review and endorse privately established performance standards for medical devices (such as electrocardiograph machines and glucose-testing products), while setting its own mandatory standards only if voluntary standards appear inadequate.[11] One could imagine EPA and OSHA using the threat of promulgating further regulations in order to induce private industrial engineers to agree upon standards for emissions control technologies — although the Justice Department unfortunately has attacked sharing of technology, in the case of automobile emissions standards in particular, as violative of the antitrust laws.

If government can sometimes stimulate private consensus on standards by the threat of regulation, it can also facilitate or cement consensus when private actors need the force of law to ensure joint action and to enforce private standards or ethical codes. The movement to regulate recombinant DNA research, for instance, seems to have evolved out of a highly competitive research environment, in which individual researchers were racing to push the scientific frontiers forward, creating new and possibly dangerous strains of bacteria. Although it was in the interests of all concerned with such research to slow the pace and agree on methods of controlling the risks, the unwillingness of individual researchers to reveal their analytic strategies in advance of publication prevented a coordinated effort. As a result, some of the leaders in the field managed, between 1973 and 1975, to build a consensus behind the idea of putting certain regulatory responsibilities in the hands of the National Institutes of Health (NIH). They fully expected, however, that the NIH would limit itself to enforcement while allowing the scientific community itself to prepare the safety standards that the NIH was to enforce.[12]

Occupational and professional licensing laws are traditional models for such governmental support of self-regulation. Sometimes poorly staffed and ineffective at the postlicensing enforcement level, and always open to the charge that they reduce competition, professional licensing schemes are probably no worse on these scores, on the average, than government regulation by nonprofessionals, and they often have been effective in ridding the field of the most blatantly incompetent and dishonest practitioners. A comparison of the National Association of Securities Dealers (NASD), which is authorized by federal law to police member firms for violations of NASD Rules of Fair Practice, with the Securities Exchange Commission (SEC), which inspects nonmember broker-dealers for compliance with comparable standards, indicated that the NASD is more diligent in its inspections, swifter in resolving customer complaints, severe in its sanctions (44 members were suspended in 1972), and generally effective in producing compliance.[13]

Nevertheless, there is always suspicion of self-regulating associations, especially that they will be dominated by larger firms that are anticompetitive in thrust and insensitive to certain consumer interests. In the case of building and construction standards, for example, unions and suppliers of certain materials have been charged with cartelizing their markets and excluding more inexpensive and labor-saving building materials by relying on local governments to enforce building codes embodying standards developed by those interests. Solving the problem of anarchy, it is feared, leads to the problem of tyranny. Yet the problem of tyranny surely is not insoluble. For the last few years the Federal Trade Commission, Congress, and the Office of Management and Budget (OMB), have been exploring possible approaches to "democratizing" the private standards-writing process, considering rules to require "adequate notice" to all interested parties, an opportunity for them to present their views, and a balance of membership on the standards-writing committees so as to include consumers, small business concerns, users, manufacturers, suppliers, distributors, employees, environmental and conservation organizations, state and local officials, labor, and so on. A recent OMB proposal would provide government grants to private standard-setting organizations whose procedures meet such guidelines and also provide "impartial mechanisms" for handling complaints or appeals by dissatisfied participants.[14]

In the Consumer Product Safety Act of 1972, which was designed to bring order — that is, safety standards — to one of the last areas of anarchy in the world of manufacturing products, the drafters paid a great deal of attention to the same issues of balanced representation, due process, and so on, while attempting to draw on the expertise and human resources of industry to produce the great raft of new standards they believed were required. Indeed, the greater danger, as Samuel Florman has argued persuasively, is that government bureaucrats intent on ensuring that no consumer interest (from more safety to cheaper products) goes unsatisfied, will encumber a private standard-writing process that has worked remarkably well with a set of time-consuming conflict-creating formal rules and adversarial procedures that would erode its essential advantage over governmental regulation.[15] Government oversight, not control, is what is needed.

Mandating Self-Regulation

A large proportion of socially harmful actions, we have argued, do not stem from attempts to "get away with" fraud or obviously inadequate or illegal safety precautions pursuant to deliberately amoral official organizational policy. In established enterprises of any size, fears of regulatory action, lawsuits, bad publicity, and customer reaction usually lead to some internal control systems to prevent major kinds of wrongdoing and harm. But these private, intraorganizational "regulatory" systems often fall far short of perfection. Irresponsible and dangerous actions continue to occur. Some stem from the drift of managerial attention: Confronted with a variety of urgent demands or organizational resources and their own limited supervisory energy, managers take calculated risks, or fail to notice problems, or forget to follow up in orders, all of which may jeopardize values that in quieter moments they actually cherish and respect. Sometimes internal supervisory and reporting systems are inadequate, so that production employees or maintenance people or department heads, motivated to meet production goals or make their jobs a bit easier, can ignore company quality-control or safety or waste-disposal rules without detection, or even prevent adverse information from getting to top management. Sometimes internal "regulators" — safety experts, quality-control engineers, environmental affairs specialists — are incompetent on some issues, or do not have enough power or early enough access to information to control harms adequately, or do not regard certain hazards as within the scope of their or their company's responsibility.[16]

These weaknesses — which are not always present, of course — suggest a set of governmental strategies to create and strengthen private intraorganizational regulatory systems as a partial substitute for direct regulation. Thus the government could enact laws and regulations that compel managers to attend to certain problems, that require installation of intraorganizational regulators and reporting systems, and that strengthen the hand of private regulators within organizations. Such requirements would be a species of governmental regulation, to be sure. But the regulation would be indirect in that it would not directly prescribe specific facilities or preventive measures but would prescribe the creation of a managerial system that would in turn devise and enforce appropriate standards for each enterprise.

To take advantage of the greater numbers and "closeness to the situation" afforded by private regulation, governmental regulatory programs often have required businesses to establish internal self-inspection systems or to hire compliance officers. An 1873 California law required every mine to employ a safety supervisor, who was made criminally responsible for accidents due to neglect of duty. An 1876 San Francisco ordinance required a licensed manager for each steam boiler. The early locomotive safety laws required railroads to establish their own inspection and safety-oriented maintenance programs; the government inspector's primary jobs were to conduct spot checks of equipment inspected by company maintenance people and to review records documenting the company's adherence to its own rules and inspection schedules. The same pattern was adopted in Federal Aviation Agency (FAA) regulation of airline safety. California regulations currently require truck operators to have a preventive maintenance program, including systematic inspection of vehicles and maintenance of records showing "the types of inspection, maintenance and lubrication operations to be performed on each vehicle and the date or mileage when these operations are due." Motor Carrier Safety Unit inspectors, consequently, are able to concentrate on evaluating the quality of the trucking company's maintenance system, and using that as a guide to the necessity for detailed and frequent governmental inspection of the trucks themselves. FDA regulations require manufacturers of intravenous solutions to establish written procedures that prescribe in detail the sanitary and quality-control routines to be used in their manufacturing processes and to establish a quality-control unit with authority to enforce them.

In some cases, the government has required enterprises to set up private regulatory systems to monitor behavior of persons or businesses outside the enterprise itself. Recent EPA regulations, for example, require producers of hazardous wastes to keep track of each load consigned to a shipper and of its ultimate interment in an authorized disposal site; if the producer does not receive a signed document from the shipper and the disposal-site operator showing that the load has been safely disposed of, it must investigate the fate of the shipment and report any discrepancies to the EPA.[17] The California Public Utilities Commission ordered electrical utilities to offer free conservation inspections to any customer that requests them, and it would not be surprising to see them become mandatory.

Government demands for self-regulatory systems occasionally extend to qualitative problems, even more difficult to control by detailed, centrally formulated governmental regulations. Federal regulations require universities that receive federal research funds to establish faculty committees and review procedures to examine research proposals, especially those involving biomedical research that might harm human subjects physically or psychologically and, if necessary, to work out with the researcher alternative methods that would avoid or mitigate such harms.[18] A recent California statute — implicitly recognizing the inability of OSHA rules to cut accidents significantly — requires all employers to establish and maintain a program of accident prevention, including training of employees on safe work practices and hazards unique to the particular job or workplace. The regulations also mandate periodic, scheduled self-inspections, and require the company to appoint a responsible management official to run the program. In a very different context, Christopher Stone has described the development of self-regulation by rock music radio stations under some not-so-gentle prodding by the Federal Communications Commission (FCC). The commission, in 1971, decided to try to curb the epidemic of popular song lyrics referring, usually by innuendo, to the pleasures of drug use. It issued a notice to licensees pointing out the problem "and then proceeded to turn responsibility for handling it back onto the broadcasting companies." It invoked the "judgment" of the licensee to determine the next steps: "The thrust of this Notice is simply that the licensee must make that judgment and cannot properly follow a policy of playing such records without someone in a responsible position (i.e., a management level executive at the station) knowing the content of the lyrics." The broadcasting companies protested, demanding firm rules, but the FCC stood its ground on imposing merely a diffuse call for "responsibility." In another notice a few months later, it wrote:

> As to the mechanics of license responsibility . . . disc jockeys could be instructed that where there is a question as to whether a record promotes illegal drug usage, a responsible management official should be notified so that he can exercise his judgment. It may be

> that a record which raises an issue in this respect is played once, but then the station personnel who have heard it will be in a position to bring it to the attention of the appropriate management official for his judgment. The Commission is not calling for an extensive investigation of each such record. What is required is simply reasonable and good faith attention to the problem.[19]

Stone reports that his own survey of rock music stations in the Los Angeles area "suggests a thoroughgoing, and not at all fractious compliance."

Designating Responsible Officers

The California employee safety-training requirement and the FCC lyrics-monitoring order both compel the enterprise to designate a specific management official to take responsibility for a self-regulatory program. This recognizes the tendency of large organizations to divide functions to the extent that no one seems individually responsible for a problem (or a mistake), or for ensuring that company rules are complied with, or for reminding employees about the human consequences of their acts and omissions. With no individual fully accountable for seeing that things go right, internal control systems easily can break down. When managers can claim they "delegated" responsibility for enforcement of programs they set in motion and were not aware of slippage, slippage is more likely to occur. As we were reminded during the Watergate affair, the interest of top officials in preserving their "deniability" suggests that methods of refocusing responsibility on particular management officials may be necessary to keep internal control systems working in accord with law or stated corporate policy.

The designation of a single individual to take primary responsibility for dealing with a problem or set of risks, on the other hand, increases the organization's constancy of attention to a problem, and makes collective evasion of responsibility more difficult. Larger manufacturers with full-time safety specialists have better worker-safety records, on the average, than smaller firms that generally do not have safety specialists. Local labor unions with full-time civil rights officers have better knowledge of antidiscrimination laws and policies and a better record of compliance efforts.[20] The chief of enforcement of California's Food and Drug Division observed that the crucial ingredient in compliance with food purity regulations is neither governmental enforcement nor whether the firm has

> a beautiful sanitation manual . . . in the plant manager's office. Rather the key is whether companies give responsibility to certain people to do something about it or somebody that oversees the whole thing. Progress has come with the development of full-time quality assurance specialists who sit equally on the organization chart with production and sales. He goes and tells the president *directly,* "We need foaming equipment" and his words are as big as the production manager who says, "We need a new sealer." He can then argue it out with the president as to the priority of the foamer or the sealer.

When market and legal pressures have not induced organizations to establish such specialized positions, therefore, it may be useful for government to require such "repersonalization" of corporate responsibility by law.

Under California insurance law, for example, each insurance company must designate some officer as the recipient of the company financial reports. Further, this officer must report the findings to the board of directors, which must document their receipt in the board's minutes. As a condition of receiving federal funds, local school administrations must appoint an official — commonly referred to as a compliance coordinator — to specialize in coordinating compliance with the requirements of federal civil rights and education-for-the-handicapped laws.[21] A consent decree among American Telephone and Telegraph (AT&T), the Department of Labor, and the Equal Employment Opportunity Commission (for women and ethnic minorities) set up a detailed system whereby AT&T must continually gather data on applicants by minority group and sex and record reasons for rejecting applicants. The decree stipulates exactly which officers in the corporation must perform which tasks in the maintenance and monitoring of the system. At the highest corporate level, the SEC has required some corporations to establish audit committees, composed of specific members of the board of directors (predominantly "outside" directors, not drawn from the corporation's own management), with specific responsibilities for ensuring compliance with laws preventing diversion of corporate funds and concealment of adverse financial information.[22] Christopher Stone has discussed requiring all large corporations to appoint and provide staffs for "public directors," who would be statutorily obligated to oversee programs designed to ensure good-faith compliance with regulations, to check the effectiveness of internal compliance systems, and in general to serve as a corporate "superego."[23] In addition, noting that the food and drug laws require pharmaceutical companies to appoint a qualified investigator to assemble all test data on drugs under development, Stone suggests that the law might require other critical corporate positions, such as chief safety test engineer for auto companies or vice president for environmental affairs in heavily polluting industries, to be filled by individuals meeting legally defined qualifications, whose functions and reporting obligations would be defined by regulation.

How can we be sure designated corporate compliance officers will take their responsibilities seriously, or push hard against intraorganizational resistance to the self-regulatory schemes they devise? One can never be sure, of course, but there are a variety of pressures on designated self-regulatory officials and others that might be devised. One is that the sheer fact of designation makes them "to blame" if their company "gets in trouble" with governmental regulatory officials or gets sued in court for failing to maintain adequate precautions against social harms. In addition, if the officers' duties were specified in some detail by law — such as the duty to file compliance reports with the government or tell regulatory officials about known product defects — or even if detailed duties were left to the corporation to prescribe in job descriptions filed with regulatory authorities — then the compliance officer would face personal liability for misrepresentation and for harms caused by his or her nonfeasance.

A related tactic is to require corporate compliance officers personally to sign official reports and records attesting to regular completion of self-regulatory procedures. The importance of the personal signature is brought out in two studies of egregious corporate misconduct by Christopher Stone — falsification of test data by a drug company that led to marketing of a dangerous drug, and test falsification by B. F. Goodrich in manufacturing aircraft brakes. "Key actors," Stone observes, "were willing to prepare distortive documents; but they drew the line at putting their names on them." A signature identifies a potential guilty party in the event of a subsequent liability suit; it exposes an individual to charges of perjury; and, as Stone puts it, "people feel a strong psychological connection between their actions and their names."[24] Thus FDA good manufacturing practice regulations for intravenous solutions not only require companies to monitor and regularly recalibrate equipment used to measure possible microbiological contamination in the factory and in various product components, but also to maintain records showing the signature of each person performing the monitoring for each product batch and the calibration of testing equipment.

Another method of increasing incentives for designated corporate compliance officers, while simultaneously trying to ensure that they meet minimal standards of knowledge and competence, is to insist that they be licensed, for then the regulatory regime requires an additional and potent deterrent — the threat of disqualification. As Stone asks, "How can we reconcile the fact that a lawyer who violated the law is likely to be suspended or disbarred, but not a safety engineer, or a chemist in a pharmaceutical house? Can anyone believe that an inept or immoral lawyer threatens more lives than an inept or immoral toxicologist?" Even without licensing, Stone points out, legislation could provide that designated "public directors," product-testing engineers, or pollution control managers found guilty of gross dereliction of duty would be legally disqualified from holding similar managerial positions or directorships in *any* company.

Changing the Balance of Power

Focusing responsibility for self-regulatory systems on individual officers or directors presumably increases their own motivation and capacity to keep the organization "on its toes," *attentive* to its legal and social obligations and to the risks generated by its operations. But what of their *power?* A quality-control system in a cannery may fall short if the chief quality-control engineer, however strongly motivated, cannot get new foaming equipment because the production manager controls the budget and wants a new sealer, or refuses to stop operations for scheduled cleaning during the peak season, or is slow to release maintenance personnel from established routines to help debug the foaming equipment. The safety director who slowed down production last week to install a new guard may be reluctant to use up needed goodwill by asking the plant managers to shut down another machine this week. One way of enhancing the effectiveness of private regulatory systems, therefore, is for the government to try to shift the intraorganizational balance of power, giving the "regulations" more power or influence.

One strategy would be modeled on the National Environmental Protection Act (NEPA), whereby Congress required governmental bodies with operating responsibilities, such as the Corps of Engineers, the Bureau of Land Management, and the Forest Service, to prepare and make public an environmental impact statement analyzing ways in which adverse environmental effects of proposed projects could be mitigated or avoided. Failure to perform this analysis in a timely and serious manner has led to court injunctions stopping planned projects. According to one careful study, NEPA and the threat of lawsuits has led to a high increase in the number, status, and influence of environmental protection specialists in the Corps of Engineers and the Forest Service. The agencies have become more concerned with environmental hazards, more knowledgeable about mitigation techniques, and more amenable to the input of outside environmental groups.[25] Expanding on this experience, Christopher Stone has proposed that business corporations about to undertake major projects or market new products should be required to prepare impact statements analyzing their probable environmental impacts and effects on human health and perhaps to make them public.[26] California law requires builders of substantial housing projects, for example, to prepare Environmental Impact Reports for consideration by zoning and planning boards — and by environmental groups — before issuance of building permits.

A more direct and intrusive method of enhancing the influence of in-house "regulators" is to change the enterprise's authority structure as a matter of law, assigning internal "regulatory" officials legally enforceable powers. For example, FDA good manufacturing practice regulations for pharmaceuticals require each plant to have a quality assurance unit with responsibility and *authority* to reject raw materials and prevent shipment of batches that do not meet quality-control standards.[27] The quality-control unit in plants manufacturing intravenous solutions, according to FDA regulations, must have those powers plus the duty and authority to "reject the design, engineering, and physical facilities" of the plant and equipment as well as manufacturing procedures and container-closure devices, "if, in the opinion of the quality control unit, it is not suitable or adequate," or "not capable of holding the product invulnerable to contamination." Conversations with several officials from one such plant indicate that quality-control officials do in fact exercise these powers.

They do routinely delay production to conduct tests, and are recognized as having the authority to override plant managers' decisions on safety issues. One could imagine extending similar duties and legal power to key officials in other settings, such as officials in chemical and certain other plants with responsibility for testing and controlling emissions or disposal of hazardous chemicals, although, as we will discuss later, it is easy to go too far in this regard.

In some instances, worker safety legislation has conferred on employees the power to override decisions by their supervisors. Federal truck safety regulations instruct drivers to check each vehicle themselves for equipment defects or unsafe loading, and authorize them to refuse to take any truck out on the road that they feel is unsafe. The Supreme Court recently upheld an OSHA rule that authorizes a worker to refuse to perform a task (and forbids the employer to discipline him or her for it), if the worker "reasonably believes" it would risk death or serious injury and if there is not "sufficient time or opportunity" to call in an OSHA inspector to assess the danger. The regulation also requires the employee first to "have sought from his employer, and been unable to obtain, a correction of the dangerous condition." The resulting "right to refuse work the employee fears is highly dangerous" enhances the power of workers to serve as self-protective regulators on many issues, although the considerable potential for abuse of this power suggests that it could lead to considerable labor-management-OSHA conflicts. Its real potential lies in stimulating more institutionalized procedures for worker-management consultation over safety issues in which the worker or the worker's representative has some degree of clout.

The Swedish experience, according to Steven Kelman, provides one model for institutionalizing worker power over job safety and health decisions. Pursuant to a 1949 law, each Swedish factory must have a "safety steward," elected or appointed by the local labor union, for each 25 to 50 production workers, depending on the size of the plant. The safety stewards — not individual workers — are empowered by law to halt operations on any machine or assignment they consider unsafe. The threat of unreasonableness is substantially moderated, however, by the extensive training provided for safety stewards and the requirement of labor-management consultation on safety issues. Both union-designated safety stewards and industrial foremen must attend 20 to 40 hours of basic health and safety training;

full-time safety stewards also receive more specialized training in chemical hazards, dust control, and the like. A job site with more than 50 workers must have a labor-management safety committee with regularly scheduled meetings.[28]

Les Boden and David Wegman of the Harvard Occupational Health Program believe that OSHA's effectiveness would increase greatly if it could follow the Swedish model.[29] They suggest (1) that one or more workers in every medium-sized and large workplace, selected by fellow employees, should take part in a governmentally run or sponsored training program in occupational safety and health; (2) that workers' representatives should be encouraged to go directly to management with complaints, rather than to OSHA, and that their leverage be enhanced by an OSHA policy of treating as a willful violation employer failure to correct a danger pointed out and documented by a workers' representative. In effect, this would give workers the clout of OSHA inpsectors without necessarily constraining them to abide by the rules that constrain OSHA inspectors. Workers would be free to be more reasonable than the rules allow, but also to be more forceful. Whether such a proposal could be implemented without risking unwarranted harrassment of management by workers can only be known after some experimentation. It seems to us that OSHA should retain discretion over whether or not to punish employer failure to follow an employee suggestion, and the sanction should be applied only if the uncorrected danger is unambiguously serious.

In fact, the Boden-Wegman proposal is simply an extension of a process already in place in the many factories and mines for which labor unions have negotiated agreements providing for employer funding of full-time union safety representatives and joint labor-management procedures for stopping operations that a worker fears are dangerous. In one aluminum plant we visited, for example, the bargaining agreement empowers a fearful worker to call in a union safety committeeman to discuss the matter with his foreman; if they can not agree, a company safety engineer and the full-time union safety officer are summoned. Failing agreement on that level, the union can call OSHA or file a grievance, although we were told this has not been necessary.

Routing complaints through the union safety specialists, moreover, seems to cut down on unreasonable employee complaints because the union specialist quickly develops a certain expertise and a sense of which hazard-abatement measures are most worth pushing for. In an auto assembly plant, a full-time union health and safety representative told us of two hazards — one involving worker exposure to lead dust, another involving fumes from glue that give workers headaches — that he was able to get abated even though there were no violations of OSHA standards in either case. The officers of one union successfully arranged for drivers to file a "gripe sheet" after each run, noting possible defects in their vehicles, thus creating written records whereby responsibility for violations of corporate maintenance rules on government regulations could be focused on particular terminal supervisors. At the time we spoke to them, they were suggesting refinements, such as requiring a response from the supervisor, and keeping separate copies of the "gripe sheet" in truck cabs to warn other drivers of problems noted by their predecessors.

The key to these apparent success stories is not that government regulations (or collective bargaining agreements) give workers uncontrolled power to stop operations they say are dangerous, but that they turn selected workers into additional intraorganizational experts on safety and health and establish systems for dialogue and dispute resolution. The model for enhancing the effectiveness of internal regulatory systems thus suggested is partly the National Labor Relations Act, which requires employers only to bargain in good faith with worker representatives (not to make any specific agreement) and partly the idea of procedural due process, whereby individuals adversely affected by governmental action have a right — enforceable in court — not to determine substantive policies but to have a hearing on their complaints and to be given a rational response.

In several other settings, government has followed this due process strategy to enhance the effectiveness of private regulatory systems. By requiring organizations to set up mechanisms for dealing with complaints openly and with some degree of procedural fairness, it is intended that individuals adversely affected by organizational policy will have greater influence over substantive policy. Under the Magnuson-Moss Act, for example, sellers of consumer goods are encouraged to establish fixed procedures to handle consumer disputes concerning the coverage of the sellers' product warranties. The incentive for sellers to do so is that dissatisfied consumers are obliged to resort to the seller's informal settlement procedure (provided it is written in the warranty and meets FTC standards) before taking civil action in the courts.[30] The courts have ruled that under the Constitution local school boards must provide due process hearings for students on a variety of issues, from disciplinary suspensions[31] to placement in classes for "retarded" students.[32] Under the Education for All Handicapped Children Act, Congress imposed vague substantive standards on local school districts — handicapped children are entitled to instruction in the "least restrictive environment" — but required districts to establish elaborate procedures for consultation with parents and formulation of written educational plans tailored to the child's needs. Adaptation of this model to controlling risks arising from corporate action is at least worthy of consideration on a case-by-case basis.

Increasing Organizational Competence

To many regulatory officials, a major weakness in some intraorganizational control systems is the incompetence of their managers or the operatives whose actions are the objects of control. Experienced truck safety inspectors, for example, complain that in some companies people without proper experience are put in charge of maintenance, often with an eye to moving on to other positions in the company as soon as they can. When maintenance management is weak and mechanics do not receive adequate training and pay, it is hard for them to be strong in insisting on proper safety procedures. One California Motor Carrier Safety Unit official says his "main problem" is "turnover in management and a lack of qualified mechanics." Regulations calling for adequate apprenticeship programs for mechanics and requiring an experienced person to be assigned to maintenance management, therefore, may be more important than reams of detailed government regulations prescribing specific maintenance procedures and equipment standards.

In fact, since 1976 Michigan has licensed automotive repair facilities and auto mechanics as well. A licensed facility is required to provide a certified master mechanic in every category of repair service the facility offers, and, beginning in 1978, "any work concerning major service or repair performed by a non-certified mechanic" was to be "inspected and approved by one who is certified in the pertinent specialty."[33] Similarly, many experienced regulatory officials agree that the most important single factor in the quality of nursing homes is not the content of the regulations or enforcement practices, but the quality and professionalism of the chief on-the-scene administrator for each facility. In California, the legislature responded to this belief by enacting a requirement that each home "must be run by a licensed administrator who meets certain training or experience requirements."

There is only so much a competent chief can do, however, if the ultimate source of danger is the actions or inactions of incompetent individual employees whose work is not entirely routinized and "checkable" by mechanical quality-control systems. The effectiveness of self-regulation systems in these cases can sometimes be enhanced, however, by mandatory training for those employees. The idea is by no means a new one. Airline pilots must be trained and retrained according to criteria prescribed by FAA regulations. Drivers for trucking companies must meet special requirements set forth in Department of Transportation regulations. Sometimes the enterprise can be required to do the training, as in the case of the Cal-OSHA regulation mentioned earlier, obligating employers to conduct regular occupational safety-training programs for workers. Sometimes the government can conduct part of the training. After the malfunction of the Three Mile Island nuclear generating plant in Pennsylvania turned out to be due in large measure to the incompetence of company technicians, who misread gauges and ignored warning devices, the Nuclear Regulatory Commission (NRC) ordered operators of similar plants to attend NRC training seminars analyzing the Pennsylvania incident. Some observers suggest more detailed and stringent regulations to govern the qualifications and ongoing training of all nuclear plant operating personnel. Externally imposed regulation and inspection regimes, they argue, never can guarantee an adequate level of safety; that goal can be achieved only by an elite, highly trained, and disciplined corps of technicians, analogous to the nuclear submarine crews that have served effectively and safely for a good number of years. Whether that is true depends on the degree to which safety precautions can be mechanized or operatives with only on-the-job training can be supervised effectively by one or two highly trained technicians — although in any case a specially trained and well-publicized corps of operators might help ease public fears about nuclear power. Our point, however, is that requirements of special training for operators in positions of special responsibility, such as drivers of trucks containing hazardous chemical wastes, might be a powerful supplement or, in some cases, even a substitute for detailed direct regulation.

Often, however, improving the competence of key personnel takes more than special training. The problem may be that market conditions deter employers from paying for training or from paying enough to motivate employees adequately. California's experience with nursing homes is an example. The inevitable frustrations of attempting to mandate elusive standards such as "humane treatment" through specific regulations and inspections led the state legislature to the finding that "quality of patient care . . . is dependent upon the competence of the personnel."[34] It also concluded that high turnover (partly due to low pay) and general incompetence of nurses' aids were major causes of poor care. Moreover, it appeared that Medicare and Medicaid fees for patients were not high enough to enable most nursing homes to pay higher salaries. A 1977 law therefore established a certification program for nurses' aides, and a statewide government-coordinated effort to supply the necessary training. As an inducement to participate, the law also provided state funds to facilities to help finance the training programs and to pay salary increases of 20 cents per hour to aides who completed the program and were certified. In 1978, the legislature increased the minimum wage law for aides (by an average of 18 cents an hour) and added another increment of 18 cents for those who stay on the job more than three months. Finally, the legislators provided a subsidy to nursing homes to help pay for those increases.[35] The focus on increasing the competence of personnel, in short, has led to state-financed training and even a state subsidy for increased salaries.

The Hazards of Over-Self-Regulation

The California nursing home law, with its mounting wage costs and governmental subsidies, highlights an important point: The logic of creating and improving self-regulatory systems easily can lead to the same "unreasonable" results as direct regulation, such as expenditures on specially trained personnel or self-inspection routines that exceed the resulting benefits, and unduly burdensome reporting and paperwork requirements. Nor is this merely a logical possibility. Despite the impression that delegating ultimate decisions or precautionary measures to private enterprises is an obviously reasonable way of achieving goals, government-mandated self-regulation schemes not infrequently operate in an unreasonable and counterproductive manner. For example, a Los Angeles City Councilman who proclaims himself "the first avowed environmentalist elected to public office in Los Angeles" and an indefatigable worker for environmentalist causes, wrote in 1978, "With accumulating experience, I am willing to say aloud what I suspect many other environmentalists may believe: *EIR's* (Environmental Impact Reports) *have grown beyond control.* Rather than a procedure to identify and deal with environmental issues, the EIR process has turned into an administrative morass costly to everyone, especially the taxpayers."[36] It is worthwhile, therefore, to examine how and why self-regulation can go awry.

The Overinclusiveness Problem Revisited

Unreasonableness in direct regulations often occurred, we pointed out, because regulatory authorities prescribed specific precautionary devices or abatement methods that, while useful in many settings, were inappropriate or unnecessary in others. Mandating self-regulation, on the other hand, would seem to avoid this trap by merely ordering enterprises to meet certain *procedural* requirements such as designating responsible personnel and installing their own control systems. The *substantive* decisions are left to each enterprise, such as deciding what problems are truly significant in its particular operation and devising appropriate remedies. But procedural requirements can be just as overinclusive as substantive ones, and sometimes just as burdensome. The delays, expense, and distortions of modern-day criminal trials are brought about by complex rules of criminal *procedure*. Each particular procedural rule, of course, was devised to close off a possible route to injustice, often one that in fact was taken in some case in the past by an unscrupulous prosecutor, a prejudiced sheriff, or an incompetent judge. But the rules are applicable to all cases, even those where the facts are clear, the police and the judge and the prosecutor entirely fair-minded, and the probability of injustice, given the entire structure of the system, very small. The cumulative effect, moreover, is that jury selection and trials average almost a week, defense strategy is preoccupied with drawing judges into procedureal error, and prosecutors promise leniency to any defendant who will plead guilty and spare the state the necessity for a trial (while threatening to seek the maximum penalty for defendants who will not bargain).

The same drive toward uniform treatment and closing of procedural loopholes through which "mistakes" might slip characterizes many mandatory self-regulation programs. The scenario should be familiar. A serious accident or other harm occurs that is traced to a weakness in the internal control system of an enterprise. The legislature or regulatory officials, however, require not just that one enterprise but all others that might cause similar harms to institute certain procedural improvements, such as to conduct more frequent self-inspections, or to appoint a full-time specialist to a key control position, or to establish a committee or a training program. The problem is that these steps inevitably will be unnecessary or nearly so in a substantial number of "good apple" enterprises that for any number of reasons already have effective internal control systems. Moreover, each time another accident occurs someplace revealing another kind of weakness, a new round of procedural prescriptions, double checks, and conformity reports or signatures will be added. The extent to which mandatory self-inspection systems can become overloaded was revealed when the Federal Railroad Administration, responding to the Carter Administration's pressure for elimination of excessive regulations, announced that it was eliminating certain "unnecessary and burdensome maintenance and [self-]inspection requirements" and that this would save the railroad industry over $100 million each year[37] ($100 million a year over the last 10 years could have bought a lot of new, safer track or rolling stock).

The drift toward overinclusive self-regulatory requirements is also illustrated by the expansion of jurisdiction of the human subjects committees that universities had to establish under pressure from HEW. Such programs necessarily entail a certain overinclusiveness, since prior clearance must be sought — and waited for — by the many careful and humane researchers as well as the handful who are careless and indifferent; but as there was no way acceptable to HEW of separating the good from the bad in advance, some level of review for all has been necessary. The real problem involves the classes of research projects that must be submitted. Originally, the concern was with experiments using drugs or medical treatments that could have adverse effects, or experiments using drugs or medical treatments that could have adverse effects, or experiments that withheld from medical subjects therapies that might help them. But HEW officials, with relentless legalistic logic, expanded the notion of "harm" that universities must prevent to its full semantic limits. HHS guidleines now require universities to establish procedures to protect research subjects from any kind of harm, including psychological discomfort, and including harm that might arise not from the experimental treatment but from possible misuse or misinterpretation of the research finding. Thus research involving the administration of written psychological or cognitive tests must first be cleared through a committee of professors because certain subjects might find certain questions disturbing or because the results might be used by some people to perpetuate discrimination against minorities.[38]

But why, the reader might ask, does not the university simply design and enforce its human subjects protection program in a flexible manner, concentrating only on the truly serious risks? After all, the advantage of self-regulation, presumably, is that it can be more flexible than direct governmental regulation. But that all depends on how the government polices self-regulatory systems on tasks they are expected to perform. It is rarely easy for government officials to evaluate the quality or effectiveness of self-regulatory efforts. Consequently, regulators write ever-more-detailed guidelines stipulating the kinds of things a good self-regulation system should contain. (Thus government requirements that employers establish safety training programs for employees — a measure that seems to decentralize the task of identifying and preventing hazards — became encumbered with detailed regulations prescribing precisely what must be taught, how often, and how.) The self-regulating enterprise, moreover, is instructed to set forth the details of its training or self-inspection or quality-control program in written form. That accomplished, government inspectors evaluate self-regulatory systems by checking the enterprise's written procedures against government guidelines and by making sure the enterprise sticks to its own written procedures and standards. The more regulators or advocacy groups mistrust the motivation of the self-regulating enterprises as a class, and the more regulatory inspectors lack the expertise to evaluate particular self-regulation systems, the more likely it is that they will insist that the enterprise adhere strictly to its own written procedures.

The result, of course, is that government guidelines come to be treated as binding rules and privately formulated procedures or standards come to be treated with the same legal sanctity as direct governmental regulations. In the human subjects protection area, for example, our university, like many others, felt compelled to write voluntary regulations that simply track the HEW all-encompassing guidelines. The university committee, then, justifiably fears that excusing some research projects from review might incur complaints from "true believers" and criticism from HEW for "violating your own rules," a criticism that could lead to a cutoff of all federal research funds to the university. Similarly, the Occupational Safety and Health Review Commission has held that employers found innocent of having violated an OSHA regulation can nevertheless be found guilty of having an inadequate safety program if the testimony reveals failure to secure continuous and literal compliance with the company's own safety rules.[39] A pending Food Safety Act quite sensibly (it seems) calls upon all manufacturers to identify critical points in their production processes, and to write up procedures for controlling and monitoring hazards of those points. But it also characterizes any food not manufactured in strict compliance with those procedures as illegally "adulterated," and makes it an offense not to report such variation to the FDA. This led a spokesman for the food industry to complain vehemently that the act "commands each processor to write his own criminal code, and never vary from it, unwittingly or otherwise."[40]

Requirements that regulated enterprises establish training programs, set up safety committees, or hire in-house experts — seemingly a *more* flexible form of regulation — can also decrease flexibility under some circumstances. The basic justification for such intrusions into management structure, as discussed earlier, is that they would be a superior *substitute* for strict enforcement of detailed, across-the-board government regulations. It is altogether too easy, however, for mandatory self-regulation measures to be imposed as an *additive* obligation on top of the enterprise's duty to adhere to all *substantive* government regulations. For example, recently updated FDA good manufacturing practices regulations for drugs require each plant to have a designated quality assurance unit, with responsibility and authority to reject new materials and prevent shipment of batches that do not meet quality-control standards. But the regulations still insist on regular FDA inspections and strict enforcement of indentical federally prescribed quality-control and facilities standards for all plants.[41] Cal-OSHA's requirement of worker safety programs in each plant does not mean employers have more discretion with respect to detailed OSHA regulations, or that inspectors have more discretion in enforcing them.

Occasionally intraorganizational improvements are traded for relaxation of direct regulation. Cal-OSHA's agreement with Bechtel Corporation to suspend enforcement on a large construction site in return for a joint union-management safety program is one example. The U.S. Department of Agriculture is planning a cutback of intensive inspection and enforcement of detailed sanitation and equipment regulations in meat-packing plants for those companies that establish competent quality-control systems, complete with their own inspectors. These "trades," however, are rarities. For regulators, it is always politically risky to take any action that could be interpreted as weakening worker or consumer protection, and repealing specific direct regulations (however ineffective, unreasonable, or both) in return for the promise of better self-regulation falls into that risky category. Moreover, some businesses, fearful of cost cutting and corner cutting by competitors, may prefer uniform enforcement of direct regulations, a situation that at least is predictable, to a regime built on self-regulation.

Similarly, it seems reasonable to require companies to hire "public" directors, specialty-trained safety or environmental managers, and so on, only if the specific firm or perhaps a segment of an industry has an especially poor record. We ordinarily do not require probation officers for citizens who are staying within the law in all important respects. Moreover, there is enough evidence of the artifical rigidities (and high costs) of "credentialism" that we should not rush into licensing every plant manager, lab technician, food handler, and brakes tester whenever a few have acted irresponsibly. But legal norms of equal treatment make *selective* imposition of such requirements difficult, except as a court-imposed penalty for serious violations of direct regulations, and there is always a possibility that legislators will overreact to serious accidents by requiring all enterprises to hire licensed compliance specialists, regardless of the costs and benefits in particular firms.

The Burdens of Documentation

When government delegates responsibility for preventing harms to individual enterprises, it remains concerned with ensuring that they actually discharge those delegated responsibilities in a serious manner. Characteristically, the enterprises are required to prove that they have complied by filing compliance plans, by reducing all their procedures to written rules and manuals, by documenting faithful adherence to their self-inspection and quality-control routines, by keeping records of all the activities and decisions of designated compliance officers of committees in order to show that they are not mere facades, and by filing reports indicating the depth of their consideration of critical problems. These measures for detailed documentation, however, conflict with the goal of making self-regulation more reasonable than direct regulation.

One of the principal aims of relying on self-regulation, after all, is to permit people close to the local situation to identify problems and discover solutions that might not be obvious to outside inspectors. We necessarily want these local actors, such as the quality-control engineer in a factory or the principal investigator in a biomedical research project, to have the discretion that permits this aim to be achieved. They cannot be completely programmed without destroying the whole purpose of self-regulation. But the regulatory officials who oversee self-regulation are expected above all to discourage or discover abuses of discretion in self-regulation systems that might cause social harm. To do so, they demand documentation — detailed justifications of how discretion is exercised, justifications organized in terms of bureaucratically preprogrammed categories listing data gathered, factors considered, and so on. These paperwork requirements tend to fall on precisely those individuals who are sufficiently talented or trained that they are given discretionary tasks in the first place; for it is only they who know the subtle nuances that might justify their own discretionary conduct. Only the physician who has studied the case and actually made the decision, for example, can know why he has ordered these lab tests rather than those, or chosen this surgical intervention in order to avoid that form of radiation therapy. And even he may not know precisely his own thought processes for, after all, "professional judgment" based on experience and hard-to-communicate intuition is bound to play a role in many cases.

If the public regulatory regime were able to distinguish categories of conduct for which less intensified documentation were permitted, or if the documentation could be executed by less valuable personnel, much of the sterile paper shuffling that increasingly afflicts professionals' work lives could be avoided. But there are limits to how much self-scrutiny of self-regulation can be tolerated by public regulators, and there is a natural tendency for the latter to err on the side of requiring more documentation rather than less. As one insightful nursing home inspector told us: "Documentation — that's the name of the game. But nurses are notoriously poor documenters; they do a lot more than they give themselves credit for." The inspector did not travel the next logical step, however, and ask why nurses had to bother "giving themselves credit" in the first place. A professional nurse *should* be more concerned with doing creditable deeds than with preparing a creditable record of them, and systematic efforts to push them toward the latter are bound to be resented when the recording takes a lot of time away from the doing. Special education teachers trained in dealing with specific learning disabilities also complain bitterly that the procedural burdens of complying with the Education for All Handicapped Children Act — documenting meetings with parents, drafting individualized educational plans for each child, filling out checklists — drastically curtail the time available for teaching. Their meetings with parents usually revolve around charges that the child's legal rights were violated by the school's failure to send out a notice written in the time period required in the law or by ad hoc modification of the agreed-to plan, rather than turning on the child's educational progress or needs. Legal appeals are common. Many special education teachers, resentful and demoralized, apparently have sought transfers into regular teaching positions.

Environmental analysts are in a similar dilemma. From our contact with these professionals in the Department of the Interior we are aware of how much the good ones shun assignments to prepare environmental impact documents. In their eyes the process is too full of busy-work to permit them to exercise their full range of talent. And from our own experience in academic hiring we are sensitive to the frustrations of having to document the many minor acts and sometimes the reasoning behind them that it might take to convince others — and particularly suspicious or hostile others — that we had conducted an energetic search for talented minority and female candidates and had chosen among all candidates by means of fair, appropriate, and universal criteria.

A second problem that arises from the elaboration of documentation requirements is organizational and personal defensiveness — defensiveness that actually works against the interests of those the newly reinforced private regulatory system is supposed to protect.

Special education compliance officers worry more about showing federal oversight agencies that filing deadlines have been met than about improving the quality of education. Agencies living under the shadow of litigation for alleged inadequacies in their environmental impact statements formalize the internal processes for preparing the documents, and write them the way agency lawyers advise in order to make sure they will withstand judicial scrutiny. In the course of this retreat into legalism, the intellectual and analytical objectives of the EIS tend to fall by the wayside. When environmental analysts are afraid to say that most risks are trivial or moderate, lest their work be attacked as a "whitewash" in court or in public hearings, it is harder for them to draw attention to the few risks they believe are really worth worrying about.

When an enterprise seeks to protect itself from lawsuits or regulatory review by emphasizing formal compliance with procedural requirements, the enterprise appears legalistic and all the more untrustworthy to the individuals or groups the procedural rules are designed to protect. Referring to "mechanically impersonal" compliance by school administrators with the Goss v. Lopez requirement of due process hearings for students charged with disciplinary infractions, David Kirp observes: "Defensiveness further erodes the strength of the school's assertion of institutional competence and the credibility of its demands for trust." One result can be a decline into adversarial battle over procedural failing — for under self-regulatory schemes procedural violations provide the main point of legal and political leverage for those who doubt the enterprise's good faith. With adversariness, the dialogue originally sought by the procedural mechanisms is cut off. According to one environmentalist observer, the National Environmental Protection Act probably has had "a negative impact on public involvement" that had been "well established long before NEPA. By tying citizen participation to a process of reviewing and filing documents, NEPA . . . sterilized and stultified the dialogue between agencies and the public that was beginning to develop in the late 1960's."[42] Another manifestation of defensiveness is the "sanitization" of written records. In the wake of student records legislation that gave parents the right to see their children's permanent files, many records were destroyed or expurgated. As Mark Yudof and David Kirp put it, the legislation "promises to promote among teachers an oral tradition which would rival the Navajo nation." In California, where the statewide association of nursing homes offers consultative services to its members to help them upgrade some of their practices, we were told that the written consultant reports are routinely filled with bland and congratulatory evaluations, while the verbal reports might mention dozens of items that need improvement. This occurs because the consultants' reports are easy targets for inspectors, who can find in them convenient leads to citeable violations.

Overcoming Unreasonableness

The preceding examples demonstrate that mandatory self-regulation programs, like direct regulation, can lead to unreasonable costs, displacement of constructive effort, and destructive defensiveness. The crucial issues, however, are whether the risks of these adverse effects are lesser or greater under self-regulation, and whether they are less or more subject to correction. We have no data, hard or soft, to help answer these questions, but there are reasons to suspect that mandatory self-regulation is somewhat more likely to avoid tendencies toward unreasonableness than direct regulation.

One reason is that key decision makers in private regulatory systems, even if subject to detailed procedural rules and legal sanctions for not following them, tend to be less susceptible to the legalistic ethos than governmental regulators. Employed and located full time in the enterprise itself, they are continually sensitive to the organization's basic mission and aware of how self-regulatory methods, if pushed too far, might have adverse consequences. While concerned with "covering the enterprise's ass," so to speak, in dealings with regulatory authorities, they are typically much less concerned than the individual regulatory official with covering their *own*. Hence they are more likely to resist literal interpretations of the rules, to accept "substantial compliance," and to fight for discretion when the requirements are inappropriate or unduly burdensome in particular cases. University professors who complain about requirements imposed by their peers on the human subjects committee or by university affirmative action officers, and production managers who castigate the chief of quality control for insisting too rigidly on adherence to certain testing requirements, undoubtedly would prefer these situations to those in which the human subjects committee and the affirmative action offices were staffed by HEW bureaucrats, or quality-control schedules were established and enforced directly by Food and Drug Administration or National Highway Traffic Safety Administration officials. When the first-line "regulators" are private professionals, the *substantive* standards are likely to be more reasonable *and* more flexibly administered, and procedural rules are more likely to be interpreted in light of their substantive consequences.

In addition, excessive procedural and documentation requirements of the kind that sometimes burden mandatory self-regulatory programs are probably somewhat easier to amend and moderate, on the average, than excessively stringent substantive regulation. One reason is that the cry of "too much paperwork" tends to be more politically persuasive than that of "too high safety standards." Even environmentalists did not protest when President Carter told Congress in an environmental message that "we do not want impact statements that are measured by the inch or weighed by the pound." Another reason is that it is often quite possible to devise simplified forms or less formal procedures and make a plausible case that they would not substantially reduce the level of protection.[43] Those who protest procedural requirements in reinforced self-regulation schemes often are professionals or specialists who have a certain claim to expertise and whose cooperation is obviously important. When nurses, industrial hygienists, quality-control engineers, and toxicologists contend that certain existing arrangements are redundant and impede their effectiveness, the spirit of self-regulation programs demands that they be given a respectful hearing, and ultimately they usually will be.

On balance, therefore, government is likely to be more flexible and responsive in dealing with reinforced self-regulation programs than in enforcing direct regulation. They will more likely succeed, therefore, in eliciting cooperation and in keeping regulatory requirements in touch with the particular needs and costs in different enterprises. Trading direct enforcement of detailed substantive regulations for the kinds of strengthened self-regulatory mechanisms described in this chapter, with the regard for the perils of documentation, represents, in our view, a fairly promising strategy for controlling social harms and reinforcing social responsibility.

NOTES

1. Melvin Hinich and Richard Staelin, "Regulation of the U.S. Food Industry," in *Study of Federal Regulation,* Appendix to Volume VI, *Framework for Regulation,*

U.S. Senate Committee on Governmental Affairs (95th Congress, 2nd Session), 1978, pp. 415, 433. At least some FDA personnel argued that the agency should respond by giving *higher* priority to problems of contamination (Ibid., p. 415).

Hinich and Staelin also note the consequences of such attacks as follows: "The regulators are unable to accurately anticipate the future political risks and benefits resulting from their actions. As a result, lower level bureaucrats try to minimize their risks. . . . As a consequence much of the effort of the agency carried out by the lower level is of the nitpicking variety and thus has little to do with consumer protection" (Ibid.).

2. Jeremy Rabkin, "Office for Civil Rights," in *The Politics of Regulation,* ed. James Q. Wilson (New York: Basic Books, 1980), p. 34, nn. 112-117, p. 445.

3. Bruce Vladeck, *Unloving Care: The Nursing Home Tragedy* (New York: Basic Books, 1980), p. 161.

4. Preliminary Staff Study (Precis), "Self-Regulation — Product Standardization, Certification and Seals of Approval," Federal Trade Commission, 1971; Samuel C. Florman, "Standards of Value," *Harper's,* February 1980, pp. 62-70.

5. Barry Mitnick, "An Incentive System Model of Organizations and Regulatory Design" (Paper presented at the annual meeting of the American Political Science Association, 1979; also issued as Working Paper 359, Graduate School of Business, University of Pittsburgh).

6. J.B. Van Cronkhite, "Please Don't Eat the Instructions," *Quality Progress,* December 1969, p. 12.

7. Albert B. Stridsberg, *Effective Advertising Self-Regulation* (New York: International Advertising Association, 1974).

8. Michael S. Hunt, "Trade Associations and Self-Regulation: Major Home Appliances," in *Regulating the Product: Quality and Variety,* eds. Richard E. Eaves and Marc J. Roberts (Cambridge, MA: Ballinger, 1975), pp. 39-55.

9. See Stan Crock, "Safety Commission Has Avoided War on Regulation," *Wall Street Journal,* 6 February 1980. This article maintains that by such tactics and being more willing to talk to business then the FTC, the CPSC has avoided the complaints to members of Congress on the political attack stimulated by the FTC's rule-making approach. But it also becomes subject to attack by consumer groups. Thus when the CPSC decided to institute a consumer education program instead of banning skateboards — a prevalent cause of serious injuries — the head of the consumer protection unit of the Americans for Democratic Action condemned the response as "totally inadequate." Consumer groups recently persuaded the Office of Management and Budget to drop a recommendation *urging* the CPSC and the FTC to give industries a chance to set their own standards before adopting mandatory standards. See "Agencies are Advised to Use Standards Set by Industry to Cut Cost to Government," *Wall Street Journal,* 18 January 1980, p. 18.

10. "U.S.-Private Coordination on Rule-Making is Urged," *National Law Journal,* 1 January 1979, p. 10. The conference rejected a resolution proposed by "Public interest" lawyers that would restrict regulatory agency cooperation with private standard-setting bodies. See also Philip J. Harter, *Regulatory Use of Standards: The Implications for Standards Writers* (Washington, DC: National Bureau of Standards, 1979).

11. The FDA estimated that voluntary standards — covering performance, testing, and labeling — would be developed for approximately 1000 medical devices, and that manufacturers would comply because hospitals and doctors would prefer prod-

ucts that meet FDA-endorsed standards. (The threat of malpractice suits undoubtedly contributes to this preference.) *HEW News,* 1 February 1980.

12. Haim Erdner, "The Emergence of the Recombinant DNA Controversy: An Organization Analysis and Public Policy Implications," Fels Discussion Paper 116, School of Public and Urban Policy, University of Pennsylvania, November 1977. See also Susan Wright, "Recombinant DNA Policy: From Prevention to Crisis Intervention," *Environment,* November 1979, pp. 34-37, and sources cited therein.

13. This is not to imply any evaluation, pro or con, of the adequacy of the NASD rules themselves. See SEC, *Report of Special Study of Securities Markets,* 4 R Doc. No. 95, 88th Congress, 1st Session, 1963; and Robert N. Katz, "Industry Self-Regulation: A Viable Alternative to Government Regulation," in *Protecting the Consumer Interest,* ed. Robert N. Katz (Cambridge, MA: Ballinger, 1976).

14. See "Agencies are Advised to Use Standards Set by Industry to Cut Cost to Government," *Wall Street Journal,* 18 January 1980, p. 8. The OMB proposal would give primary jurisdiction and grant-giving authority to the Commerce Department, and allow the FTC to serve as adviser.

15. See Samuel C. Florman, "Standards of Value," *Harper's,* February 1980, pp. 62-70. After reading the FTC's compilation of "abuses in the standards process, Florman identified about 30 cases (including alleged hasty approval of new materials, too much deliberation, too much emphasis on economy, and too much emphasis on safety) and observed that "the processing of more than 20,000 standards has resulted in fewer than 100 dissatisfied parties. . . . What other institution, I wondered, public or private, has done so well?" (p. 68). Florman also points out that there are a number of alternatives by which dissatisfied parties can publicize their grievances, and that the FTC now can challenge individual standards under its existing legal authority to prevent antitrust violations and unfair trade practices.

16. A study of environmental scientists and toxicologists in large chemical companies, for example, recently concluded that "specialized corporate staffs have yet to make major in-roads on influencing the environmental behavior of line managers beyond fulfilling legal requirements, and promotion incentives for the line managers continue to pivot on maintaining high levels of production at minimum cost." Moreover, these specialized staffs generally have not been active in locating potentially serious problems not specifically the subject of government regulations or proposed regulations; they rarely undertake studies of how contractors or customers dispose of wastes, how the biosphere near plants is affected, or whether there are undetected patterns of illness among workers. Office of Toxic Substances, EPA, *Voluntary Environmental Activities of Large Chemical Companies to Assess and Control Industrial Chemicals* (Springfield, VA: National Technical Information Service), p. 5.

17 "EPA Issues Record-Keeping Rules as Part of Broad Filing Plan for Harmful Wastes," *Wall Street Journal,* 27 February 1980, p. 8.

18. At the University of California, the office of the general counsel has announced that the university would not feel obliged to defend a researcher from liability claims if the researcher has not complied with the university regulations concerning protection of human subjects.

19. Christopher Stone, *Where the Law Ends* (New York: Harper & Row 1975), pp. 218-219.

20. See Michelle Hoyman, "Coercive and Noncoercive Mechanisms for Compliance with the Civil Rights Act of 1964" (Paper delivered at the meeting of the Midwest Political Science Association, 1974).

21. The requirements include a series of self-regulatory actions, such as (1) filing formal assurances of compliance with the federal regulations, (2) conducting a self-evaluation of school district practices in dealing with disadvantaged groups, and (3) establishing a formal grievance procedure for dissatisfied parents. See Paul T. Hill et al., *A Study of Local Education Agency Response to Civil Rights Guarantess* (Santa Monica, CA: Rand Corporation, 1979).

22. "It is increasingly accepted that . . . the independent auditor (and the internal auditor, where there is one) should have direct access to the board's audit committee." Bayless Manning, "Thinking Straight About Corporate Law Reform," 41 *Law and Contemporary Problems* 3, 28 (1977). Even without specific regulatory requirements to do so, many corporations have voluntarily established audit committees, and at least 35 major corporations have established "public responsibility committees" of the board to deal with issues such as affirmative action, community relations, pollution, product quality and safety, and occupational safety and health. Michael Lovdal, Raymond Bauer, and Nancy Treverton, "Public Responsibility Committees of the Board," 55 *Harvard Business Review* 40, 60 (1977).

23. Stone, *Where the Law Ends,* ch. 15. Partly in response to criticisms of the inadequacy of supervision by the boards of directors, most major corporations now have a majority of "outside" directors. In addition, women are now found on the boards of 28 percent of major manufacturing companies and 41 percent of nonmanufacturing companies. The corresponding figures for black directors, according to the same survey, are 17 percent and 32 percent. The Conference Board, *The Board of Directors: Perspectives and Practices in Nine Countries,* 1977; cited in William Van Dusen Wishard, "Corporate Response to a New Environment," *Law and Contemporary Problems* 41 (Summer 1977): 228. Whether or not these outside and "minority" directors have taken more interest in corporate governance than any other directors, or have more effectively influenced internal self-regulatory programs, is still a matter for guesswork, however.

24. Stone, *Where the Law Ends,* p. 195.

25. J. Serge Taylor, "Environmentalists in the Bureaucracy" (Ph. D. dissertation, University of California, Berkeley, 1979).

26. Stone, *Where the Law Ends,* pp. 221-227. Stone is not specific about when such reports should be required, to whom they should be disclosed, and whether or by whom lawsuits could be brought to challenge their inadequacy (and on what grounds) — all decisions that could make the requirement either ineffective or highly unreasonable.

27. *HEW News,* 25 September 1978.

28. Steven Kelman, *Regulating America, Regulating Sweden: A Comparative Study of Occupational Safety and Health Regulations* (Cambridge: MIT Press, 1981), pp. 199-203.

29. Les Boden and David Wegman, "Increasing OSHA's Clout: Sixty Million New Inpectors," *Working Papers for a New Society,* May/June 1978. They argue that "the basic reason for OSHA's ineffectiveness . . . is its excessive reliance on enforcement of health and safety standards." Instead, "by educating and training

workers, and by increasing their responsibilities for and control over workplace hazards, OSHA can significantly improve its effectiveness."

30. See Laurence P. Feldman, "New Legislation and the Prospects for Warranty Reform," 40 *Journal of Marketing* 41, 44 (1976).

31. Goss v. Lopez, 41a U.S. 565 (1975). See generally David L. Kirp, "Proceduralism and Bureaucracy: Due Process in the School Setting," *Stanford Law Review* 28 (1976), p. 864. The Supreme Court further increased the leverage of students (and their parents) in Wood v. Strickland, 420 U.S. 308 (1975), which held that school board members (and by implication school officials) are liable in money damages for denying students "unquestioned constitutional rights."

32. The consent decree in Pennsylvania Association for Retarded Children (PARC) v. Commonwealth of Pennsylvania, for example, has led to an elaborate structure of dispute resolution for parents who believe their children were wrongly labeled as retarded or were deprived of "appropriate" educational placement. At the first level there are administrative hearings with an impartial hearing officer, decisions based exclusively on evidence introduced into the record, and so on. At the second level there are appellate reviews of hearing outcomes, intended to ensure that due process is observed at the lower level and to promote a certain uniformity of outcomes in factually similar cases through adherence to precedent. See, generally, David L. Kirp et al., "Legal Reform of Special Education," 62 *California Law Review* 40 (1974).

33. Ruth W. Woodling, "Auto Repair Regulation: An Analysis," Institute of Government, University of Georgia, February 1976, pp. 14-15. The Michigan approach of permitting noncertified mechanics to remain in the market neatly avoids many of the cartelization problems implicit in the usual licensing approach, wherein nonlicensed personnel are prohibited from furnishing services altogether. On improving the quality of auto repair generally, without detailed direct regulation, see Eugene Bardach, "Where to Get a Good Fix," *Policy Analysis,* Spring 1977.

34. Assembly Bill 3619 (Duffy Bill; 1977).

35. Assembly Bill 1426 (1978). There are conflicting reports on whether turnover has in fact decreased.

36. Dick Kirschten, "Paperwork is Having a Big Impact on Environmental Statements," *National Journal,* 16 July 1977, p. 1119. See also Bernard Frieden, *The Environmental Protection Hustle* (Cambridge: MIT Press, 1979).

37. Burt Schorr et al., "Relaxing Rules: Federal Agencies Ease, Lift Some Regulations That Burden Business," *Wall Street Journal,* 4 September 1979, p. 1.

38. We probably violated our university's regulations by interviewing regulatory officials and businessmen for this study without first filing a protocol with the campus human subjects committee and without getting signed "informed consent" forms from our respondents. The committee, had we filed, presumably would have approved our proposal and not required any forms, recognizing that the kinds of people we interview are quite accustomed and quite able to protect themselves both before consenting to be interviewed and in answering any question. But we were happy to avoid the considerable delay, annoyance, and paperwork (remember, paperwork almost always involves clerical expense) involved in even submitting a protocol. We were able to do so because, unlike most professorial projects, our financing for this research was not governmental and was not administered through the university.

39. Robert Moran, "Employer Protection Against OSHA Inspections," *Foundry Management and Technology,* April 1979, p. 112. A federal judge noted that this creates disincentives for highly specific company safety programs. Cape and Vineyard Div. of New Bedford Gas Co., v. OSHRC, 512 F. 2d 1148, 1154 (1st Cir. 1975).

40. Eugene Lambert, "Dancing with the Gorilla," *Food, Drug and Cosmetics Law Journal,* July 1975.

41. *HEW News,* 25 September 1978. FDA Commissioner Kennedy insisted, "All pharmaceutical firms must meet identical standards for quality control."

42. Sally K. Fairfax, "A Disaster in the Environmental Movement," *Science,* 17 February 1978, p. 746.

43. Eugene Bardach and Lucian Pugliaresi, "The Environmental-Impact Statement vs. the Real World," *The Public Interest,* Fall 1977. The human subjects protection machinery is so overextended and unreasonable that it would not be hard to propose many ways to make it more reasonable and more effective. The human subjects protection committee of the Berkeley campus of the University of California in fact came up with one such proposal in 1975. It was turned down flat by representatives from HEW who wanted more, not less, formalistic surveillance by the committee. Affirmative action, on the other hand, represents a case in which reducing unreasonableness would probably lead to a reduction in "effectiveness" as well, if effectiveness is taken simply to mean "more" (minority students admitted, say, or women hired by university departments). If other interpretations of effectiveness were accepted, however, perhaps the two goals might turn out not to be in conflict.

PART III

Prospects for Regulatory Reform

11

Regulatory Reform in the Large and in the Small

DAVID HARRISON, Jr.
PAUL R. PORTNEY

The Reagan Administration is clearly proceeding as if it has a mandate to make major changes in U.S. economic policy. This is attested to by the substantial cuts the administration has proposed and won in both federal taxes and spending. At the same time it was proposing these radical changes in fiscal policy, the Reagan Administration also instituted less radical but nevertheless potentially significant changes in another determinant of economic activity — regulatory policy.[1] The most visible of these latter changes were the creation of a President's Task Force on Regulatory Relief, to be chaired by Vice President Bush, and the issuance of Executive Order 12291 concerning federal regulation.[2]

President Reagan's Executive Order 12291, which revoked President Carter's Executive Order 12044, is noteworthy in the requirements it imposes on the federal regulatory agencies. Specifically, in Section 2, it requires that, to the extent permitted by law:

> (b) Regulatory action shall not be undertaken unless the potential benefits to society outweigh the potential costs to society; (c) Regulatory objectives shall be chosen to maximize net benefits to society; (d) Among alternative approaches to any given regulatory objective, the alternative involving the least net cost to society shall be chosen; and (e) Agencies shall set regulatory priorities with the aim of maximizing the aggregate net benefits to society, taking into

> account the particular industries affected by regulations, the condition of the national economy, and other regulatory actions contemplated for the future.[3]

Indeed, these requirements would appear to be bliss for any literal-minded cost benefit analyst interested in federal regulation.

In addition to placing these requirements on the federal regulatory agencies, the Executive Order implicitly imposes responsibilities on the President's Task Force and on the Office of Information and Regulatory Affairs (OIRA) within the Office of Management and Budget (OMB). A reading of E.O. 12291 suggests that these responsibilities will include, but will not be limited to:

- ascertaining whether each agency has correctly identified "major" rules (those imposing an annual cost on the economy of $100 million or more, or ones that result in major increases in prices for consumers, individual industries, federal, state, or local government agencies, or geographic regions);
- reviewing all preliminary Regulatory Impact Analyses (RIAs) prior to agencies' issuance of notices of proposed rule-making, and all final RIAs prior to issuance of final rules (this includes estimation of benefits and costs — both quantifiable and nonquantifiable — as well as identification of alternative approaches to those taken by the agencies);
- postponing any proposed or final rule makings if the preliminary or final RIAs are inadequate;
- reviewing RIAs that agencies are required to prepare on the *existing* regulations that agencies must designate for review;
- determining whether a proposed regulation is consistent with congressional intent and within legal authority;
- reviewing the factual record that the agency must submit with a proposed rule to ensure its accuracy;
- monitoring the regulatory agendas the agencies submit to determine whether all major rules are included;
- preparing standards to which RIAs must conform and developing cost and benefit estimation methodology;
- identifying regulatory overlap or duplication; and
- monitoring compliance with the requirements of E.O. 12291.

This is an ambitious list of responsibilities, to say the least. It is also vaguely familiar. Although the duties of President Carter's interagency Regulatory Analysis Review Group (RARG) were not as sweeping as those listed above, that group was assigned many of these reponsibilities. As George Eads has recently pointed out,[4] RARG confined itself to reviewing between 10 and 15 major rule makings per year, never intending to give thorough scrutiny to all the major rules, much less the minor ones, coming out of the regulatory agencies. This selectivity on the part of RARG was a direct result of the relatively limited resources available to regulatory oversight in the Carter Administration. Basically, RARG was staffed with several people from the Council of Economic Advisers, perhaps 20 analysts from the now-defunct Council on Wage and Price Stability (COWPS), and a handful of people from other offices of the White House and executive branch.

If OMB — through OIRA — is now to subject *all* existing and proposed rules to scrutiny and, at the same time, discharge the other responsibilities it is given under E.O. 12291, it will have to be given considerably more resources than those assigned to regulatory oversight in previous administrations. Yet it is clear that these resources are not forthcoming. In fact, the personnel available for regulatory analysis and oversight in the new administration are virtually the same as those available under the Carter regime. They have been partially consolidated under one roof at OMB, and this may help somwhat, but, at full strength, OIRA will have but 90 slots, many of which will be filled by people monitoring paperwork burdens and reporting requirements. Even if all 90 worked around the clock reviewing preliminary and final RIAs and performing the other functions E.O. 12291 entrusts to them, it is hard to see how they could be a match for the federal regulatory establishment. The Environmental Protection Agency (EPA) alone has approximately 11,000 employees and a yearly operating budget in excess of $1 billion: it issues hundreds of regulations each year, many if not most of which are the result of congressional directive rather than agency initiative. When one considers the other social regulatory agencies — the Occupational Safety and Health Administration (OSHA) and the National Highway Transportation and Safety Administration (NHTSA), for instance — as well as the independent regulatory agencies — which include the Interstate Commerce Commission, the Federal Communications Commission, and others — it quickly becomes clear that neither OIRA nor any other comparably sized body could do all that is required by E.O. 12291. Not only are the office's physical and human capital limited, so too is its political capital. That is, it simply cannot afford to "go to the mat" on each and every regulatory issue that comes before it.

Another factor will complicate the regulatory oversight efforts of the administration — the presence of other actors on the stage of regulatory reform. For at the same time that E.O. 12291 puts in place certain administrative reforms, the Senate has before it a bill (S. 1080), currently cosponsored by 80 members, that would make a number of significant changes in the Administrative Procedure Act governing the regulatory process. While certain features of the bill would codify those portions of E.O. 12291 dealing with benefit-cost analysis, other features would give the administration other tools that might be used to reform regulation. Included among these is a provision that would enlarge the scope of judicial oversight of federal regulation.

In addition, of course, the administration also has the opportunity to make changes in the laws that authorize and empower agencies to issue regulations. For example, the Clean Air Act is up for reauthorization this year,[5] and other important environmental, safety, and health statutes will likewise require reauthorization over the next several years. These reauthorizations provide a convenient opportunity for proposal of fundamental changes in the enabling statutes, changes that can limit or expand the kinds of activities that can be regulated as well as alter the form that regulation can take. Thus this avenue offers regulatory reform opportunities to this or any other administration.

In other words, those wishing to reform regulation in the Reagan Administration will be forced to do what those before them have done — allocate scarce resources among competing ends. Not only must they deploy physical and political capital in pursuit of regulatory oversight, but they must also determine how much time and effort to devote to other kinds of regulatory reforms. These can include changes in the enabling statutes under which regulations are written as well as more fundamental changes in the process by which regulations are prepared, overseen, and reviewed by both the legislative and judicial branches of government. The selection of approaches to regulatory reform will be dictated by three considerations: what each kind of reform can expect to accomplish, what objectives the reformers have in mind, and the cost of pursuing each of these approaches.

Our purpose in this chapter is to bring some order to the discussion of regulatory reform. This we attempt to do in three ways. In the first section we identify a number of recent or proposed changes in the way social regulation is carried out in the United States. More importantly, we place each of these proposals in one of three categories, depending on whether the proposal would: (1) alter the process by which a regulation is prepared, promulgated, and enforced; (2) change the substance of the enabling statute or the way it is interpreted; or (3) affect in a major and structural way the focus of control over regulation. Accordingly, we refer to the constituents of these three generic categories as process, substantive or structural reforms.

There are two difficulties with this approach. First, certain proposals may be intended to address more than one aspect of the regulatory system — in such cases, our "filing system" may provoke disagreement. Second, there will be considerable intragroup variation; that is, not all process reforms will be alike. This will make it difficult to generalize about the strengths and weaknesses of the generic categories. Nevertheless, the advantages of our classificatory approach outweigh its limitations.

In the second section of the chapter, we identify the criteria most often used to evaluate reforms. Typically, these criteria are revealed by individuals or groups when they say, "How can you favor *that* proposed reform? It wouldn't accomplish X." The criteria we identify are the Xs that turn up in such discussions. Here, too, there are limitations to our approach. For example, we do not pretend to be exhaustive in our identification of criteria. However, we do feel that we have identified the rationales behind most currently proposed reforms.

In the third section, we discuss each of the generic kinds of reform proposals in light of the identified criteria. In essence, we attempt to determine which kinds of proposals will accomplish which ends. Our purpose here is prescriptive as well as descriptive: Given one's primary evaluative criteria, we suggest which kinds of reforms one ought to embrace and which kinds are unlikely to satisfy such goals. A brief final section draws some inferences about regulatory reform strategy in the Reagan Administration.

Regulatory Reforms

The list of regulatory reforms considered here is far from exhaustive. Proposals on which there is substantial agreement are not included. For example, virtually everyone would favor EPA's recent efforts to consolidate the permit process ("one-stop shopping") and thereby shorten delays. Similarly, OSHA's attempt over the last several years to concentrate on serious health hazards (in lieu of regulating toilet seats) appears to enjoy nearly unanimous support. The focus here is on important reform proposals on which there is substantial disagreement.

Process Reforms

Of the regulatory reform proposals to be discussed here, almost all of those that have actually been put into effect are what we refer to as process reforms. That is, they have changed in some way the process by which regulation is proposed, reviewed, made final, and eventually enforced. The success rate of adoption of process reforms may be due to their appearance — they seem to be the simplest and the most innocuous. As we will later point out, however, process reforms do not necessarily command widespread support.

We have already discussed what are probably the most well-known process reforms — those arising out of E.O. 12044 in the Carter Administration and E.O. 12291 in the Reagan Administration. Both add important steps to the process agencies must follow in promulgating rules, steps having to do with the consideration of alternatives in pursuit of goals and the evaluation of costs and benefits associated with those alternatives. In addition, the process was modified in the Carter Administration to include a new actor (the Regulatory Council), whose primary purpose was the preparation of a calendar of upcoming regulations (a function to be performed by OIRA in the Reagan Administration).

The intent behind both of these Executive Orders is clear. By subjecting the proposed rules (and, in the case of E.O. 12291, certain existing rules) of agencies to greater internal analysis and outside review, it was felt that these agencies would take extra care in designing rules. Thus social goals might be accomplished in less burdensome ways, conflicting rules and regulations might be eliminated, and questionable scientific data might be given shorter shrift in rule making.

Process changes embody more than enhanced oversight, however. They also include modifications designed to ensure that certain topics receive special attention in rule making. Taking a cue from the existing requirement for environmental impact statements, a number of proposed reforms have called for the creation of other types of impact statements to accompany new regulations. Specifically, various proposals have called for the indentification of the impacts of new regulations on small business, industry competition in general, urban areas, and prime agricultural farmland. Each of these proposals would have regulatory agencies prepare special analyses as part of the rule-making process. For example, by forcing explicit consideration of urban impacts — in addition to overall economic impacts — one proposal attempts to ensure the selection of the regulatory alternative that is least disruptive to urban areas (however that might be divined). These proposed or recently enacted reforms share a common characteristic: They add another "hoop" to the sequence that agencies must now pass through as they move from proposed to final regulations.

Still another process reform is a requirement for enhanced public participation in rule making. This participation most often takes place during the public comment period. In theory, of course, a final rule reflects not only the data and analysis the promulgating agency developed to support the proposed rule, it also reflects the comments that the affected industry, environmental groups, and others submitted during the comment period. These comments may be submitted by mail or they may be delivered at public meetings the agency may hold to solicit opinions on the proposed rule. In fact, several regulatory agencies currently cover the expenses of certain individuals or groups who wish to comment on proposed rules but who may not have the financial wherewithal to do so.

The process reforms identified here may seem unremarkable, hardly the stuff of which violent disagreement is made. Can these really be the regulatory reforms everyone seems to be arguing about? Certain of these process reforms indeed have been and will continue to be the subject of heated debate. For example, the creation of the Regulatory Analysis Review Group was bitterly resisted and condemned by environmental and public interest groups. Its creation was seen as another attempt to water down regulations on their way to promulgation; environmentalists also saw RARG as a conduit for industry's point of view on the proposed regulation even after the public comment period was over. Some members of Congress have opposed White House oversight and other process reforms not necessarily because they opposed the objectives of the reforms, but because they opposed the possible loss of congressional control over regulatory agencies. These same objections are sure to be raised against the oversight mechanism established in E.O. 12291. In fact, since OMB involvement will take place less informally and off the record, there will no doubt be even louder cries of sub rosa involvement by business in the rule-making process and greater concern that congressional prerogatives are being compromised.

Federal funding of public interveners in the regulatory process has also drawn considerable fire, in this case from business and industry representatives. Why, they have asked, should tax dollars be used to help advance the causes of public interest groups opposing industry positions? This use of tax dollars puts industry in the position of financing not only their own efforts to influence regulations as they are developed, but also the efforts of their "opponents."

In short, even apparently unexceptional process forms can strengthen — or appear to strengthen — the hand of one or another participant in the regulatory process. Because of this possibility, these reforms will continue to be opposed by those groups that feel threatened with diminution of power.

Substantive Reforms

Substantive reforms of regulations are those that alter the mandate of enabling legislation under which regulations are written. We focus here on two related substantive reforms that economists have advocated for some time — the introduction of benefit-cost principles in standard setting where it is now forbidden or not required, and the use of decentralized economic incentive schemes rather than command-and-control regulations. The former is concerned with the choice of goals in social regulation; the latter addresses the question of how these goals are met.

Perhaps the most well-known prohibitions on the balancing of benefits and costs in social regulation are the Delaney clause in the Federal Food, Drug, and Cosmetic Act (where the prohibition is explicit) and Section 109 of the Clean Air Act, which authorizes EPA to establish national ambient air quality standards for certain air pollutants. Under the Delaney clause, "no additive shall be deemed safe [and hence permitted] if it is found to induce cancer when ingested by man or animal. This provision raises serious difficulties when the additive may prevent deaths from other health-related problems (as saccharin is alleged to do). Thus it has been proposed on several occasions that the Delaney clause be stricken from the act and replaced with language encouraging balance of benefits and costs.

Although the Clean Air Act is less clear in prohibiting trade-offs between health benefits and economic or other considerations, the courts have not been at all ambiguous in rendering such interpretations. In its recent decision on EPAs ambient standard for lead,[6] the District of Columbia Circuit Court of Appeals made it clear that such balancing is not permitted under the Clean Air Act and the Supreme Court recently let stand that decision. Substantive proposals have been advanced to amend the Clean Air Act to require that economic considerations be taken into account in standard setting.

Substantive reform may be required to obtain cost-benefit comparisons even where existing statutes appear to allow for the inclusion of economic factors. Agencies often consider short-term economic impacts — price increases, plant closures, or layoffs — rather than the long-run resource costs emphasized by economists. For example, the 1977 Amendments to the Clean Water Act require EPA to set effluent guidelines for toxic substances discharged into waterways based on the "best available technology economically achievable" (BAT), a criterion EPA has interpreted as "what the industry can afford." This is different than requiring a cost-benefit or cost-effectiveness comparison, since an industry's ability to afford large pollution expenditures does not guarantee that benefits are commensurate with costs.

Proposals such as those to amend the food and drug and clean air laws would be even more controversial were it not for one thing: benefit-cost comparisons are *required* in the preparation of regulations under other enabling legislation, the most notable example being the Consumer Product Safety Act. Thus substantive reforms that would extend such balancing to all regulatory statutes can hardly be thought of as revolutionary, even when they are strongly opposed.

Substantive reforms can deal with means as well as ends. Decentralized economic incentive schemes — such as effluent charges or marketable permits — are seen by economists as the logical extension of the economic approach to rule making. The distinguishing characteristic of each of the decentralized substantive reforms is the particular decision it would decentralize. For instance, a pure system of effluent charges (or a system of fully marketable pollution rights) would leave the desired level of pollution up to the individual discharger. Polluters could discharge all they wanted so long as they are willing to pay the per-unit charge or secure the appropriate number of discharge permits. Substantive reforms at this level of decentralization have not been undertaken in the United States to date.

A lesser kind of decentralization has taken place, namely, certain regulatees have been given the flexibility to meet predetermined standards (for occupational safety, pollutant discharges, and so on) in whatever way they see fit. Although this is a less sweeping reform than adopting charges or marketable permits, it is a step in the direction of decentralization. EPA's "bubble policy" is such a substantive change. It allows a firm to alter the origin of pollutants at a conglomeration of individual sources so long as the environmental performance of all sources taken together is at least as good as it would be if each source were regulated separately. Similarly, proposals to allow auto companies to average mileage improvements or emissions reductions across product lines are designed to accomplish the same end — to achieve some overall energy or environmental goal while leaving at least some of the means up to individual economic actors.

Substantive changes can take other shapes, of course. For example, former EPA Administrator Douglas Costle has suggested another kind of change in the Clean Air Act. Rather than expand the role of economic and other analysis, he would reduce it by replacing the national air quality standards with a set of technology-based discharge standards that would presumably apply to all sources. The logic behind such a proposal is quite straightforward: Not only would such discharge standards eliminate the favorable treatment existing sources receive relative to new sources; this approach would also eliminate the need for states and the EPA to determine the contribution of individual sources of pollution to air quality problems in each control region. Hence, technology-based standards are seen as simplifying air quality management while at the same time strengthening it and making it more uniform.

Our discussion of substantive reforms, however, does not include such proposals as Costle's. There is a radical difference between the greater flexibility in pollution control that economic incentives would permit and the loss of flexibility that technology-based standards would necessitate. Lumping them together in the same generic category would make it impossible to generalize about the strengths and weaknesses of what we call substantive reform. Therefore, we have restricted this category to proposals that would introduce benefit-cost analysis or cost-effectiveness analysis into standard setting and implementation, or that would replace command-and-control regulation with economic incentive schemes.

Structural Reforms

Structural reforms can be thought of as the heavy artillery in the deregulatory battle. We focus on three major structural changes. Their common characteristic is an intention to change the ultimate locus of control of the regulatory process; they can be distinguished from one another according to which branch of government would be given enhanced power at the expense of the regulatory agencies.

The Bumpers Amendment (after Senator Dale Bumpers of Arkansas) would shift the locus of power in regulation to the judicial branch. This shift would be accomplished by directing courts to make no initial presumption of validity of the facts underlying federal regulations that are challenged in suits before the courts. (Currently, courts presume such validity and confine their decisions to questions of interpretations of enabling statutes and questions of procedural regularity.) If judicial review is expanded, courts will clearly assume some of the authority heretofore vested in the regulatory agencies.

Another structural reform, the congressional or legislative veto, would weaken the authority of regulatory agencies and enhance the power of the legislative branch. Under this proposal all regulations emanating from agencies would be subject to veto by one or both houses of Congress during some specified period following issuance of a final regulation. In fact, while blanket legislative veto authority was proposed in several bills during the 96th Congress, certain regulations are already subject to such a restriction. For example, all final EPA pesticide regulations can be overturned within 60 days of issuance, as can the ruling of the Federal Trade Commission.

Still another structural reform about which much has been heard, the regulatory budget, could shift power away from regulatory agencies to the executive branch. Under a regulatory budget, some administrative authority — perhaps the Office of Management and Budget — would establish limits on the new compliance costs that regulatory agencies could impose on the private and public sectors each year.[7] This cap, or limit, would serve the same purpose now served by the current federal expenditure budget. That is, it would force regulatory agencies to operate not only within their own means, but also within the means of those regulatees whose money they now can effectively spend without limit.

Whichever branch of government established the compliance-cost limitations (or budgets) would, of course, capture some of the power now held by regulators. This might be the executive branch, as suggested above, or it might be Congress, since it ultimately authorizes and appropriates funds for the direct expenditure budget. In either event, while a regulatory budget would change certain of the rules of the game, in other respects it would not usurp as much power as would either judicial or legislative review of all regulation. This is because once a regulatory agency's compliance-cost budget was established, the agency would presumably be free to issue any new regulations it wished so long as it stayed within its budget constraint. Unless coupled with some sort of review procedure, the regulatory budget would allow regulatory agencies the same flexibility they enjoy now, save for the absolute limit. It is noteworthy that President Reagan's Executive Order 12291 is not silent on the subject of the regulatory budget. Section 6(a)(6) of that order indicates that one of the reasons that OMB should develop procedures for agencies to follow in estimating benefits and costs is "for the purpose of compiling a regulatory budget."[8]

Criteria for Judging Reforms

Three criteria used to evaluate regulatory reform proposals stand out in the public discussion of reform: *less* regulation, *more certainty* in regulation, and *more efficient* regulation.

First, there can be little doubt that many advocates of regulatory reform, mainly those in the business community, have one thing in mind — less regulation. These individuals do not necessarily act out of pure self-interest (even though their interest would be well served by a rollback of regulations). Nor do they necessarily object to all regulation. They may believe fervently in regulation where it is justified by its benefits, but believe at the same time that evidence of such benefits does not support the current extent of regulation. Whatever their reasons, their goal in regulatory reform is a reduction, and perhaps a substantial one, in the amount of regulation.

Even those who would not take great issue with the extent of regulation might object to its capriciousness and delay. That is, they may desire some assurance that standards governing effluent discharges, occupational exposures, or vehicle mileage requirements, for instance, will be set on some consistent basis and without interminable delays. In other words, another important criterion against which proposed reforms are judged is that of more certainty in regulation. Reform proposals that provide a stable milieu for individual, governmental, and business decision making will of course rate well against this criterion. Those proposals that have the opposite effect will rate poorly.

When economists discuss regulatory reform, they generally have in mind another criterion. Among such individuals, more efficient regulation is often the major goal of regulatory reform. Reform proposals will be favored according to this criterion if they increase the likelihood that the social benefits associated with particular regulations will exceed the costs, or if they reduce the costs of meeting some predetermined standard, where benefits and costs are measured according to the precepts of modern welfare economics. Proposed reforms that have the opposite effects, or that are not at all concerned with costs and benefits, will do poorly when viewed from the standpoint of more efficient regulation.

There is another criterion one might use to evaluate regulatory reform proposals — that of *equity,* or *fairness*. No criterion is as open to differing interpretations as this one, however. For example, one form of equity with which observers are concerned is geographical. That is, they might ask whether the proposed reform would do anything to address the perceived geographical inequity of current regulations (which may discriminate in favor of middle-western or western coal, or discriminate against new sources likely to be located in the West or Southwest to the benefit of older, eastern or middle-western sources).[9]

Equity can take other forms, as well. Regulation and its reforms can be judged according to principles of horizontal equity (how similar is the treatment of identically situated regulatees?); vertical equity (are firms, individuals, or communities that are in a position to spend more on regulation required to do so?); transitional equity (are regulatees on whom the rules are suddenly changed given some consideration?); and procedural equity (is everybody given a fair shot in the process by which regulations are prepared, discussed, and made final?).

We fully recognize the importance of equity (or distributional considerations) as a criterion by which policy changes are judged, and both of us have addressed these issues elsewhere.[10] Equity considerations are as relevant for regulatory reform proposals as they are for proposed changes in tax or expenditure programs. Nevertheless, for several reasons we do *not* include them among the criteria we use to judge our generic reform proposals. First, as indicated, there are many notions of equity — a proposal that might reduce geographic disparities might at the same time be seen as horizontally inequitable. Moreover, it would be difficult to pinpoint the effects of certain reform proposals even if one specific interpretation of equity were used. For example, the imposition of effluent charges (a substantive reform) may reduce, leave unchanged, or exacerbate an unequal distribution of income, depending on the pattern of industrial activity and the pattern of consumer preferences. Thus it would be difficult to evaluate how certain kinds of reforms would do when measured against this metric. For these reasons, we limit our discussion to an evaluation of each category of reform proposals against the criteria of less regulation, more certainty in regulation, and more efficient regulation.

The Regulatory Reform Match-Up

In this section we discuss the potential of each of the major reform categories. Each of the three reform categories is evaluated in terms of its performance on each of the three criteria. This discussion provides the data for our concluding remarks.

Process Reform

The process reforms we have discussed are designed to improve regulation by providing openness and greater analysis. The premise is that decisions will be better if all interested parties are involved and if the regulatory agency is held to a high standard of analysis. How likely are these changes to be successful as measured by our criteria?

Less Regulation

Enhanced oversight such as that mandated in Executive Orders 12044 and 12291 can have an effect on the number of regulations issued and the costs of complying with them. This is so for several reasons. First, a requirement for more regulatory analysis changes the "price" to an agency of issuing a rule — additional analysis invariably requires more staff and/or contract resources. Thus, fewer rules can be issued unless the agency's budget for standards development is increased. Second, review of regulatory impact analyses will take time. If OIRA in OMB decides that an analysis must be redone, that will add both time and expense to the issuance of a regulation. In the Ford and Carter administrations this price effect was small. It remains to be seen whether the Reagan Administration's changes will raise the price of regulation to the extent that it materially reduces the flow of new rules.

The oversight process — such as the RARG, OIRA, or other White House review procedures — could also reduce the number of regulations or reduce overall cost by improving cost-effectiveness. But this effect of oversight is limited.[11] For one thing, because of physical limitations, comprehensive reviews can only be performed for a small percentage of regulations. Although agencies were required under Carters Executive Order 12044 to prepare a regulatory analysis for any regulation imposing annual costs of more than $100 million, RARG reviewed fewer than 20 regulations per year. While COWPS commented on other major regulations, it was simply not possible to analyze and follow up all major regulations. This will no doubt also be true of the new OMB regulatory review process, which is not much more than an amalgam of preexisting COWPS and OMB review personnel.

An even more important constraint, however, is that oversight is confined to very limited issues because many of the statutes on which the regulations are based provide little support for cost-effectiveness tests. Air quality regulations provide a good example of these constraints. In the Carter Administration RARG reviewed two proposed revisions of national ambient air quality standards — the ozone standard in February 1978, and the carbon monoxide standard in November 1980. Both reviews criticized the exclusion of cost considerations from the standard-setting process. The change in the ozone standard from 10 ppm in the proposal to 12 ppm in the final rule was regarded by some commentators as an example of White House weakening of environmental standards. But EPA officials denied that cost-benefit considerations played a role in the decision. Since EPA's mandate is to set standards at levels which, "allowing for an adequate margin of safety, are requisite to public health" — rather than to balance the costs and benefits of control — EPA officials have a plausible case.

Automotive emissions standards provide another example of the inherent limitations of review procedures of process requirements. The Clean Air Act Amendments of 1970 required that automotive emissions be reduced by 90 percent from precontrol levels. While there is some leeway in determining the baseline, test procedures, and timing of these requirements, there is no choice but to live with the standards and the costs they entail regardless of benefit-cost considerations. The same general limitations apply to the effluent limitations EPA is to impose on industrial water polluters. The 1977 Amendments to the Clean Water Act require EPA to establish standards for toxic water pollutants based on the best available technology economically achievable (BAT). The amendments also specify what industries are to be subject to BAT controls and what substances are to be controlled. While it may be possible to reduce costs to industry by reviewing specific effluent guidelines, the bulk of the costs of this program are probably set once the substances and industries are listed.

More Certainty in Regulation

Increasing the number of actors involved and the number of issues to be addressed in the regulatory process virtually guarantees that process reforms will decrease rather than increase the certainty of business about their regulatory obligations. For example, much of the criticism from industry of the environmental impact statement (EIS) requirement centered on the uncertainty it created for project approval. The statements tended to be large, technical documents, the adequacy and scientific accuracy of which became the subjects of court battles. Uncertainty was also increased by a lengthy and somewhat inconclusive court debate on whether the National Environmental Policy Act imposed an obligation on government agencies to assign more weight to environmental objectives in decision making, or whether the statute simply required full disclosure.[12] The Council on Environmental Quality recently modified the EIS requirements to reduce the possibility of unwarranted delays and to increase their usefulness. Other intra-agency process reforms — public participation, urban impact, and regulatory analysis — have been discussed less than the EIS requirement, but there seems little doubt that to the extent they become a part of agency procedures, they add to delays and uncertainties in promulgating regulations.

Executive branch oversight and review add to uncertainty in two ways. First, uncertainty is created simply by adding more options to the regulatory decision, options that typically must be specified in more detail and evaluated by the agency. For example, the 1980 RARG review of NHTSA's regulations on fuel efficiency standards for light-duty trucks recommended that NHTSA consider a revised method of calculating fleet-average fuel economy that would permit companies to achieve more cost-effective improvement of their entire fleets. NHTSA reopened the rule making to permit comments on the RARG proposal. This delayed the rule making and created additional uncertainty, since industry could not know whether NHTSA would adopt one of its original alternatives or the alternative proposed by RARG.

Executive branch oversight can also add to uncertainty if the agency actually adopts certain kinds of recommendations. For instance, more cost-effective alternatives typically require the agency and the regulatee to use discretion rather than follow more rigid — but potentially more wasteful — procedures. This is illustrated by EPA's draft policy on airborne carcinogens, which required the agency to identify substances that have a high probability of being carcinogenic and to regulate certain sources of those substances to levels corresponding to the "best available technology" — a phrase whose general meaning has been revealed in past EPA rules. The RARG review suggested that the agency use cost-benefit principles to establish emissions limitations — principles that would almost certainly have required greater analysis and judgment. Businesses and other regulatees that place a high weight on certainty may well prefer the EPA draft approach, which, though it may involve greater control expenditures, may provide an earlier estimate of what is required of them.

More Efficient Regulation

Some process reforms have efficiency as their major objective. While often justified as anti-inflationary or productivity-enhancing, executive branch reviews are not intended simply to reduce regulatory costs, but rather to increase the efficiency and cost-effectiveness of regulations. In some cases, these reviews may even recommend modifications that might increase the cost of complying with a regulation. For example, the RARG review of EPA's hazardous waste regulations made the point that the exclusion of some small firms from safe disposal requirements may be unwarranted if these firms produce very toxic substances. Therefore to the extent they are successful (and this is difficult to determine), certain process reforms do rank highly in terms of economic efficiency.

It is interesting to speculate on the circumstances under which process reforms are likely to be most effective. They are likely to have the greatest impact when a single decision "settles something." For example, EPA's setting a single national ambient air quality standard or automoblile emissions standard generally involves a single number (although there are admittedly complications over averaging, test procedures, and the like that complicate even these cases). Thus White House review can focus on the specific requirement. Any change in the standard that increases calculated net benefits is, ipso facto, an efficiency improvement. Other regulatory issues are much less specific and difficult to monitor. Consider the setting of air pollution standards for existing sources in nonattainment (dirty) areas. The Clean Air Act requires that existing sources in such areas install "reasonably available control technology" (RACT) as determined by the states. Those concerned about efficiency would prefer that EPA review the state-imposed RACT standards to ensure their flexibility to the costs and benefits of control. But how would one monitor whether EPA was performing the necessary reviews? Presumably one would have to follow the agency's individual decisions, an impossible task given the number of standards, states, and sources.

Other process reforms seem designed to add nonefficiency criteria to the decision process and thus may actually decrease the efficiency of regulation. Requirements for assessing environmental and urban impacts and for full public participation may generate decisions based on impacts on particular groups rather than on overall costs and benefits. Distributional considerations need not necessarily conflict with efficiency, however. Attention to detailed effects may in fact point the way to efficiency-enhancing modifications. For example, one of us has argued for some time for a "two-car strategy" for automotive emissions control (stricter controls in dirty areas), a strategy whose efficiency benefits are particularly apparent when one estimates the differential benefits and costs of uniform standards on different geographic and income groups.[13] The EIS requirement may also alert agencies to environmental costs (or benefits) whose incorporation in decisions will improve efficiency properly defined.

Substantive Reform

Changing statutes to permit cost-benefit comparisons or the expanded use of economic incentives is the most direct way to introduce economic principles into regulation. How do such substantive proposals stack up against our evaluative criteria?

Less Regulation

Requiring cost-benefit comparisons in standard setting would almost certainly result in less regulation than we now have. For one thing, since the benefits of control are often difficult to identify, much less quantify, it would be difficult to prove that benefits exceed cost — this would probably result in some reduction in regulation. In addition, standards that are currently set without regard to cost could only be weakened when cost-benefit comparisons are permitted. Consider the ambient air quality standards that EPA has established for major pollutants. As mentioned, the standards are now set to protect the public health with an adequate margin of safety, which EPA has interpreted as requiring the agency to identify that threshold concentration below which there are no adverse health effects. Modifying the mandate to require a balancing of costs and benefits would result in weaker ambient standards, which in turn would result in less stringent regulations imposed by the states in their state implementation plans (SIPs).

This argument is less clear in the case of standards that are set on affordability criteria, such as the water effluent guidelines. If agencies now avoid setting costly standards for industries that cannot afford them — which implies that the cost and demand conditions in the industry do not allow the firms to pass the added costs on to consumers — changing to a cost-benefit test would generate more stringent regulations for some and more lenient standards for others. Nevertheless, we suspect that on balance the cost-benefit approach would lead to fewer and less stringent regulations.

What about the substitution of economic incentives for more traditional forms of regulation? At first glance, one might be tempted to say that it will do away with regulation altogether, and it will if one takes a narrow enough view of regulation. At a deeper level, however, the effect is less clear. Effluent charges or marketable permits can reduce regulatory compliance costs by allowing firms the option of eschewing pollution control in favor of paying for the right to pollute. Such a system is most likely to reduce the overall financial burden on a firm (compliance costs plus payments to pollute) when the firm is not required to pay the charge or purchase permits for the pollution that previously was "free" under the more conventional regulatory approach of setting discharge standards. In other words, under such a regime the substantive reform under discussion here could be seen as reducing the amount of regulation. However, most effluent charge schemes and many marketable permit systems envision no "free" pollution whatsoever. Fees would apply to *all* emissions (rather than to some "excess" level) in the former; *all* pollution permits would be auctioned off under the latter. Hence, once a firm toted up both the cost of avoiding the fee or permit price and the payments for the pollution that remains after all economical control actions are taken, it may find that the total private cost of the incentive approach exceeds the private costs of command and control.[14] In such a case, a firm would be justified in complaining that that substantive reform led to more, not less, regulation.

More Certainty in Regulation

Substantive reforms of the sort discussed above are likely to increase the complexity of the regulator's task and thus, at least initially, decrease certainty. Consider a requirement to balance benefits and cost in standard setting. Standard setting already requires discussions with the industry, preparation of contractors' reports, intra-agency discussion of proposals, public comment, intra-agency discussion of final rules, and (sometimes) interagency debate and high-level review. For large or otherwise important regulations, the government — and indeed the agency — is not always of one mind on the proper regulation. Some of the differences and regulatory uncertainty revolve around interpretations of science, statutory mandates, or permissible flexibility. Adding judgments about the proper balancing of costs and benefits is likely to extend the debate and — according to critics — threaten to paralyze the process. Indeed, the difficulty of using judgment in reviewing regulations has led some to suggest that agencies adopt less flexible, rather than more flexible, rules. One proposal, discussed in the introduction, is to substitute for the current state-by-state, source-by-source approach a set of uniform technology-based controls on all existing air pollution sources. The major benefit of such a proposal would be to increase regulatory certainty.

Substituting economic incentive schemes for traditional regulations may, at least in the short run, create even greater uncertainty. Requiring agencies to consider costs and benefits in setting regulations, though difficult and inherently imprecise, is at least within the context of the current command-and-control approach. Giving agencies mandates to tax an offending activity or to auction off some fixed amount of it is bound to create additional confusion. Setting a "correct" price is far from straightforward, particularly since the price would have to vary, at least for emissions in different locations. Marketable permits may create even greater administrative uncertainty, since the agency would have to decide how much pollution to market, who should receive the original allocations, how to trade off emissions in various locations, and how the market should function. Moreover, even relatively simple markets take time to reach an equilibrium and adjust to changed circumstances. While such markets for pollution may eventually function quite easily, the initial experiments are bound to be awkward and markets may never provide the certainty that fixed discharge standards would.

More Efficient Regulation

Efficiency is, of course, the fundamental objective behind the two kinds of substantive reforms we suggest. To the extent that these substantive changes are adopted, therefore, efficiency will be enhanced. Such efficiency gains include obtaining maximum environmental, health, or safety benefits for given control expenditures and, over time, lowering control costs by providing incentives for technological improvements in pollution control.

These general expectations are straightforward and, we think, accepted by virtually everyone in the regulatory reform debate. What is less clear is the potential magnitude of the efficiency gains, although the gains will in general depend both upon the prereform regulatory alternative and the responses of regulated industries to changed rules. Gains will be greatest where marginal costs per unit of activity vary widely and where the command-and-control system is, in fact, rigid.[15]

Structural Reform

It is more difficult to assess structural reform proposals. There are virtually no "real-world" applications of the regulatory budget and of greatly expanded judicial and congressional oversight, thus their strengths and weaknesses cannot be tested by actual results.

Moreover, since the structural reform proposals are relatively new, their a priori characteristics have not been mulled over by a generation of scholars as in the case of effluent charges. Nevertheless, it is possible to speculate on some of their likely effects. Most of our discussion concerns the regulatory budget, the most sweeping of the proposed structural reforms.

Less Regulation

All structural reforms are likely to lead to reductions in the scope and overall size of regulation. In the case of the legislative veto and expanded judicial review, this result is unambiguous since neither of these reforms can do anything but reduce agency rule making. Under a regulatory budget, an agency could in theory be allowed a budget large enough to expand its rule making. As a practical matter, however, it too would likely be intended to constrain agency rule making.

Assessing the impact of the regulatory budget on the overall cost of regulation is difficlt, however. This is so because agencies may respond to the imposition of a regulatory budget by changing the nature of the regulations they issue. In particular, agencies whose statutory mandates are unchanged will tend to regulate in ways that avoid the budget system. For example, establishing a regulatory budget for direct-control expenditures on plant and equipment may well result in agencies prohibiting new activities or products. Since such bans do not force firms to install control equipment and hire workers to operate and maintain it, direct costs of regulation may appear small. But indirect costs — in the form of forgone consumers' surplus — may be very large. If these indirect costs were not charged against the budget, total costs might *rise* when the budget was implemented.

More Certainty in Regulation

Structural changes would invariably add to uncertainty in the short run as the overall regulatory system adjusted to the change. But there are reasons to expect that uncertainty for industry would increase in the longer term as well. For one thing, simply adding another actor to the regulatory process increases uncertainty. Consider the legislative veto. An industry would have to wait first for the regulatory process to be concluded and then for the legislature to consider a veto if the regulation were major. Of course, the Congress can already override regulations by changing statutes, and has done so in several celebrated cases (those of saccharin and interlock devices for seat belts, for example). But these are extremes. If a legislative veto were in effect with the express purpose of containing costs and avoiding improper rules, the number of regulations that would be brought up for consideration — and thus the uncertainty of the overall process — would invariably increase.

Uncertainty would also increase under the regulatory budget proposal if, as we discussed above, wide disagreements over costs bedevil efforts to actually implement a regulatory budget. Not only will there be disagreements over methodological issues — such as the choice of a discount rate, wage rates, and so forth — but there will be disagreements over the cost and effectiveness of various technological options. Moreover, agencies will have incentives to understate the cost of each regulation they propose (so they can carry out more programs within a given budget) and industries will have incentives to overstate the costs. White suggests solving the latter problem by instituting a "truth in regulatory costs" scheme that is based upon the use of noncompliance fees.[16] Since the industry would be able to avoid compliance by paying the fee, the agency would not understate the cost because it would permit regulatees to escape compliance too cheaply.

Another way of reducing uncertainty over the regulatory budget is to develop cost-measurement procedures before the budget concept is imposed. The Office of Mangagement and Budget has circulated among agencies a proposed Regulatory Cost Accounting Act, which would develop such procedures. The proposal distinguishes direct compliance cost — expenditures made to comply with regulations — from indirect costs, such as the costs of prohibiting firms from locating in certain areas or marketing certain products. Agencies would be required under the proposed act to measure direct costs using standardized rules, while they would be required to measure indirect costs only to the extent that it is "reasonable and practical to do so."

More Efficient Regulation

Whether the structural reforms increase the efficiency of regulation will depend upon whether efficiency is an important goal of the actor whose authority is enhanced — the courts in the case of enhanced judicial oversight, the Congress in the case of the legislative veto, and the agency and Congress in the case of the regulatory budget. While some legal scholars argue that the courts implicitly use efficiency as their decision criterion in common law cases,[17] the judicial perspective in interpreting statutes or administrative rules is often thought to be noneconomic. For example, Stewart argues that the courts have tended to amplify the narrow agency focus on costs and benefits to give greater weight to factors such as ecological diversity and procedural fairness.[18]

The weight that Congress gives to efficiency in regulatory matters is difficult to determine. The major instances of congressional override of regulatory actions — such as limitations on the Federal Trade Commission's investigations of the funeral industry, or overturning of the FDA's ban on saccharin — suggest that the Congress overturns regulations that either a large percentage of the public believes are uncalled for or that are directed against a well-organized group represented in most congressional districts. These motivations may or may not be consistent with the efficiency objectives of eliminating regulations whose costs are greatly disproportionate to their benefits.

Agencies' concern for efficiency is also difficult to determine. The efficiency rationale behind the regulatory budget is that, as DeMuth puts it, "agencies would measure the costs and benefits of individual regulatory proposals in order to further their own organizational interests."[19] Moreover, the agency would have to entreat a budget authority and a congressional committee for regulatory appropriation, which would involve demonstrating that their past expenditures were beneficial. While regulatory agencies may well take this approach — trying to provide the greatest environmental benefits or safety benefits from programs under their jurisdiction — one can certainly imagine other responses. An agency may, for example, focus its control on industries with little political power or on substances and activities that appear to threaten large numbers of persons.

Conclusion

Table 11.1 summarizes the likely success of each reform category as measured against the criteria discussed in this chapter. Perhaps surprisingly, the table suggests that one of the generic categories — substantive reforms — dominates the other two.[20] In no case do either process or structural reforms do better measured against a particular criterion, and substantive reforms dominate the other categories with respect to at least one criterion.

TABLE 11.1 Reforms Rated Against Three Criteria

Reform Category	*Less Regulation*	*More Certainty*	*Efficiency*
Process	maybe	no	maybe
Substantive	yes	no	yes
Structural	yes	no	maybe

Why is this surprising? Simply because to date no administration has made much effort to effect substantive changes in the statutes under which environmental, safety, and health regulations are written. For instance, during the Ford Administration, Congress passed the Resource Conservation and Recovery Act, a major piece of environmental legislation that did not contain much language that would permit benefit-cost or cost-effectiveness comparisons. Similarly, the 1977 amendments to the Clean Air and Clean Water Acts did little to expand the use of benefit-cost analysis and cost-effectiveness analysis,[21] and both sets of amendments were supported by the Carter Administration. While it is still premature to judge the Reagan Administration on this count, preliminary indications on the Clean Air Act are that this administration, too, may eschew substantive reform in favor of the process reforms typified by Executive Order 12291. Thus it appears that the two prior administrations (and perhaps the current one) may be guilty of failing to make use of the most effective route to regulatory reform, in spite of their professed commitment to that goal.

There are several respects in which we must qualify this observation. First, we wish to reemphasize our earlier warning about the difficulty of grouping reforms into broad categories. Not only do our process reform and structural reform categories embrace considerable variation, but particular kinds of process reforms, say, will vary between administrations. Consider, for instance, executive branch oversight as provided for in Executive Orders 12044 and 12291. The success of this kind of oversight depends in large part on the likelihood that the president ultimately would back the reviewers in a showdown with the regulators. We believe it fair to say that this possibility was unlikely in the Carter Administration. In fact, White has documented several instances where the opposite occurrred.[22] This made it unlikely that agencies would go further in the direction of efficiency in regulation than they wanted to go. Such a showdown may be less likely in the Reagan Administration. The appointed heads of the social regulatory agencies may not take strongly opposing positions to those of the regulatory reformers and, if they do, President Reagan may side with his oversight staff. Thus all attempts at oversight by executive order, even where the goals are apparently the same, cannot be grouped together indiscriminately. This must be taken into account when one considers our view of the potential success of process reforms.

Second, the reform categories we identify may have very different political costs attached to them. That is, in spite of the opposition to executive branch oversight, it is probably easier to accomplish than substantive reform, and probably considerably less costly than structural reform. Therefore, even if process reforms may accomplish less than substantive reforms, they may be more politically cost-effective. In other words, success per unit of political capital expended may be greater in effecting process reforms than elsewhere. This logic no doubt lay behind the push for process reform.

There is one important qualification to this point. However large the costs may be of making substantive changes in statutes, most of these costs are behind the administration once the laws are changed. Once the balancing of benefits and costs is permitted, much of the battle has been fought. To be sure, it is necessary to be vigilant and ensure that a proper balancing is taking place, but once the principle is established, it need not be reestablished time after time. The costs of oversight-type process reforms are continuing, however. Each episode raises anew questions about the legitimacy of this oversight, the lengths to which it can go, and the results it accomplishes. Thus neither this administration nor future ones should be deceived by the apparently low "front-end" costs of process reforms.

The attraction of process reforms may be waning for a third reason. Recent decisions by the Supreme Court have made it clear that the Court will not permit benefit-cost comparisons in regulatory standard setting when the statute requires another test.[23] The implication of this is clear. While regulatory agencies may be compelled via executive order to estimate and compare benefits and costs, in many instances they cannot set standards based on this balancing. This surely defeats one of the major purposes of the executive order, since there is no special virtue in making benefit-cost comparisons unless they somehow affect decision making. Therefore both the current and future administrations may be forced to work for changes in legislation — that is, substantive reforms — if they want explicit comparisons of costs and benefits. The court rulings do not appear to affect cost-effectiveness analysis.

One final note: None of the reforms we have discussed deal effectively with the problem of regulatory certainty. One can, of course, imagine changes that would meet this criterion. For example, the Congress might require that all regulations remain unchanged for a fixed period (say, ten years) to provide a stable target. Such changes may fare poorly in terms of efficiency and effectiveness, and thus not be considered reforms by most observers. But most reforms will actually increase regulatory delays and business uncertainty over the rules that must be followed. Indeed, the push for regulatory reform comes just as the current process has become more certain — major regulatory programs are being implemented and ambiguous phrases such as "best available technology economically achievable" are taking on well-established meanings. These considerations suggest that a major impediment to reform is that reform means change.

NOTES

1. For a discussion of the effects of regulation on macroeconomic activity, see Henry M. Peskin, Paul R. Portney, and Allen V. Kneese, eds., *Environmental Regulation and the U.S. Economy* (Baltimore: Johns Hopkins University Press, 1981).

2. *Federal Register,* 17 February 1981, pp. 13193-13198.

3. Ibid., pp. 13193-13194.

4. George Eads, "Harnessing Regulation: The Evolving Role of White House Oversight," *Regulation,* May/June 1981, pp. 19-26.

5. For a detailed discussion of the possibilities regarding this reauthorization, see David Harrison, Jr., and Paul R. Portney, "Making Ready for the Clean Air Act," *Regulation,* March/April 1981, pp. 24-31.

6. See Lead Industries Association, Inc. v. Environmental Protection Agency (D.C. Circuit Court, June 27, 1980).

7. See Christopher DeMuth, "Constraining Regulatory Cost — Part II: The Regulatory Budget," *Regulation,* March/April 1981, pp. 29-44.

8. *Federal Register,* 17 February 1981, p. 13196.

9. For an excellent discussion of this point, see Bruce Ackerman and William Hassler, *Clean Coal/Dirty Air* (New Haven, CT: Yale University Press, 1981).

10. See David Harrison, Jr., *Who Pays for Clean Air: The Cost and Benefit Distribution of Federal Automobile Emission Standards* (Cambridge, MA: Ballinger, 1975); and Paul R. Portney, "The Distribution of Pollution Control Costs," in *Report*

of the Environmental Research Assessment Committee (Washington, DC: National Academy of Sciences, 1977).

11. For an evaluation of the effectiveness of regulatory oversight in the Ford and Carter administrations, see Thomas Hopkins, Thomas Lenard, John Morrall III, and Elizabeth Pinkston, "A Review of the Regulatory Interventions of the Council on Wage and Price Stability, 1974-1980," mimeographed (Washington, DC: Council on Wage and Price Stability, 1981).

12. "Cost-Benefit Analysis in the Courts: Judicial Review Under NEPA," *Georgia Law Review,* Winter 1975, pp. 417-453.

13. David Harrison, Jr., "Controlling Automotive Emission: How to Save More than $1 Billion per Year and Help the Poor Too," *Public Policy* 25 (1976): 527-553.

14. For a discussion of these issues, see David Harrison, Jr., Steven Kelman, Albert Nichols, Robert Repetto, and Thomas Schelling, "Incentive Arrangements for Environmental Protection: A Critical Examination" (Report to the U.S. Environmental Protection Agency, February 1981).

15. Ibid.

16. Lawrence J. White, "Truth in Regulatory Budgeting," *Regulation,* March/April 1980, pp. 44-46. For a discussion of other ways to induce truthful revelation of compliance costs, see Jon C. Sonstelie, "Economic Incentives and the Revelation of Compliance Costs" (Report prepared for the Council on Environmental Quality, January 6, 1981).

17. Richard Posner, *Economic Analysis of Law* (Boston: Little, Brown, 1972).

18. Richard Stewart, "The Development of Administrative and Quasi-Constitutional Law in Judicial Review of Environmental Decisionmaking: Lessons from the Clean Air Act," *Iowa Law Review,* February 1977.

19. DeMuth, "Constraining Regulatory Costs," p. 36.

20. Such dominance assumes that the reform categories' "scores" have the same importance — for example, that all categories are equally poor when judged by the criterion of certainty. Since our objective is to provide a rough evaluation of reform proposals, we have not tried to refine the scoring system.

21. Two notable exceptions were the codification of EPA's "offset" policy in the Clean Air Act and the substitution of a cost-reasonableness test for industrial pollution in the Clean Water Act.

22. Lawrence J. White, *Reforming Regulation: Process and Problems* (Englewood Cliffs, NJ: Prentice-Hall, 1981).

23. American Textile Manufacturers' Institute et al. v. Raymond Donovan et al. (U.S. Supreme Court, June 17, 1981).

12

The Political Feasibility of Regulatory Reform

How Did We Do It?

ALFRED E. KAHN

At the start of Jimmy Carter's term in office, few political analysts or economists would have predicted that by 1981 the federal government would have deregulated or substantially deregulated trucking, the airlines, the railroads, and financial markets, and made some progress toward deregulating communications. These accomplishments have surely demonstrated that regulatory reform *is* politically possible. For those of us who recognize how very much remains still to be done, the interesting questions are: What lessons can we learn from those past successes? What made those achievements politically possible? What light do they shed on the prospects for continuing regulatory reform during the next several years?

I have come to recognize increasingly that such successes as we had were essentially political in nature. (So, by the way, were our failures.) That is to say, they consisted more in getting these changes through the political and administrative processes than in devising novel economic prescriptions; most of the prescriptions were already there in the literature, waiting for us to apply. It seems to be important therefore to give more systematic thought than I have until now to *how* we did what we did. How and why did it happen?

AUTHOR'S NOTE: I would like to acknowledge, with thanks, the assistance of Steven Booth and Scott Lindsay in the preparation of this material.

Economic Versus "Social"

The answers to these several questions will differ depending on whether we are thinking of what may be loosely characterized as economic regulation on the one side, and social or protective regulation on the other — the former concentrating explicitly on price, entry, and output to specific industries, the latter seeking to preserve such values as public health and safety, and the quality of the environment.

There are, of course, very important economic and political differences between these two. At the same time, the distinction must not be drawn too sharply. For one thing, although the most striking victories have been won in the former area, there have been some very significant reforms or beginnings of reforms in the latter as well. For another, the differentiation encourages the erroneous popular view that an economic calculus is not equally applicable to both. Finally, while of course simple deregulation is the proper prescription only in situations where competition can work — and it does not work in the presence of severe market failures — regulatory reform in the social and protective field *too* must consist very largely of an effort to emulate the competitive market. What must be done, and what we were attempting to do in the Carter Administration, is to adopt regulatory techniques that make the fullest possible use of the incentives and mechanisms of the market — the bubble, transferable rights, auctions, emissions taxes, and white markets.[1]

If the traditional distinction between these two kinds of regulation is often overdrawn, it is also sometimes insufficiently refined. There *are* generalizations that can legitimately be drawn from the whole range of regulatory experience — for example, that regulators have a very high preference for stability and tidiness, and a high marginal propensity to meddle, to prescribe, to cross-subsidize, and to identify their missions with the interests of particular client groups. Moreover, my own experience over the last few years gives me an especially poignant recognition of the importance of extending the concept of economic regulation to embrace such interventions as parity price supports, the minimum wage, the Davis-Bacon Act, antidumping statutes, and the many exemptions from the antitrust laws.

There is, however, a danger of oversimplification. Many of the people who have written in this field in the last 25 years have gone astray trying to draw generalizations about Regulation, with a capital

R, and about the behavior of Regulators, again with a capital R, as though the same generalizations and prescriptions apply equally to the fields of civil rights, fair competitive practices, occupational safety, and the provision of telephone service. This has produced some overly simple generalizations that recent experience has in some measure confounded.

The Revisionist Literature and Its Limitations

When I was a student of economics, I believed, or assumed, that regulation was simply a beneficent response to defects in the operation of unregulated markets. I recognized, of course, the phenomenon of special interest legislation — government interventions to subsidize particular parties or to protect them from competition — but such protectionism was not the same thing as regulation. By and large, regulation was imposed to protect the public interest. Until very recently, that was evidently the popular view: Witness the continued, indeed accelerated, multiplication of regulatory interventions and agencies during the Ford and Nixon administrations.

During the last 25 years or so, however, we have experienced an outpouring of revisionist scholarship — by historians, economists, and political scientists emulating economists — presenting quite a different view. Its major themes are that regulation all too often (probably most of these scholars would say "typically") runs counter to the public interest because it promotes economic inefficiency; that these failures are not accidental or the result of human error but inherent in the institution; that regulation is properly understood not so much as the government constraining the exploitative exercise of private power as the use of government authority for private gain, principally of the regulatees, at the expense of the public at large; that, correspondingly, the behavior of regulators can best be understood in terms of the pursuit of self-interest — whether that be defined as maximizing prestige, voter support, bureaucratic power, or simply tenure in office; and, finally (completing the logical circle), that the self-interest of regulators coincides with that of the politically well-organized private client groups, whom they serve with ever more pervasive, economically inefficient intervention.[2]

That short summary hardly does justice to a burgeoning literature, and I do not intend, in any event, to deny the many ways in which it has enriched our understanding of the phenomenon. I think it is fair to say, however, that these revistionist interpretations did not prepare us to predict or even understand the wave of deregulation and the more modest reform of regulatory techniques that we have experienced during the last few years — some of which tendencies will surely continue through the early 1980s as well. The reason, I suggest, is that the literature gives inadequate recognition to a number of other powerful determinants of public policy. An understanding of these, and of the ways in which they change over time, is the key to understanding the recent reforms and assessing the prospects for their extension.

Ideas

The first of these is the ever-changing conception of what constitutes good public policy. As James Q. Wilson has observed:

> We must be struck at every turn by the importance of ideas. Regulation itself is such an idea; deregulation is another . . . The value of regulation by command-and-control as opposed to regulation by the alteration of market incentives requires an assessment of the competing ideas. . . . To the extent an agency can choose, its choices will be importanly shaped by what its executives learned in college a decade or two earlier.[3]

Michael Levine provides an illuminating example of this phenomenon in the imposition of regulation on the airlines back in 1938 and their recent deregulation:

> All of these awkward facts are consistent with a story that goes something like this: In 1938 it appeared to the general public and the Congress that uncontrolled markets did not work very well for the public over the long run. Although markets produced low prices during the Depression years, many producers went out of business. The airline business was relatively new, Congress had little experience with it, and there was no reason not to apply general skepticism about markets to airlines. Doubts about airline markets were reinforced by the fact that firms were continuing to attempt entry. . . . It seemed to Congress that mistakenly optimistic entrepreneurs were seeking profitable operations where none were possible, draining away resources needed for further extension of the airline system in fruitless and profitless competitive struggles for existing business. Firms that had invested substantial resources in pioneering air transportation would become the innocent victims of still another example of market competition run riot.

> It was therefore not difficult for the airline industry to persuade Congress and the public that the fledging airline industry would go the way of many other Depression-era firms and the full potential of aviation could not be developed in a free-market environment. . . . Whatever its vices, this story has the singular virtue of being consistent with the legislative history of the 1938 act . . . This history . . . contains numerous statements . . . which seem to suggest that Congress was not intentionally freezing entry nor thereby creating a cartel for the sole benefit of the airlines and a few isolated geographic areas. . . . This modified [public interest] theory says that airline regulation was imposed by a Congress which, while attempting to act in the public interest, made a mistake.[4]

It is interesting to observe that in most of these assertions Levine is, in effect, paraphrasing Justice Brandeis's dissent in New State Ice Company v. Liebman,[5] and the report of the coordinator of transportation to President Roosevelt in 1935 about trucking.

I will not duplicate Levine's persuasive account of how the climate of public opinion changed, how an altered conception of the public interest led in the turn to the appointment of a different breed of regulators, who were prepared to confound the revisionist theories by introducing profound changes in the direction of economic efficiency, at the expense of the authority of their agencies and of their own tenure as regulators. The airline example clearly illustrates the role of changing *ideas* in the development of regulatory policies.

In the same way, while the Interstate Commerce Act and its subsequent amendments were in part supported by the railroads, they were also the fulfillment of planks in the platforms of the Granger movement and the Populist party. The fact that electric companies themselves promoted regulation as the price they had to pay for exclusive, franchised monopolies is only part of that particular story: Public utility regulation was promoted also by the Progressive movement, reflecting prevailing political philosophies and conceptions of the public interest. And "rationalization" of the motor carrier industry through regulation was espoused earnestly — if also mistakenly — by early theorists of the New Deal.

The Economic Climate

These examples clearly suggest a second explanatory factor that I think the revisionists have tended to underestimate: the changing condition of the economy at large.

It was obviously not a coincidence that the deregulations of the last few years reversed legislation passed in 1933, 1934, 1935, and 1938 — the Banking, Communications, Motor Carrier, and Civil Aviation Acts. Both the governing statutes and the regulatory philosophy shaping these industries more or less consistently for the following 45 years were forged during, and by, the Great Depression. Nor was it mere coincidence that these deregulations were effected in an era of stagflation.

These two fundamental determinants — the condition of the economy and the governing economic philosophies — obviously interact very closely. The Great Depression seemed to justify a thorough reexamination of the microorganization of our economy and a widespread skepticism about unregulated markets. (Remember, this was before the distinction between micro- and macroeconomics came into vogue.) In his famous dissent in New State Ice v. Liebman,[6] Justice Brandeis — who thought he was speaking for the public interest, and not as a tool of the ice companies — expounded the view that unregulated competition might be responsible for the business cycle, i.e., for cycles of overexuberant investment, leading in turn to excess capacity and destructive price-cutting (which he saw as the mechanism for destructive general deflation). And it was this attitude, as well as the depth of the depression, that led to the cartelization of the entire economy under the National Recovery Act, of which program the specific regulatory statutes so recently overturned were an integral part.

The remarkable resurgence of western capitalism in the 1950s and '60s led to a rediscovery of the virtues of the market, and progressively discredited the notion of the superiority of central planning; but the latter view persisted for a long time. For example, Americans were very worried in the late '50s about the "growth gap" between the Free World and Communist Countries. It has only been in the last fifteen years that that notion has been discredited by the remarkable economic progress of countries like South Korea, Taiwan, Hong Kong, Singapore, and Japan, not to mention Western Europe, while the collectivist countries have tried to find ways of reinventing the market.

The final, decisive push toward deregulation was supplied by stagflation. This is not the place to analyze substantively the relationship between regulation and inflation, and the related question of what place regulatory reform has in a program for combatting inflation. It is clear, however, that social regulation is one of the ways in which the public places demands on the economy, thereby contributing to the imbalance between the sum total of demands and aggregate supply that constitutes inflation. To the extent, also, that cartellike, protectionist regulation compels inefficiencies or interferes with the dynamic pressures that competition would otherwise exert to improve efficiency, it has contributed to the stagnation of productivity, which has further aggravated this progressive imbalance in the last several years. Finally, to the extent that competition-suppressing regulation has contributed to the perverse behavior of wages and prices — and there is evidence that suggests it has, especially in the '70s[7] — then clearly it has contributed to the unresponsiveness of prices to macroeconomic restraint, which is a very important part of our stagflationary dilemma.

Whatever the validity of that connection is a matter of economics, there is no doubt of the political fact that the general economic environment of the last decade has made the job of regulatory reformers easier than it would otherwise have been. Whereas in the 1930s the general conception was that we were suffering from poverty in the midst of plenty, that our resources were unlimited, and all we had to do to solve the problem of poverty was to put idle labor and capital to work, we have now rediscovered the economics of scarcity. And that has made the time ripe for the application of more rigorous tests and more efficient techniques to regulatory interventions, as well as for subjecting protectionist regulations that suppress competition to much more critical scrutiny.

In addition to the condition of the economy at large, the changing circumstances of the particular industries subjected to regulation have had an important influence in determining the nature of the regulation imposed and, recently, in generating pressures for regulatory reform. The special difficulties confronting the automobile and steel industries are obvious cases in point — though whether the result will be to promote more cartelization or less is by no means clear.

The wage concessions in 1980 by the United Automobile Workers to save their jobs at Chrysler have justly received a great deal of attention. Less widely noticed was another substantial concession in the regulatory area. The Occupational Safety and Health Administration (OSHA), with the strong support of the unions, had previously adopted the general principle — a policy now reversed by the Reagan

Administration — that safety on the job may not be assured by requiring workers to wear protective equipment; instead, plants had to be engineered or reengineered to this end, regardless of the respective costs of the two safeguards. At the time of the auto companies' deepest distress, regulations were under consideration for protecting workers against arsenic and lead that would have required a very costly reengineering of the plants. In consideration of the industry's competitive difficulties and extreme need for capital to provide capacity for the smaller, more fuel-efficient cars that buyers were demanding, the UAW and OSHA agreed instead to have the workers wear protective equipment. Just as the general rediscovery of scarcity has encouraged the introduction of an economic calculus into regulation in the economy at large, so the adversity that has befallen the automobile industry, placing jobs in jeopardy, induced its workers to accept regulations stipulating somewhat less comfortable, but also a good deal less costly, means of protecting their health.

Shifting Interest-Group Configurations

Besides underestimating the influence of changing economic circumstances and prevailing ideas about proper public policy, the revisionist literature has, I believe, been excessively simplistic, as well as static, in its characterization of the interests of the parties most directly affected by regulation. In fact, at any given time those parties will often have highly divergent interests — there are always the outsiders and the insiders, for example, whenever entry is restricted — and the interest configurations change over time. The coalitions that succeed in introducing a particular government regulatory regime — like the ones that set up private cartels — are rarely permanent. As circumstances change, the component interests diverge.

The coalition that put together the Interstate Commerce Act, for example, was not simply a group of railroads — in fact, many railroads were opposed — but consisted also of shippers who believed that they were being subjected to discriminatory treatment or exploitation, localities worried about geographic discrimination, and farmers who wanted discriminatorily favorable treatment. Most of these groups also favored extending regulatory cartelization to the motor carriers in 1935; and the farmers were content to go along, *provided* the carriage of agricultural commodities was exempted. When, however, this cartelization interfered with the ability of the railroads to regain lost business by pricing down toward incremental costs on competitive traffic, and to earn enough on captive traffic to keep them financially healthy, the railroads deserted the coalition and ultimately succeeded — in 1980, in a much-changed intellectual and economic environment — in achieving a large measure of freedom.

I believe, similarly, there would never have been airline deregulation if it had not been that United Airlines became increasingly discontented with the way the Civil Aeronautics Board (CAB) was systematically denying it the opportunity to enter new markets and to leave old ones; and that Pan American progressively found itself subjected to competition on international routes from other carriers, who were in a position to feed themselves passengers from their domestic routes, while Pan Am was denied the right even to pick up passengers to fill empty seats on the domestic legs of its international flights. There were carriers, in short, who were beginning to conclude that regulation was causing them more pain than pleasure. Once the process of liberalizing entry began, gradually, case by case, the tensions mounted. Companies previously protected within their historic markets found themselves subjected to additional competition within those markets but not free to exploit new opportunities themselves — to add promising new routes or drop old nonprofitable ones. Company after company concluded that, under the circumstances, it would be better off with no regulation at all.

The condition of the industry and of the economy were also very propitious for deregulation in the late '70s. The period 1970-1975, when regulation was at its most restrictive, was also a period of dismally low airline profits: The return on equity of the trunk carriers was slightly over 3 percent over the 6 years.[8] The industry was suffering the consequences of competitive overscheduling and a scramble to acquire wide-bodied jets just as the rate of growth in traffic was falling off. For that very reason, 1976-1978 were ideal years for the introduction of deregulation. First of all, there were all those empty seats that could be filled at near-zero marginal costs; competitive price reductions could confer benefits on both the traveling public and the airlines. Moreover, the economy was in a period of cyclical recovery, which offered the opportunity for a great deal of additional business: New entrants would not merely be bidding for a share of an unchanging pie. And if freedom of entry was to be accompanied by greater freedom of exit, it would offer established carriers opportunities to rationalize their route structures — to cut costs, drop loss-generating operations, and develop new, more profitable ones.

It was not just the interests of the airline companies, however, that produced deregulation: Most of the industry and the related unions remained bitterly opposed. For the rest of the explanation it is necessary to return to my first two factors: the changing philosophical and political environment, and inflation. These various factors helped produce an immensely diversified and ultimately irresistible coalition of politicians and private and public interest groups across the country — Senators Edward Kennedy and Howard Cannon, Presidents Ford and Carter, the Consumer Federation of America, Common Cause, Ralph Nader and his various followers, the National Association of Manufacturers, along with such established airlines as United and Frontier, and aggressive would-be entrants like Southwest. The campaign for trucking deregulation had the support also of an association of minority businesses, who were speaking for small business people excluded by regulation from the opportunity to get into trucking; the National Federation of Small Businesses (which did yeoman work in the cause): the Food Marketing Institute; farm groups chafing at restrictive interpretations of the agricultural commodities exemption; and some very large industrial and mercantile shippers. Only so broadly based a coalition could have prevailed against the concerted opposition of the American Trucking Association and the Teamsters.[9]

There are signs of a change in the attitudes of hitherto complaisant regulatees in another industry that may augur important reforms in the next several years, and that is the electric utility industry. I came to the chairmanship of the New York Public Service Commission (PSC) in 1974 with the conviction that the industry needed to move forthrightly in the direction of marginal-cost pricing. In view of the fact that, because of inflation, marginal costs in time of peak demand seemed clearly far above average costs (or revenue requirements) as traditionally defined, I was surprised to find that the electric companies were generally opposed to any kind of time-of-day rates, and most of all to any attempt to base rates on the elastic components of their markets on the basis of high current incremental costs. Why were they so opposed? As far as I could tell, they still believed (apparently for the typical reasons outlined by Harvey Averch and Leland Johnson)[10] that they were better off with expanded capacity, which higher charges on peak would render less necessary. They were clearly motivated also by fear of the unknown: Might a radically revised rate structure, particularly one bearing most heavily on their demand-elastic business, cause them to fall even further short of earning their cost of capital? They were probably also indulging the pride of engineers in providing the most reliable, gold-plated service possible; and perhaps they wanted to maximize sales rather than profits. Finally, they were probably victims of sheer bureaucratic inertia.

A remarkable change has taken place in the last five years, however, primarily because inflation and regulatory lag have resulted in such attrition of profits that it has obviously ceased to be in the interest of most electric companies to build additonal plant. Time-of-day rates and marginal-cost-based pricing have become more widely accepted, and many electric companies are looking actively for ways to discourage new customers from coming in line. Even more radically, some of them, severely oppressed by regulation in time of inflation, have become increasingly receptive to freer entry into electricity generation, by customers, cogenerators, or even independent central station generators selling at wholesale. Some of these public utility monopolists may become converts to freer competition and deregulation in the 1980s, just as the Bell System did, however reluctantly, in the late 1970s.

Membership in the coalitions of regulatory reformers and resisters varies, of course, from one situation to the next. In the future, this variability will become especially obvious as the focus of reform efforts shifts form the economic to the social and protective sphere. Environmentalists, for example, who played a very useful role in supporting marginal-cost pricing of energy, crude oil and natural gas deregulation, and transportation reform, are far less supportive of the application of the same economic principles to environmental protection.[11] Consumer organizations, who were very active in the struggle to deregulate trucking and the airlines, bitterly opposed deregulating crude oil. Senator Kennedy clearly exemplified this (at least partial) contradiction in his primary campaign for the presidency. Indeed, regulation and regulatory reform, neither more nor less than politics generally, produce strange bedfellows. One of the strangest of these liaisons was the one that produced the 1977 Amendments to the Clean Air Act — as Bruce A. Ackerman and William T. Hassler have aptly characterized it, the coalition of proponents of clean air and dirty (Eastern) coal.[12]

Technology

The first reaction of the complete regulator to technological change, with the threat it usually poses to the existing order, is to try to bring it under control. Consider the reaction of the Federal Communications Commission to the new competition between cable TV and local broadcasters, or of the ICC to the spread of trucking, with its threat to railroads and their historical rate structures — persuasive illustrations of what James W. McKie has referred to as the "tar baby" effect.[13]

But technological change — the fourth determinant of changing regulatory policy — is no respecter of regulatory boundaries, and it cannot be contained indefinitely. It has rendered obsolete the distinctions — drawn under the Communications Act of 1934 and the American Telephone and Telegraph antitrust consent decree — between written and voice communication, cable and satellite, video and telephone, data processing and communications. Obliteration of what remains of these regulatory boundaries, which make no sense under modern technology, is a leading item on the reform agenda for the 1980s.

Conclusions: The Prospects for Regulatory Reform

I have no interest in suggesting a new theory of regulation — a revision of revisionism, as Michael Levine puts it[14] — which in a few years would almost certainly prove again that economists are much better at predicting the past than the future. What economists *are* good at, in politics, is pointing out the benefits of economically efficient arrangements.

That fact that a policy is rational from society's standpoint is, of course, no assurance it will be adopted. It is helpful, nevertheless, that regulatory reform is not a zero-sum game. The trick is to introduce it at times and in ways that demonstrate that fact: that everybody — or almost everybody — can win.

For example, as chairman of the New York PSC I had the job of defending the commission's decision to permit the New York Telephone Company to introduce charging for directory assistance, against the loud complaints of so-called consumer representatives and a fair number of demagogues that we were taking something away from people that was previously free. Because the commission had had the wisdom to introduce the change *not* in the context of a general rate increase, but in a separate proceeding, in which there was no issue of increased revenues for the company, and since any reduction in information calls resulting from the charge would save the telephone company money, it was possible to provide refunds to subscribers who made few such calls per month and to promise that the net effect of introducing the charges would be a $20-25 million reduction in bills for the year. This is exactly what happened. The tariff provided for 3 free information calls a month plus a 30 cent rebate, with a charge of 10 cents for each call in excess of 3. The result, within 2 months, was a 40 to 45 percent reduction in the number of such calls, with 85 percent of the subscribers receiving the full refund. Within only a few months, the opposition disappeared.

Technological progress has helped make improvements like this possible. Metering of telephone calls is progressing so rapidly that it is now very cheap not only to count but also to time local calls in most parts of the country. So more and more, we are likely to see charging by the minute and the mile as well as the message, instead of a flat monthly charge for unlimited calls over wider and wider areas — with positive marginal costs but no additional charge. There will be opposition, but it will be possible to demonstrate that the result will be very large savings for the great majority of users.

Because this type of reform is *not* a zero-sum game, and because the possibilities for cost savings are enormous, I believe that the most productive regulatory reform activity in the next several years will be in introducing marketlike techniques that will enable us to achieve given regulatory goals at minimum cost. This is the beauty of the Environmental Protection Agency's bubble and its experimentation with transferable rights. Here is a cause to which both proponents and opponents of environmental and other kinds of social and protective regulation could fruitfully subscribe, if only they could submerge their mutual distrust about each other's ultimate intentions, and concentrate instead on these innovative regulatory techniques.[15]

Ultimately regulatory reform depends on the emergence of coalitions of public and private groups with a strong interest in pressing for it. The possibility of moving closer to social efficiency constitutes a very favorable precondition, but it will take effective political leadership to take advantage of that opportunity and mobilize the requisite forces. The Reagan Administration is in an excellent position to assume this kind of leadership in dealing with social and protective regulations because of the differences between its constituencies and those of the Democratic party — unless it fritters away the opportunity by attempting simply to turn back the clock.

Unfortunately, ideological preconceptions about states' rights may cause the administration to abandon the leadership role the Carter forces attempted to assume, with the president's explicit support, in a regulatory reform program at the state and local level. One part of that effort was an attack on state and local regulations that grossly inflate construction costs — complicated, duplicative, and unconscionably time-consuming permitting requirements, and unreasonably restrictive building codes and land-use limitations. In cooperation with the National Association of Homebuilders and the Office of the President's Advisor on Inflation, the Department of Housing and Urban Development (HUD) set up demonstration projects in four localities in which state and local officials agreed to institute expedited, one-stop permitting and to relax excessively onerous regulations. In three of the four cases — the fourth, unfortunately, was right near Mt. St. Helen's and was not a great success — it took only four to five months from the filing of initial applications to complete the projects. The estimates of HUD — confirmed by the builders, and informally by conversations with two purchasers of the first houses — were that this cooperation cut 20 to 30 percent of the cost of the houses, with the principal savings resulting from the reduction in permitting time. I understand that there have been inquiries about the recent HUD report on these demonstrations[16] from hundreds of cities that want to replicate them.

My greatest worry about the prospects for regulatory reform under the new administration, however, is in the economic field. The Republican party has historically had a split personality on the subject of free competition — part eighteenth-century liberal, part eighteenth- to twentieth-century protectionist. Reflecting the latter was the letter that Governor Reagan wrote to the American Trucking Association, shortly before the election and after his endorsement by the Teamsters, in which he promised that his ICC appointees would have direct experience in the industry. There are similiar indications that the new FCC will be much more protective of the broadcasters than its predecessor; and the administration is trying to limit imports of Japanese cars.

Finally, I want to reemphasize the power of the first two critical factors that I have identified: ideas and the economic climate. In some considerable measure there is airline deregulation today because of ideas set forth in an article Michael Levine wrote many years ago,[17] and because of some hearings that Steven Breyer conducted for Senator Kennedy.[18] Similarly, the writings of Allen Kneese and Charles Schultze on transferable rights and pollution taxes,[19] Julian Simon on airline bumping,[20] and Ronald Coase on spectrum allocation[21] have contributed substantially to the regulatory innovations being initiated and proposed today.

It gives me a certain amount of amusement and pleasure — and I hope it does them as well — to contemplate the influence the revisionists' ideas about the inherent, ineluctable tendencies of regulation have had in the real world. Those ideas have contributed in important measure to the qualification, if not refutation, of their own theories! (In this way they have in a sense re-proved the Heisenberg principle, which says that one cannot observe a phenomenon without changing it.)

As for the second factor — external economic circumstances — a great deal of credit for the regulatory reforms already adopted, I have already pointed out, goes to inflation. My advice to regulatory reformers is, therefore, pray for continued inflation!

NOTES

1. See the references in note 15 below.

2. I have drawn heavily here on Michael E. Levine, "Revisionism Revised? Airline Deregulation and the Public Interest," *Law and Contemporary Problems* 44 (Winter 1981): 197-195, which also contains citations to this literature. For an exceptionally interesting appraisal of the "capture" and other theories of regulatory behavior, and a development of a more complex and also more persuasive explanation, in the context of detailed studies of changes in the regulation of electric utilities in New York and California in the 1970s, see also Douglas D. Anderson, *Regulatory Politics and Electric Utilities* (Boston: Auburn House, 1981).

3. The Politics of Regulation (New York: Basic Books, 1980), p. 393.

4. Levine, "Revisionism Revised?" pp. 191-192.

5. 285 U.S. 262, 292 (1932).

6. Ibid., especially pp. 307-308.

7. See Milton Kafoglis and Oliver Grawe, "A Reconsideration of the Efficiency of Regulation" (Paper presented to the American Economic Association [Association for the Study of the Grants Economy], December 1979).

8. Calculated by the Bureau of Economic Research, Civil Aeronautics Board, from Form 41 reports.

9. My former deputy for regulation, Ron Lewis, has pointed out that several other factors played an important role in trucking deregulation, in addition to the

widespread general frustration with excessively intrusive government regulations (of which we made good use by publicizing the manifestly absurd restrictions typically incorporated in Interstate Commerce Commission certificates). For one thing, the administration consciously attacked airline regulations first, recognizing that the political opposition there was weaker. And the dramatic and highly visible fare reductions produced by that reform helped pave the way for trucking deregulation — but for which we would not have succeeded in liberating the railroads as well.

Also in combatting the folklore surrounding trucking regulation, we made a conscious effort to develop specific kinds of information to help us combat some of the traditional rationalizations, such as that it helped ensure service to small towns. We found, for example, that the ICC had never denied an application by any carrier to discontinue service to any town, and, indeed, had no record of who was producing service where. The Department of Transportation undertook studies of small-town service, and found it was typically provided not through internal subsidization, but mainly by exempt carriers — private carriers, carriers of agricultural commodities, and United Parcel — and, in lesser degree, by a few specialized certificated carriers who found it remunerative.

Finally, we had the unwavering commitment of the president, who appointed enthusiastic deregulators to the ICC and then assured Congress that he would veto any unacceptable bill it might be tempted to produce, leaving the industry to the tender mercies of his appointees — the same kind of one-two punch as deregulated the airlines.

10. "Behavior of the Firm under Regulatory Constraint," *American Economic Review* 12 (December 1962): 1052-1069.

11. See Barry R. Weingast, "Regulation, Reregulation, and Deregulation: The Political Foundations of Agency-Clientele Relationships," Washington University Center for the Study of American Business, Working Paper 62 (St. Louis: 1980).

12. "Beyond the New Deal: Coal and the Clean Air Act," *Yale Law Journal* 89 (July 1980): 1466-1571.

13. "Regulation and the Free Market: The Problem of Boundaries," *Bell Journal of Economics* 1 (Spring 1970): 9.

14. Levine, "Revisionism Revised?"

15. See my "Regulation and the Imagination," in U.S. Regulatory Council, *Innovative Techniques in Theory and Practice, Proceedings* (Washington, DC: 1980). Also, U.S. Regulatory Council, *Regulating with Common Sense: A Progress Report on Innovative Regulatory Techniques* (Washington, DC: 1980): U.S. Environmental Protection Agency (EPA), *Controlled Trading, Putting the Profit Motive to Work for Pollution Control* (Washington, DC: 1980); and EPA *Smarter Regulation,* drawing on a forthcoming article by William Drayton (Washington, DC: January 1981); also notes 19, 20, and 21, below.

16. *Housing Cost Reduction Demonstration,* 606-H (Washington, DC: December 1980).

17. "Comment, Is Regulation Necessary? California Transportation and Regulatory Policy," *Yale Law Journal* 74 (July 1965): 1416-1447.

18. U.S. Senate, 94th Congress, 1st session, Committee on the Judiciary, Subcommittee on Administrative Practice and Procedure, *Oversight of Civil Aeronautics Board Practices and Procedures* (Washington, DC: 1975).

19. *Pollution, Prices and Public Policy* (Washington, DC: Brookings, 1975); and Charles L. Schultze, *The Public Uses of Private Interest* (Washington, DC: Brookings, 1977).

20. "An Almost Practical Solution to Airline Overbooking," *Journal of Transport Economics and Policy* 2 (May 1968): 201-202; "Airline Overbooking: A Rejoinder," *Jounal of Transport Economics and Policy* 4 (May 1970): 212-213; and with G. Visvabhanthy, "Auction Solution for Airline Overbooking," *Journal of Transport Economics and Policy* 11 (September 1977): 277-283.

21. "The Federal Communications Commission," *Journal of Law and Economics* 2 October 1959): 1-40.

13

Conclusions

LeROY GRAYMER
FREDERICK THOMPSON

There is one key point upon which all the contributors to this volume agree: The *methods* now used to deal with the problems addressed by the new social regulation are often inappropriate and frequently contradictory, and seldom reflect the most efficient means to achieve the program goals. Responsibility for promoting a cleaner, safer, healthier environment has been concentrated in the hands of regulatory officials who have frequently failed to consider alternatives to uniform application of design standards or to command-and-control types of regulation. More often than not the approaches chosen or required by law have failed to target monitoring and enforcement activities where they would have the greatest payoff. Regulators are generally more attentive to those who benefit from the agency's activities than to those who are likely to be harmed. Finally, it seems that Congress is largely responsible for this state of affairs, not only because legislators chose the methods the regulators use and created many of the inconsistencies that cause regulations to work at cross-purposes, but also because of their continuing influence on the regulatory agencies' behavior. The regulators behave the way they do, in large part, because that is how Congress (or at least the small number of legislators who oversee their activities) wants them to behave. The predispositions of the regulators reflect the predispositions of their sponsors in Congress.

Consequently, if we are to reform the new social regulation, we must persuade Congress to make substantive changes in regulatory legislation and to modify its oversight efforts in such a way as to promote more reasonable regulation. But how does one persuade Congress? The answer to this question depends, of course, on the reasons for Congress's preferences. If Congress simply does not understand what it has wrought, the answer lies in demonstrating the flaws in the existing regulatory apparatus. However, to the extent that the existing regulatory apparatus reflects the real interests and preferences of key elected officials, even irrefutable demonstration of its drawbacks may not eventuate in substantive reform. Since it seems quite likely this is the case — that it is frequently no accident that the methods used by the regulators are often unsatisfactory — does this mean that reform of the new social regulation is not possible? On the contrary, we agree with a comment made by Darius Gaskins, who observed:

> I don't have much patience with people who talk to me about political unfeasibility; I think that the issue of political feasibility is generally a smokescreen put up by someone who, for whatever reason, doesn't want to entertain the possibility of change or wants to resist the change itself. . . . I think lots of things are politically feasible *if you are clever enough to figure out what you want and attempt to get it.*[1]

What this means is that reform will not be easy; reformers first must figure out exactly what they want and how to get it.

In this concluding chapter, we will address the following issues: the flaws in the existing regulatory apparatus, Congress's responsibility, and the obstacles to reform and some steps that might be taken to overcome them.

Flaws in the Existing Regulatory Apparatus

The critiques of the existing regulatory apparatus by the contributing authors contain both diagnosis and prescriptions. For example, they prefer performance standards to engineering standards, in large part because they assume that industry personnel are better situated and motivated to determine how to meet regulatory targets than are engineers located in Washington. This same logic underlies their support for many of the innovations in the environmental regulatory area — bubbles, offsets, and so on — as well as their advocacy of smog taxes, marketable emissions permits, and the like. Furthermore, these preferences are fairly well supported by careful, empirically based analyses of existing and alternative organizational processes — motivation and incentive systems, performance measurement and standards, and recruiting and promotional practices.

Why is it that bureaucratic risk avoidance leads to overregulation and inflexibility on the part of regulatory agencies? Why is it that risk avoidance is very nearly a master principle of bureaucratic organizations? In this volume, Bardach and Kagan have identified several examples that demonstrate how these "organizational principles" operate in the regulatory environment. It is frequently difficult to monitor an individual inspector's performance; however, it may be relatively easy to monitor his or her adherence to standard procedures. Moreover, in the absence of satisfactory performance measures, a manager does not know whether subordinates will use their discretion advantageously. Deviation from standard procedure, even when justified, is discouraged because it reduces a manager's ability to control the inspectorate. Since managers prefer inspectors to "go by the book," they reward those who do and punish those who do not. Hence the inspectorate tends to adhere to the rules, whether they result in the desired consequences or not.

Why do program administrators behave this way? One may infer that they face only limited external pressure to improve performance but face negative incentives when it comes to undertakings that improve the efficiency with which regulatory objectives are obtained, but that also may involve some risk. For example, an administrator who adopts a standard enforcement strategy may not be criticized for failing to maximize overall efficiency. On the other hand, if the official undertakes nonstandard procedures to increase overall efficiency and something goes wrong, he or she may be out of a job. The acceptance of standard performance that does not increase efficiency, combined with the high risks associated with error, simply does not provide bureaucratic officials with incentives to try to improve public-sector performance.

Why is this risk avoidance particularly the case with respect to regulation? Can something be done about it? The explanation usually given for the lack of incentives for efficiency in the public sector (that is, inability to measure the consequences of an organization's activities) is not very satisfactory. As far as social regulation is concerned, performance can be measured—environmental quality, imperfectly, emissions, more satisfactorily; workplace exposures to chemical hazards, accidents, and the like, quite accurately. Furthermore. regulatory performance often *is* measured, and when it is, these measures frequently appear to influence regulators' decisions, especially with respect to the design and execution of regulatory programs. Thus how can we explain the absence of incentives for overall efficiency or the disincentives that have led to risk avoidance?

The answer is that efficient choice requires *both* cost and performance measures. This is the case because the absence of cost measures is seldom at issue. Nevertheless, proper incentives are just as likely to be absent where performance can be measured, but costs cannot be or are ignored, as where costs are measured, but performance cannot be or is ignored. This, it seems to us, is the key to the "unreasonableness" of the regulators — they are held accountable only for those costs that appear in the governmental accounts. This is the unique problem of regulatory decision making: The bulk of the costs asssociated with the design and execution of regulatory programs, the costs of complying with regulations, are borne outside the regulatory agency budget and thus are not part of the performance evaluation within the agency.

The proposals for tradable emissions permits such as those described by Hahn and Noll in this volume represent highly plausible solutions to this problem. For example, a tradable permits system would in theory create a system of incentives that should lead industry decision makers to seek overall efficiency. Moreover, the Hahn and Noll proposals demonstrate that incentive mechanisms can be designed to deal with the problem of excessive emissions, and that these mechanisms can be implemented so that they work nearly as well in practice as they sound in theory. (Furthermore, their proposals avoid some of the political liabilities associated with emissions taxes.)

Congressional Responsibility

The preceding diagnosis does not necessarily imply anything at all about congressional intent. If anything, it would appear to imply that the most appropriate, direct response to ineffective and inefficient regulation would be to improve regulatory methods by setting performance standards for the regulators or by changing organizational incentives to motivate regulators to make better decisions. However, past attempts to regulate the regulators have not been particularly effective in inducing them to behave more wisely, effectively, or consistently.

An equally plausible response would be to shift control of the regulatory process to the executive branch or to Congress. This is the thrust of the so-called omnibus proposals, as well as of the regulatory cost accounting and budgeting proposals and legislative veto proposals. Indeed, much of the attention of regulatory reformers in Congress has been directed at these kinds of structural or procedural changes. The chapter by Harrison and Portney contains a discussion of several of these reform proposals.

Over a dozen omnibus bills were introduced in the 96th Congress. For the most part they called for increased cost and/or benefit analysis along with appropriate modifications in the administrative law system, increased federal funding of public participation in the rule-making process, and centralization of oversight authority. They differed in terms of degree, kind, and timing of the analysis required, the scope of judicial review, and the location of oversight authority. At the one extreme, the Dole Rulemaking Improvements Act would actually have: required agencies to base their rule-making decisions on *ex ante* cost-benefit analysis; extended this requirement to all regulating agencies; made satisfactory performance subject to judicial review; vested oversight of regulatory activities in a powerful regulatory council.

The Brown-Bentsen Federal Regulatory Budget Act envisioned the development of a regulatory budget parallel to the expenditure budget. Under this proposal, the Office of Management and Budget would forward to Congress an estimate of the direct compliance costs for the existing and proposed regulations of each agency. Congress would then "appropriate" a maximum limit on the cost of compliance resulting from each agency's regulations for the next fiscal year.

Various legislative veto proposals have also been introduced. These would permit Congress or a committee of Congress to overturn by resolution specific rules issued by regulatory agencies.

There is, in our view, no immediate prospect for the enactment of any of these proposals. Nevertheless, it is worthwhile to review some of the motivation behind them. It appears that legislators like to claim that the regulators have run amok and are doing outrageous things never contemplated by Congress. Perhaps this is so, but in most cases regulators do what the legislation stipulates.

Not infrequently there is a real conflict between reason and statute. For example, the Department of Transportation (DOT) recently issued regulations that would be five or six times as costly, on a per ride basis, as provision of taxi service to the handicapped in specially equipped vehicles. Not surprisingly, Congress has called into question the common sense of regulators in the DOT who administer the law. However, the statute in question, Section 504 of the Rehabilitation Act of 1973, clearly states that "no otherwise qualified handicapped individual . . . shall . . . be excluded from participation in . . . any program or activity receiving federal financial assistance." Clearly the breadth of this law is unwise. However, as reluctant as Congress is to have such laws enforced, it is more reluctant to repeal or withdraw a "benefit" previously granted to a specific and probably mobilized subgroup within the population. Instead it would prefer to shift the responsibility for such changes to the agency or the courts.

This desire to adjust decisions concerning the allocation of benefits to interest groups without appearing actually to be doing so may underlie the appeal of omnibus proposals calling for a cost-benefit test for proposed regulations. Omnibus proposals that permit judicial review of the decision-making / rule-making procedures may be particularly attractive, since a judicially enforceable analysis requirement would provide an action-forcing mechanism to get the executive or the courts to do what legislators are reluctant to do. To date, however, none of these omnibus proposals has been enacted; according to Harrison and Portney, this reflects good sense on the part of Congress.

Central review of the effects of, and the alternatives to, all regulations promulgated in the United States (about 7000 a year) would be an administrative nightmare. Harrison and Portney imply that it simply is not appropriate to overcome the deficiencies of existing laws by omnibus legislation. Instead, they suggest that what we should aim for is an effective decentralized decision-making system—one in which regulators consider a wider array of approaches and are induced to make better decisions.

Ultimately, this is the purpose and function of the regulatory budget. The unique problem of regulatory decision making is that, although the cost of complying with government regulations is a cost of government decisions, it is not treated as a cost *to* government. Consequently, these costs are unconstrained by the systematic mechanisms of public finance. In theory, a regulatory budget would provide the same kind of incentives to regulators to set priorities as is provided by the expenditure budgeting and control process.

Both the legislative veto and the regulatory budget are in part attractive because they would give Congress a second chance at fine tuning what they have wrought without requiring formal rejection of their legislative handiwork. This mechanism is explicit in the case of the legislative veto. The budget process allows a similar form of self-control. Where public expenditures are concerned, Congress can pass authorizing legislation promising a great deal, but can choose to appropriate funds to support only a portion of what is authorized.

Harrison and Portney point to several questions that must be answered before a decision can be made to adopt a regulatory budget. The first set of these questions has to do with its feasibility, the second with its incentive effects.

To realize the full benefits of a regulatory budget, it would be necessary to measure the costs of compliance as they are incurred and to allocate these costs to regulatory program accounts. It would also be necessary to estimate accurately the incremental direct costs of compliance with proposed new regulations. Furthermore, these estimates would have to rely on information provided from industry, and it is clear that industry estimates tend to be biased upward. Therefore, a mechanism must be created that would correct this bias. Solutions are not now available for these problems.

The second set of concerns associated with the regulatory budget is potentially more serious. The purpose of the regulatory budget is to motivate people to make the right decisions — to correct the tendency to pay far more attention to administrative costs than to compliance costs, despite the fact that the latter far exceed the former. (OMB analysts estimate that the ratio of staff and managerial review effort is currently weighted 6 to 1 in favor of administrative costs.) However, a regulatory budget can only hope to reflect the *direct* cost of complying with regulations. As is the case with an expenditure budget, indirect costs and benefits would not be reflected in the regulatory accounts. We know that this exclusion frequently leads administrators to act contrary to the manner that would be suggested by applied welfare analysis. Budgeters, for example, generally seek to minimize total costs rather than to maximize net benefits. Since this problem is characteristic of expenditure budgeting, one may infer that it would also characterize the regulatory budget. The issue here is whether or not the regulatory activities of government generate or have the potential to generate indirect costs far in excess of those produced by expenditure programs. If so, the bias inherent in excluding these consequences from the regulating budget would be very serious, as the imposition of a regulatory budget would tend to move regulatory agencies toward programs in which indirect costs predominate. For example, the Environmental Protection Agency could realize its goal of "no deterioration in air quality" simply by prohibiting all new sources of emissions; such a policy would entail substantial indirect costs, but minimal direct compliance and administrative costs. At present, it is not possible to evaluate this issue.

Harrison and Portney conclude that neither procedural reform nor structural reform represents a promising approach to reforming the new social regulation. Improved oversight and review may correct some of the excesses of overzealous or overcautions regulators; indeed it already has. A regulatory budget might or might not correct some of the more perverse incentives facing the regulatory bureaucracy. But to get at the fundamental problems of the new social regulation, substantive reform of the enabling legislation is required.

Overcoming the Obstacles to Reform

What are the prospects for substantive reform of the new social regulatory legislation? At this time it seems to us that the principal obstacles to reform are political. Hence, the key questions now are: Can the political obstacles to reform be overcome? And, if so, how?

To answer such questions, academics tend to turn instinctively to the plentiful literature on political and administrative processes. However, many of those who have examined the politics of regulatory reform have relied far too much on interest group theory, and too little on political experience with recent efforts to enact reforms. In making this observation we are not rejecting interest group theory. Interest groups play an undeniable role in policy formulation and implementation. But it is an error to treat interest group politics as if it encompassed the entire realm of politics that relates to regulatory reform.

Interest Group Politics

To show the limitations of interest group theory, first it is necessary to outline its general themes. According to the interest group theory of politics, the role of government in general, and of regulation in particular, has always been and must inevitably be that of arbiter among competing economic claimants.[2] Hence regulatory policies are simply a "fulcrum upon which contending interests seek to exercise leverage in their pursuit of wealth."[3] In other words, the purpose of regulation is the redistribution of income to specific groups. Interest group theory further implies that the gains from regulation will tend to go to a small fraction of the community, that most others will be excluded from these gains, and that the gains will come at the expense of economic efficiency. In turn, these arguments rest on the belief that special (that is, narrowly focused) economic interests are at an advantage in dealing with the public goods problems that militate against interest group formation. They also rest on the assumption that only the losers or potential losers in competitive private market transactions are likely to seek redress in the political arena.

It is impossible to refute such claims by appeal to theory. Neither can they be rejected as incompatible with the facts of political conflict, which tends to involve a broader public in the determination of outcomes and not merely that portion of the public having a direct or immediate interest in them.[4] In part, this is because exclusive special interests can triumph by disguising themselves in such a way as to obtain the support of the broader public. Cynics imply that where regulation is concerned, income redistribution has succeeded in its disguise, many of the purported benefits of regulation are no more than successful masquerades, and the growth of regulatory activities has occurred because these masquerades have reached new levels of sophistication and effectiveness.

It is not possible to insist that the new social regulation is somehow exempted from this indictment. Of course, because industry has opposed so much of the new social regulation and because it has been supported by public lobbies, as well as because the new social regulation is directed at real market failures, it is natural that we might believe that it is somehow different from the "bad old" direct economic regulation. However, when one looks carefully at the new social regulation as it is in practice and especially at the etiology of the flaws in the regulatory apparatus identified in this volume, one must regretfully conclude that it is not. Many, if not most, of the discrepancies between regulatory ideal and regulatory practice in this area reflect precisely the same kind of bias that is so characteristic of direct regulation: small, well-organized, special interests triumphing at the expense of diffuse, unorganized interests. Here, too, efficiency is a public good; and here, too, as is the case with many public goods, it is undersupplied.

Anomalies

Still, if we apply conventional interest group theory to regulatory policy, we are struck by some rather serious anomalies. As Kahn and Levine observe in their chapters, many of the regulatory reforms that have taken place are inconsistent with the predictions of the interest group model. Total or substantial deregulation has occurred in such areas as air freight, passenger air travel, securities brokers' commissions, "fair trade" legislation, broadcasting and cable television, oil and natural gas pricing and allocation, and trucking. Weighed against the overall scope and domain of government regulation of economic activity in the United States, these reforms are, perhaps, not very significant. But weighed against the predictions of the interest group theory of regulation, they are very surprising.

In drawing attention to these anomalies, it is not our intention to discredit interest group theory. We merely wish to indicate that it has definite limits. Clearly, interest group theory is a powerful tool of political analysis. It is powerful precisely because the everday politics of Congress is interest group politics. Indeed, the general utility of the interest group theory of congressional politics is so palpable that students of the legislative process seldom ask why it is that legislators are so responsive to interest group demands.

Congressional Versus Presidential Politics

That American legislators are quite tolerant of inefficiency in government, on the one hand, and responsive to interest group demands, on the other, is largely explained by the system of geographic representation.[5] Furthermore, the consequences of geographic representation are reflected in and reinforced by the internal organization and decision-making rules of Congress.

Geographic representation results in an orientation toward the specific interests of constituents. Since activities on behalf of efficiency generally produce benefits that are widely diffused, the direct payoff to the individual legislator from such activities tends to be small. That is, the individual legislator cannot hope to get credit for influencing the welfare of his or her constituents in any signicant way by improving the performance of government and the economy in general. What he or she can do is secure benefits for identifiable groups of constituents, reward supporters, and trade favors with lobbyists. Not surprisingly, that is for the most part what is done by rational legislators. Indeed, inefficiency in government offers the enterprising legislator extensive opportunities to provide highly valued services to influential constituents by cutting through red tape or obtaining relief from niggling, arbitrary rules or regulations.[6]

In addition, there are certain characteristics of the American legislative process that reinforce the legislators' propensity to respond to interest group demands. First, party discipline is weak. Second, legislative decision making is highly decentralized. The everday business of Congress takes place in committee, where logrolling and vote trading are highly visible. This means that the individual legislator can take personal credit for grants made to identifiable groups by his or her committee or subcommittee(s). At the same time, it is equally difficult for legislators to avoid individual responsibility for denying grants to special interests. Specialization in Congress, therefore, tends to promote special interest legislation. Third, with some obvious exceptions, ideological commitments are either weak or widely shared by members of Congress. This means that most issues are viewed as negotiable.

Hence, the granting of favors to special interests in exchange for political support is a characteristic of most legislation. It seems to us, however, that the value of the favors conferred by regulation is often unusually high. If so, this may be attributable to the haste with which so much of the regulatory legislation was enacted — a particular characteristic of the new social regulation. As we noted earlier, it may also be because, where grants are provided to special interests through regulation, Congress cannot easily or gracefully withdraw them simply by not appropriating funds to support everything promised in the authorizing legislation.

In any case, congressional politics is usually interest group politics and interest group politics is inimical to regulatory reform. The Carter Administration's efforts on behalf of deregulation and regulatory reform, however, should remind us that the president and bureaucracy may act on behalf of the unorganizable many. Furthermore, if the president leads, Congress may follow. Indeed, when the president can mobilize resources and gain broad public support, it is nearly always in the interest of a majority of Congress to follow. Of course, Congress must be persuaded that the president has, in fact, mobilized public support, or that he could if Congress fails to support him.

Presidential politics is to some extent party politics. Ultimately, the perceived performance of government is what party politics is all about. To the extent that the president is interested in reelection and in the success of his party, he ought to be interested in promoting allocative efficiency through government action.[7] The president can also invoke his role as leader of *all* the people and seek coalitions with the core of his party and supporters in the opposition party.

The observation that the president has an interest in promoting efficiency or that executive leadership may overcome interest group politics does not, however, explain why it is that the Carter Administration promoted deregulation so zealously. Nor does it explain why it was ultimately successful in several instances, but not in others. And these questions must be answered before we can say whether or not the recent experience with deregulation is germane to the question of the political feasibility of reforming the new social regulation.

Explaining U.S. Deregulation

How then do we explain instances of deregulatory success in the United States? It appears to us that the necessary and sufficient conditions for the success of the Carter Administration's reform efforts include three factors exogenous to the political process and three endogenous to it. According to Kahn the three exogenous factors are the condition of the economy, technological change, and the resurgence of promarket ideas.

These factors may indeed promote a predisposition to regulatory reform, but they do not guarantee it. The fact that the Carter Administration had both successes and failures leads us to ask what other factors account for these different outcomes. Here three factors endogenous to the political process appear to be particularly significant: presidential leadership, the attention of Congress, and compelling evidence that regulatory reform is in the public interest.

Presidential Leadership

Someone must initiate the process of regulatory reform, and, as we have seen, Congress cannot and will not. On the other hand, we have argued that the president has a political interest in promoting economic efficiency (and good macroeconomic performance) in general. Improving the efficiency and effectiveness of regulations and removing those that impose costs greater than the social benefits they provide can make an important contribution to the president's perceived need to improve the performance of the economy.

It is not sufficient, however, for the president to announce that he is in favor of regulatory reform, to order regulators to "regulate better," or to shrink the regulatory bureaucracy in size. Nor is it enough to "twist a few arms" (or "reason together") on behalf of regulatory reform legislation. Effective leadership must ultimately be aimed at the lawmakers in Congress. The president must adopt a plan of attack, including a list of targets and their priority, and a strategy of persuasion. In those cases when the Carter Administration was successful as with airline deregulation and trucking there was a sequential attack on a limited number of targets.

One of the main lessons to be learned from the successes of the Carter Administration is that appointments to regulatory bodies matter a great deal. If the president appoints advocates of special interests — such as business, labor, consumers, or the environment — to senior policy-making positions in regulatory agencies, the agencies in question will protect those interests. On the other hand, when the president wants allocative efficiency, he should appoint economists with prior records as advocates of efficiency[8] — they are the "shock troops" with which to fight the battles of deregulation.

Study of the roles played by Alfred Kahn and Elizabeth Bailey in achieving airline deregulation, or Darius Gaskins in promoting greater competition in the surface freight industry, reveals their commitment to efficiency and skill in dealing with the industries involved and in goading Congress to take legislative action. Given the right individuals, the right organizational roles, and, to be sure, the right external circumstances, experience suggests that economists with strong backing from the president can make the case for regulatory reform successfully.

Getting the Attention of Congress

The successful reform efforts of the Carter Administration captured the attention of Congress. The unsuccessful ones did not. In the cases of both airline and trucking deregulation a substantial number of legislators and particularly legislative leaders became interested enough in understanding the issues to pay attention to the arguments made on both sides.[9] Where the issues remained relegated to a handful of committee members and their staffs (as with the 1977 Clean Air Act Amendments),[10] legislative outcomes were dominated by interest group politics. As we have noted, this meant that substantive reform was very unlikely; the results were as expected (as when special interest legislation favored the eastern producers of dirty coal).

Compelling Evidence that the Regulatory Reform Is in the Public Interest

In the airline and trucking cases, having gotten the attention of Congress, it was then necessary for Kahn and Gaskins to persuade Congress to deregulate. How did they do it? Here the story of airline deregulation is particularly instructive.

First, analysts in the administration and on congressional staffs were able — on the basis of a substantial body of empirical research[11] — to show the adverse effects of regulation and to characterize the consequences of deregulation in such a way as to strengthen the political coalition in its favor. Supporters of airline deregulation, for example, repeatedly explained that price and entry regulation in the domestic airline industry had raised the prices paid by the consumer well above what they would have been had price and entry been determined by the market and, as Stephen Breyer has observed, "lower prices" are far more arresting than "more efficient use of aircraft."[12] Furthermore, this explanation was supported by highly plausible evidence. According to James Q.Wilson:

> If there was a single fact that was of crucial significance in making persuasive the argument that price and entry regulation had adverse effects on consumers, it was the comparison of rates charged by unregulated airlines (for example, those linking San Francisco and Los Angeles) with those charged by regulated interstate airlines (for example, those connecting Boston and Washington, D.C.). Even so it was necessary to look carefully for other factors besides regulation that might have affected prices (there were some, but they were not decisive).[13]

The apparent value of this further research should also be stressed. It was needed: to explain both the original justification for regulating the industry and the objective it came to serve; to understand the position of the major actors associated with industry and the effects deregulation would have on their positions, that is, to identify winners and losers; and because "the detailed investigation (was) itself necessary to convince others that the proponents of reform (were) serious, thorough, and (had) made their case."[14] This last point reflects one of the key tenets of the rhetoric of persuasion.

Finally, it was necessary for the advocates of reform to show how to get from "there to here." It was not enough to show that regulation was inefficient. Proponents of deregulation had to develop a plan that appeared "practical and fair to allow a transition from the regulated regime to the new system."[15]

In contrast, we would observe that reform of the new social regulation has not attracted the attention of the press or of Congress. It is probably true that increased efficiency and regulation in general are not in the abstract very arresting issues. Perhaps proponents of incentive mechanisms in such areas as health and safety regulation ought to pay more attention to characterizing the consequences of reform in attention-grabbing terms. More important is the fact that, unlike Kahn or Gaskins, policy makers in the social regulatory agencies have not, so far, sought by their actions to direct the attention of Congress to issues of substantive reform.

Even if they could get the attention of Congress, however, it is not obvious to us that the proponents of incentive mechanisms are prepared to persuade Congress to follow their advice. To a considerable degree the kind of hard, credible evidence available for use by the advocates of airline deregulation, for example, is not available to those who wish to redirect the new social regulation. To cite examples of effective alternatives to existing regulatory regimes, the proponent of incentive mechanisms must draw on examples from outside the United States — from Great Britain or Scandinavia, as critics of the Food and Drug Administration do; from Canada, as supporters of accident taxes can; or from Europe, as supporters of effluent fees must. Unfortunately, these examples are by the very fact of their foreignness unfamiliar and suspect to Americans. Finally, supporters of alternatives to current methods of regulation are not now able to put forward detailed, practical implementation plans. Faced with the costs of change and uncertain benefits, most people, including legislators, prefer to stay with "the devil they know." (The work by Hahn and Noll can help to supply empirical evidence that could help bring the case home to the United States.)

These are a few of the lessons to be learned from the Carter Administration's victories and defeats. What do they tell us about the prospects for reform of the new social regulation? First, they tell us that if the president really wants to reform social regulation, he probably can. Second, an effective strategy that includes both a plan of attack — including a list of targets and the order in which they are to be addressed — and a plan of persuasion must ultimately be directed at Congress. The question is, does President Reagan really want to reform the new social regulation or does he want to suppress it? It is still too early to answer this question; the administration could go either way.

NOTES

1. Darius Gaskins, commentary made at the Conference on Reforming Government Regulation: Alternative Strategies to Social Regulatory Policy, presented by UCLA Extension, Santa Barbara, California, February 1981.

2. See, among others, David Truman, *The Governmental Process* (New York: Knopf, 1951); V. O. Key, *Political Parties and Pressure Groups,* 5th ed. (New York: Crowell, 1965). More recent works on interest groups and lobbying include Terry M. Moe, *The Organization of Interests* (Chicago: University of Chicago Press, 1980); Richard Wagner, "Pressure Groups and Political Entrepreneurs: A Review Article," *Papers on Non-Market Decision Making* 1 (1969): 151-170; and Norman Frohlich, Joe A. Oppenheimer, and Oren R. Young, *Political Leadership and Collective Goods* (Princeton, NJ: Princeton University Press, 1971).

3. Sam Peltzman, "Toward a More General Theory of Regulation," *Journal of Law and Economics* 19 (1976): 211-248.

4. See E.E. Schattschneider, *The Semi-Sovereign People: A Realist's View of Democracy in America* (New York: Holt, Rinehart & Winston, 1960), p. 35; here Schattschneider states, "The flaw in the pluralist heaven is that the heavenly chorus sings with a strong upper-class accent. Probably about 90 per cent of the people cannot get into the pressure system." Our point is that interest groups are concerned with issues and policies. Most voters pay no attention to, have no knowledge of, and are unaware of the consequences of most policies. Voting is largely retrospective, not prospective. At the macro level, national elections — presidential and congressional — appear to be little more than referenda on the management of the economy.

5. See, for example, R. Douglas Arnold, "The Local Roots of Domestic Policy," in *The New Congress,* eds. T. Mann and N. Ornstein (Washington, DC: American Enterprise Institute, 1981), pp. 250-287. See also Barry Weingast, "Regulation, Reregulation, and Deregulation," *Law and Contemporary Problems* 44 (Winter 1981): 147-177.

So far the preoccupation with macroeconomic issues has preempted the Reagan Administration's attention and resources. While the objective of economic efficiency associated with regulatory reform is relevant to macroeconomic concerns, the president so far has not chosen to expend political energy on a major regulation reform effort with Congress. Instead, he has been preoccupied with budget deficits, budget cutting, and tax reform issues. It will be interesting to observe over the next few years whether an administration that has expressly committed itself to regulatory reform will integrate these efforts into its long-term strategy to improve the economic performance of the country.

6. Morris P. Fiorina, *Congress: Keystone of the Washington Establishment* (New Haven, CT: Yale University Press, 1977).

7. This argument was first advanced by Gerald Kramer in "Short-Term Voting Fluctuations in U.S. Voting Behavior, 1898-1964," *American Political Science Review* 65 (1971): 131-143. Kramer argued that "if the performance of the incumbent party is 'satisfactory' according to some simple standard, the voter votes to retain the incumbent party in office to enable it to continue its present policies; while if the incumbent's performance is not 'satisfactory,' the voter votes against the incumbent" (p. 134).

In other words, Kramer claims that elections are referenda on the economic performance of the governing party, and that voter expectations about future performance are positively correlated with recent performance. William Niskanen has provided a more rigorous formulation of the incumbency hypothesis in which voting is characterized as utility-maximizing behavior under binary-choice conditions; see Niskanen, "Economic and Fiscal Effects on the Popular Vote for the President," in *Public Policy and Public Choice,* eds. D.W. Rae and T.J. Eismeier (New York: Russell Sage, 1979), pp. 93-120.

These and other studies consistently show that the most powerful predictor of electoral success is the change in real per-capita net national income. These results are not now seriously questioned; see S.J. Lepper, "Voting Behavior and Aggregate Policy Targets," *Public Choice* 18 (Summer 1974): 67-81; and Edward Tufte, "The Determinants of the Outcomes of Midterm Congressional Elections," *American Political Science Review* 69 (June 1975): 812-826.

However, the interpretation of these results is still being debated. For example, George Stiger rejects the macroeconomic explanation of political behavior, and asserts that "the economic basis for political affiliation must be sought in the area of income redistribution"; see Stiger, "General Economic Conditions and National Elections," *American Economic Review* 63 (May 1973): 167. However, he has not presented empirical support for this assertion. Furthermore, Niskanen tested Stiger's proposition and found no evidence of a distributional effect on the popular vote for the president. Indeed, Niskanen suggests that standard cost-benefit analysis ought to be a sufficient guide for most decisions made by a president seeking re-election and that it should be sufficient to explain most decisions of the presidency, except when other groups, such as Congress, on which the president is dependent are concerned about (distributional) effects; Niskanen, "Economic and Fiscal Effects," p. 110. Furthermore, incumbents are evidently aware of the relationship between economic conditions and electoral outcomes and act accordingly, albeit sometimes in a wrongheaded manner. See William Nordhaus, "The Political Business Cycle," *Review of Economic Studies* 42 (1975): 160-190.

8. The outstanding examples are the appointments of Alfred Kahn and Elizabeth Bailey to the Civil Aeronautics Board and of Darius Gaskins to the Interstate Commerce Commission. As Kelman explains, economists are effective in these

situations not because they are wiser or smarter than other people, but because they have an intense, often irrational, commitment to efficiency. See Steven Kelman, *What Price Incentives?* (Boston: Auburn House, 1981).

9. See Michael E. Levine, "Revisionism Revised? Airline Deregulation and the Public Interest," *Law and Contemporary Problems* 44 (Winter 1981): 174-175.

10. See Bruce Ackerman and W. T. Hassler, *Clean Coal/Dirty Air* (New Haven, CT: Yale University Press, 1981).

11. See, for example, W. A. Jordan, *Airline Regulation in America* (Baltimore: Johns Hopkins University Press, 1970); M. E. Levine, "Is Regulation Necessary? California Air Transportation and National Regulatory Policy," *Yale Law Journal* 74 (1965); T. E. Keeler, "Airline Regulation and Market Performance," *Bell Journal of Economics and Management Science* 3 (Autumn 1972): 399-424; George Douglas and James E. Miller III, *Economic Regulation of Domestic Air Transportation* (Washington, DC: Brookings Institution, 1974).

12. Stephen G. Breyer, "The Genesis of Airline Deregulation: The Role of the Kennedy Hearings and Report" (Paper presented at the National Conference on Airline Regulation, sponsored by the Institute for Research on Public Policy and the American Enterprise Institute, Ottawa, June 17, 1979).

13. James Q. Wilson, "Policy Intellectuals and Public Policy," *Public Interest,* Summer 1981, p. 41.

14. Breyer, "Genesis of Airline Deregulation," p. 4.

15. Ibid., p. 7. Potential "losers" (small cities that lost services and employees that lost their jobs) were provided with a "safety net" in the form of direct subsidy programs. To date, the amounts expended have been far less than anticipated.

About the Authors

EUGENE BARDACH is Professor of Public Policy at the Graduate School of Public Policy, University of California, Berkeley. He was formerly Assistant Professor of Politics at Brandeis University, and has also served as a Policy Analyst for the U.S. Department of the Interior. He received his B.A. from Columbia College and his Ph.D. from the University of California, Berkeley. He is the author of several books on public policy issues, including (with Robert A. Kagan) *Going by the Book: The Problem of Regulatory Unreasonableness* (Temple University Press, 1982); *The Implementation Game: What Happens After a Bill Becomes a Law* (MIT Press, 1977); and *The Skill Factor in Politics* (University of California Press, 1972).

ROY N. GAMSE became Deputy Associate Administrator for Policy and Resource Management of the U.S. Environmental Protection Agency in July 1981. He has served the agency since 1973, as Acting Assistant Administrator for Planning and Management (1981), Deputy Assistant Administrator for Planning and Evaluation (1977-1981), and Director of the Economic Analysis Division (1973-1977). He holds a B.S. in economics from the Massachusetts Institute of Technology and an M.B.A. from Harvard Business School. In 1980 he received the Senior Executive Service Presidential Rank Award for Distinguished Executives.

LeROY GRAYMER is Head of the Public Policy Program at UCLA Extension and President of the Institute for Policy and Management Research in Santa Monica, California. Previously he has served as Associate Dean, Graduate School of Public Policy, University of California, Berkeley; Professor of Political Science and Vice President, California State University, Dominguez Hills; and Assistant Director of the Institute of International Studies, University of Oregon. Since developing the Public Policy Program, which is designed to link the resources of the research community to the needs of policy makers, he has conducted conferences on tax and expenditures limitations, federal budget and tax reforms, and water and energy policy, as well as the conference on reforming government regulation from which this book was developed.

ROBERT W. HAHN, a Research Economist at the California Institute of Technology, has also held positions as an economist for the U.S. Council on Environmental Quality and the World Bank. He was awarded B.A. and M.A. degrees in economics from Brown University, and an M.S. and Ph.D. in social science from the California Institute of Technology. His publications include *An Assessment of the Determination of Energy Needs: The Case of Nuclear Power,* "On the Applicability of Market Solutions to Environmental Problems," and "Designing Market Mechanisms to Control Pollution."

DAVID HARRISON, Jr., Associate Professor, John F. Kennedy School of Government, Harvard University, was Senior Staff Economist for Regulation to the President's Council of Economic Advisers in 1979-1980. He has also been a consultant to the Environmental Protection Agency, the Department of Housing and Urban Development, and the Massachusetts Department of Environmental Quality. He holds a B.A. from Harvard College, an M.Sc. from the London School of Economics and Political Science, and an M.A. and Ph.D. in economics from Harvard University. He is the author of *Who Pays for Clean Air* (Ballinger, 1975) and coauthor of *The Automobile and the Regulation of Its Impact on the Environment* (Oklahoma University Press, 1975) and *Incentive Arrangements for Environmental Protection: A Critical Examination* (MIT Press, forthcoming).

ROBERT A. KAGAN is Associate Professor of Political Science at the University of California, Berkeley. Prior to joining the faculty there he was active in a variety of fields, including serving as Assistant to the Chairman of the Federal Price Commission in 1971-1972; he also has been Vice President of the Kagan-Dixon Wire Corporation (1966-1969) and practiced law with the firm of Shanley and Fisher, Newark, New Jersey (1962-1966). He received his B.A. from Harvard

College, his LL.B. from Columbia University, and his Ph.D. from Yale University. His publications include journal articles on the history of state supreme courts, and a book entitled *Regulatory Justice: Implementing a Wage-Price Freeze* (Russell Sage, 1978); he is also coauthor, with Eugene Bardach, of *Going by the Book: The Problem of Regulatory Unreasonableness* (Temple University Press, 1982).

ALFRED E. KAHN is Robert Julius Thorne Professor of Economics of Cornell University and Special Consultant to National Economic Research Associates, Inc. He is a Fellow of the American Academy of Arts and Sciences. From 1974 through 1980 he was on leave from Cornell University while serving in several government positions. In 1979 and 1980 he was Advisor to the President on Inflation and Chairman, Council on Wage and Price Stability; in 1977 and 1978 he served as Chairman of the Civil Aeronautics Board; and in 1974-1978 he was Chairman, New York State Service Commission. He holds an A.B. and M.A. from New York University and a Ph.D. from Yale University; he also has been awarded three honorary LL.D. degrees. Among his important books are *Great Britain in the World Economy* (Columbia University Press, 1946; reprinted in 1968); *Integration and Competition in the Petroleum Industry,* with Mervin G. DeChazeau (Yale University Press, 1959; reprinted in 1971); and *The Economics of Regulation,* 2 vols. (John Wiley, 1970 and 1971).

JAMES E. KRIER, Professor of Law at the University of California, Los Angeles, and formerly a member of the law faculty at Stanford University, was the first Visiting Scholar at the General Counsel's Office of the Environmental Protection Agency. After receiving his J.D. from the University of Wisconsin he served for one year as law clerk to the Chief Justice of the California State Supreme Court, and then became an Associate in the firm of Arnold & Porter, Washington, D.C. He has coauthored several books, among them *Pollution and Policy,* with Edmund Ursin (1977); *Environmental Law and Policy,* with Richard B. Stewart (1978); and *Property,* with Jesse Dukeminier (1981). He is a member of Phi Kappa Phi and the Order of the Coif.

MICHAEL E. LEVINE became Executive Vice President, Marketing, of Continental Airlines in mid-1981. Prior to that he served concurrently as Henry R. Luce Professor of Law and Social Change in the Technological Society, California Institute of Technology, and Professor of Law, University of Southern California. He has also held several positions with the U.S. Civil Aeronautics Board, including that of General Director, International and Domestic Aviation (1979); while serving in that capacity, he was given the CAB Award for Excellence and Distinguished Public Service. After receiving his B.A. from Reed College, Portland, Oregon, and his LL.B. (J.D.) from Yale University, he spent a year as a Law and Economics Fellow at the University of Chicago Law School. He has published several significant articles on airline regulation, most notably "Is Regulation Necessary? California Air Transportation and National Regulatory Policy," which first appeared in the *Yale Law Journal* in 1965, and "Revisionism Revised: Airline Deregulation and the Public Interest," *Law and Contemporary Problems* (January 1981).

JOHN MENDELOFF, Assistant Professor of Political Science, University of California, San Diego, has served as a consultant of the President's Task Force on Work Place Safety and Health, the U.S. Department of Labor, and the Occupational Safety and Health Administration, and as an analyst for the California Department of Industrial Relations. After receiving an A.B. from Harvard College, he earned M.P.P. and Ph.D. degrees at the Graduate School of Public Policy, University of California, Berkeley. He is the author of several articles related to public policy, including "Welfare Procedures and Error Rates," *Policy Analysis* (Fall 1977), and "Toxic Substances: Does Overregulation Cause Underregulation?" *Regulation* (September/October 1981). His book, *Regulating Safety: An Economic and Political Analysis of Occupational Safety and Health Policy,* was published by MIT Press in 1979.

WILLIAM A. NISKANEN was appointed a Member of the President's Council of Economic Advisers in 1981. He had been a Professor in the Graduate School of Management, University of California, Los Angeles, from 1980 to 1981, and Director of Economics at Ford Motor Company from 1975 to 1980. He has also served on the faculty of the Graduate School of Public Policy, University of California, Berkeley, from 1972-1975. He received a B.A. from Harvard College, and an M.A. and Ph.D. from the University of Chicago. His several publications, including *Bureaucracy and Representative Government,* are critical analyses of the appropriate roles for government in a democratic society.

ROGER G. NOLL, Professor and Chairman, Division of Humanities and Social Science, California Institute of Technology, has also been a Senior Economist at the President's Council of Economic Advisers and a Senior Fellow at the Brookings Institution. He received his B.S. from the California Institute of Technology and his Ph.D. from Harvard University. The many public service committees on which he has served include the Advisory Commission on Regulatory Reform of the Senate Committee on Government Operations (1975-1977) and the National Commission on the Agenda for the Eighties. He has published extensively in scholarly journals and has written two books on regulatory policy: *Reforming Regulation* and *Economic Aspects of Television Regulation;* the latter was honored by the National Association of Educational Broadcasters as the best book on communications policy published in 1974.

PAUL R. PORTNEY, Senior Fellow at Resources for the Future, served as Senior Staff Economist at the Council on Environmental Quality in the Executive Office of the President (1979-1980). He has been a Visiting Professor, Graduate School of Public Policy, University of California, Berkeley, and Research Fellow at the Brookings Institution. He holds a B.A. from Alma College, Alma, Michigan, and an M.A. and Ph.D. from Northwestern University. He was editor of *Current Issues in U.S. Environmental Policy* (1978) and coeditor of *Environmental Regulation and the U.S. Economy* (1981). His most recent article, "Housing Price, Health Effects, and Valuing Reductions in Risk of Death," was published in the *Journal of Environmental Economics and Management*.

FREDERICK THOMPSON became an Associate Professor in the Graduate Program in Public Policy and Administration, School of International and Public Affairs, Columbia University, in 1981. During 1980-1981 he was a Visiting Associate Professor, Graduate School of Management, University of California, Los Angeles; he has also recently served as Senior Research Consultant for the Economic Council of Canada's inquiry into government regulation. He received his B.A. from Pomona College and his Ph.D. from Claremont Graduate School. His recent articles include "More and Better Analysis? The Case of Health, Safety, and Environmental Regulation," in *Government Regulation,* edited by W. T. Stanbury (1980): "Reforming Regulatory Decision Making," *Sloan Management Review* (Winter 1981); and "Control and Controls: A Reexamination of

Control Patterns in Budget Execution," *Policy Sciences* (Winter 1981).

DAVID LEO WEIMER, Assistant Professor of Political Science and Public Policy Analysis, University of Rochester, recently served as a Visiting Economist in the Office of Energy Security, U.S. Department of Energy. He received a B.S. in engineering and a B.A. in urban studies from the University of Rochester, and an M.A. in statistics and an M.P.P. and a Ph.D. in public policy from the University of California, Berkeley. His most recent publications include "Federal Intervention in the Process of Innovation in Local Public Agencies: A Focus on Organizational Incentives," *Public Policy* (Winter 1980); *Improving Prosecution?* (Greenwood Press, 1980); and *Wise Virgins: An Analytical History of the Strategic Petroleum Reserve Program* (forthcoming).

W. R. Z. WILLEY, Staff Economist for the Environmental Defense Fund, Inc., Berkeley, California, has also served as Technical Advisor to the Egyptian Academy of Sciences and as Project Specialist, Resources and Environment, for the Ford Foundation. He received his Ph.D. from the University of California, Berkeley, where he was awarded the Flood Fellowship in Economics (1968-1969) and a Special Career Fellowship in Economics (1969-1971). He has written in many areas of relevance to the formation of public policy, including "Electricity Consumption and Investment Finance in California," in *California Energy* (U.S. Federal Reserve Bank, 1976); "Barriers to the Diffusion of Integrated Pest Management Programs in Commercial Agriculture," in *Pest Control Strategies,* edited by D. Pimentel and E. Smith (Academic Press, 1978); and "Economic and Environmental Aspects of Alternative Investments in California's Water Resource System," in *California Water Policies and Problems* (Institute of Governmental Studies, University of California, 1982).